TYNE VIEW.

A WALK AROUND THE PORT OF TYNE

TYNE VIEW

A WALK AROUND THE PORT OF TYNE

MICHAEL CHAPLIN

ILLUSTRATIONS BY **BIRTLEY ARIS**   PHOTOGRAPHS BY **CHARLES BELL**   POEMS BY **CHRISTY DUCKER**

*For Chris and Billie —
Enjoy the Walk!
Michael Chaplin
November 2016*

Words © Michael Chaplin 2012
Photographs © Charles Bell (www.saatchionline.com/charlesbell)
Illustrations © Birtley Aris
Poems © Christy Ducker

First published by New Writing North in 2012
This edition published 2013

New Writing North
PO Box 1277
Newcastle upon Tyne
NE99 5BP
www.newwritingnorth.com

Supported by Port of Tyne

Port of Tyne
Maritime House
Tyne Dock
South Shields
Tyne & Wear
NE34 9PT
www.portoftyne.co.uk

ISBN 978-0956655165

ADDITIONAL PHOTOS
Cover, pages 16
and 366 – courtesy of
North News & Pictures.

Pages 60 and 62 –
courtesy of David Tiernan.

Graphic design by David McClure
www.velcrobelly.co.uk

Typeset in Minion Pro and Trade Gothic

Printed and bound in north east England by Martins the Printers
www.martins-the-printers.co.uk

To my grandchildren: Thames-siders Eve and Ella;
and Ollie and Poppy, the Tynesiders
⚓ Michael

To all the members of my family who served in the Merchant Navy
⚓ Birtley

To my children Danniella, Wesley and Jasmine, my mother Joy,
my sister Anne and to the memory of my father, William Bell,
who grew up on the steep southern banks of the Tyne above Blaydon
⚓ Charles

To my family
⚓ Christy

PORT *of* TYNE

WELCOME TO TYNE VIEW...

The Port of Tyne is a major deep sea port, connecting the people and businesses of the North East of England to all five continents across the globe.

Huge volumes of cargoes are handled across its quays: from cars and waste paper to coal and steel; from retail goods and parts for manufacturing to giant subsea machinery. Hordes of ferry and cruise passengers pass through, either visiting or setting off on holiday.

This is all vital to the region's economy, supporting 9,500 jobs, and it's our responsibility to ensure that the Port that has existed since Roman times continues to be fit to meet the ever-changing demands of business and industry, for now and the future.

This means we invest in infrastructure, making sure the river is deep enough and the quays are strong enough to accommodate most of the world's biggest cargo and cruise ships, and we seek out new business opportunities. We believe a thriving local area is important for our business to succeed, so we also support local communities in many different ways.

Having the esteemed Michael Chaplin as our very popular writer-in-residence has helped us ensure that we spread the word about the Port ever wider. So when he suggested a walk around the jurisdiction of the Port of Tyne – 21 miles upriver and the same coming back – I said please feel free.... And I even joined him – for some of the way, at least!

The stories and images gathered by Michael, Charles, Christy and Birtley on the walk are such a good read, as well as a unique record of the life of the River Tyne, that we were delighted to support the publication of *Tyne View* by our friends at New Writing North. I do hope you enjoy the book.

Andrew Moffat
Chief Executive Officer

⚓ CONTENTS

BEFORE

⚓ BEFORE

This is an account of a journey, undertaken close to home in the month of July 2011, tracing the jurisdiction of the Port of Tyne, an area of water stretching from a point three miles off the two piers at its mouth to the river's tidal reach 21 miles upstream.

Since I and my companions – artist Birtley Aris, photographer Charles Bell and poet Christy Ducker – didn't fancy the swim, we started our walk at the lighthouse at the tip of the South Shields pier, made our way along the south bank of the river to Wylam, crossed over its bridge and then returned seawards to the point of the Tynemouth pier.

As expeditions go, it's not exactly epic. In ten days on the hoof, we can't have walked more than 50 miles, but all of those days were filled with rich experiences, visiting factories, workshops, museums, churches, community centres and schools, but equally importantly, meeting people who had interesting things to say about their lives and work, community and culture, most especially their river. These Tynesiders, many of whom we almost literally bumped into on the riverside path, were unfailingly open and eloquent, but many asked us a question of their own: why exactly are you doing this?

Which is a fair enough enquiry, and I'm going to try to answer it – in a slight circular way – by asking one back: can you remember your first glimpse of the River Tyne?

In my experience, people usually do, though I have to confess I don't, but I'll come to that shortly. Among those who wrote down their first impressions were distinguished visitors like Charles Dickens, Arnold Bennett and the decidedly grumpy JB Priestley, who still managed to write:

'There is, you see, something bracing about the Tyne. After you have seen it, you realise it is not for the likes of us to be sorry for ourselves.'

However, it was the fond recollection of another writer that has stayed with me, for understandable reasons. As a teenage boy, my dad, the novelist Sid Chaplin, first visited the city in the early 1930s, travelling from his home in Ferryhill 30 miles away, and like many visitors and returning pilgrims, saw it from the vantage point of a train idling on the King Edward Railway Bridge. That first sight of the river and the great gorge it had cut over many millennia to separate Newcastle and Gateshead rather took his breath away, as he recalled many years later:

I looked down into the mighty trough. On one side was a little wonder of a Swing Bridge and high above the great High Level. It was the turn of the tide and the brown Tyne from the hills was pushing through black waters the sea had siphoned up from the slakes and the sewers. The Swing Bridge called to a ship and the gulls went up with a clap of wings. There was a puff of white smoke from Robbie Stephenson's High Level. Downriver the brave ships rode at anchor while one-eyed giants on wheels raked out their holds; fleets of drift-wood jostled ready to set sail; and the great noble city went up the river in steps and stairs. There she sat, like a conference waiting for its picture to be taken, and the big open smile was all the better for a blackened stump or two – the Keep, the Black Gate, the Cathedral with its lantern of stone. Because I hadn't learned to swear, I remember saying to myself: 'By gum, I'd give two years off the back end of my life to come and live in the heart of all this…'

This is about as vivid as a description of a place can get, though in fairness it should be said that it presents a rather Newcastle-centric view of the river scene. There are many places on the Tyne that offer grand perspectives of water and landscape, and I can think of at least one that tops it: the sight of the mouth of the Tyne from the deck of a ship approaching safe harbour – the embrace of the crab legs of its two piers, the smudgy horizon of distant hills, the cranes of the middle river, the white markers of the High and Low Lights at North Shields, the waving of the ever-present sightseers on the Spanish Battery. Throughout the bulk of the 2,000 years since Tyneside was first settled, this is how most people arrived in this place: Roman centurions and the traders who brought them goods from the impossibly distant Mediterranean; Vikings with a more sinister intent; barques bringing pit props from the Baltic shore; colliers plying back and forth to London and continental ports; warships in sail and steel; giant supertankers and tiny fishing cobles; and the *City of Port Elizabeth*, a cargo vessel that had taken its new fifth engineer – my brother Chris – to South Africa and back in the mid-1960s, when I was among that morning's crowd on the Battery. They all passed this way, like the distinctly unromantic, box-like ferry that returned me from a weekend in Amsterdam many years later, when I was so moved by this matchless early-morning panorama of home.

By the time Chris came home from the Indian Ocean that morning in the mid-1960s, I'd been living in Newcastle for the best part of a decade. In 1957 my father kept the promise he'd made to himself all those years before to take up residence in the city by the Tyne, and the family moved from Essex to an Edwardian house perched above a municipal dump in the then-unfragrant Jesmond Vale. I was five years old, which offers some excuse for why I don't actually remember crossing the river for the first time, though I do recall lying in my tiny front bedroom at night, in the darkness, listening to the distant hooting of ships working upriver, and the occasional ghostly boom of the Shields foghorn. The sense of curiosity this aroused led not long afterwards to an adventure on the Ouseburn. The tributary of the Tyne was a noisome, smelly ditch back then – there was still industry upstream in Gosforth to pollute it – but it did have dozy sticklebacks in the pool above the waterfall by the white bridge. Often a fishing expedition led to a wander upstream into Jesmond Dene, but one day I had the idea of turning right instead of left and following the Ouseburn downstream. My pals and I – I suppose we were about seven – had never done this before.

The remaining course of the river had only a mile to run, but our expedition turned out to be as mysterious and hazardous as searching for the source of the Nile. Mysterious, because a quarter of a mile from the white bridge, the Ouseburn disappeared into a grate on the side of a hill, forcing us to search for the place where it emerged again; hazardous, because the journey involved crossing into Shieldfield, whose battle-hardened lads greeted Jesmond boys with grim amusement and twirling bicycle chains. The Ouseburn meanwhile moved mythically on beneath the streets, then undergoing slum clearance, emerging into the light under the Byker bridges, in what's now yet another of Newcastle's numerous cultural quarters. At that time the Ouseburn Valley was a pungent sink-hole of abandoned mills, leadworks and hideaways for gentlemen of the road, incidentally also the stamping ground of Arthur Haggerston, my dad's chancer anti-hero in the novel he was writing at just this time, *The Day of the Sardine*. Through this silent, spooky landscape, we moved like nervous US cavalrymen in a Sioux burial-ground, or trigger-happy GI's in the war about to begin in Vietnam, but finally we were through it, observing the tide moving up our stream, gently rocking the ancient motor boats by a pub perched under a bridge. Finally we passed between the long sheds belonging to the Tyne Improvement Commission and reached our destination: a few hundred yards downstream of those mythic bridges, the Ouseburn said hello to its Big Daddy, the Tyne, to us as vast and mythic as the Mississippi, with cranes dipping, hooters blaring, ships turning in midstream for the sea. We didn't stay long. It stank to high heaven and was kind of scary. In any case we had to get home for tea, and the Lone Ranger on the telly.

But something was set. Around this time I started taking Sunday morning walks with my dad as he gathered material for his Newcastle novels. Often these wanderings ended by the Quayside's weekly market. Here big men in braces stood on the backs of trucks, barking out the benefits of nylon sheets to slab-faced headscarved women, heavily drawing on un-tipped cigarettes. But I was drawn to the river, where I'd stare at the disconcerting speed of its oily current, down or indeed up, depending on the tide. Once I saw a dead dog and shivered at the stiff legs proud of the water, wondering where its body would finally rest. Dad saw it too: the sight was recorded at the climax of *The Day of the Sardine*.

Thus the Tyne became part of my world, a border between my home town and that alien place on the other side; more than that, a central feature of the mental map I carried inside my head of all the places that mattered to the growing boy, along with Heaton Grammar School, the People's Theatre, the Jesmond Picture House, St James's Park and the Handyside Arcade. Later, after university, I returned to work on *The Journal* as a reporter, and the Tyne became part of another world, of stories that might make the paper, among them launches of ships from yards downriver. On one assignment I saw an Esso super-tanker going down the slipway at Swan Hunter, accompanied by various lost vignettes: gaffers in bowler hats and visiting dignitary, dead animal draped on shoulders and confections of chiffon perched above; cheap champagne hitting plate steel; dancing chains restraining the ship and madly-capering rats running for cover; most impressive, the heart-stopping spectacle of the ship gathering speed as it was received into the water of Tyne.

Another destination for the young journalist had its own, rather grimmer rituals: the Coroner's Court, then found in a squat stone building at the northern end of the Swing Bridge. Not many people went down that way then; it was the mid-70s and the Quayside seemed to be quietly dying too. Inside the smoky room where inquests were held, it was cold and dark whatever the season, and it wasn't only the fingerless gloves often worn by the coroner's clerk that put one in mind of Dickens' *Our Mutual Friend*, since what brought us all here was that book's leitmotif: the corpses of human beings, some of whom had met their end, in suicidal despair or drunken stupor, in the black river flowing thickly 30 feet below our feet. I didn't know it then, but this place of bleak little endings was offering something of an omen for the Tyne as a whole.

In 1977, I was offered a job as a current affairs researcher at London Weekend Television, and 20 years after my dad made the journey in reverse, I crossed the bridge going south to live by another river, the Thames. It was to be almost 30 years before we came back to make a new home. In the interim we returned many times: for holidays by the sea, countless football matches, the occasional family wedding, rather more funerals (my dad's among them), and another ritual as I morphed from television producer into writer, the openings of plays at Live Theatre, a converted mediaeval warehouse a few yards from the Tyne. During this time there was wholesale change on the river, mostly for the worse, as its shipyards closed one by one and the coal trade that had been so vital to its growth and enrichment withered and died. Of course I knew about these apparently inexorable events, but followed them from a distance. I didn't see or indeed feel them, until a day in the summer of 2001 when I celebrated my 50th birthday with friends and family on a pleasure cruise from Newcastle Quayside down to the sea. Like many before and since, I was quietly shocked by what I saw, even more by what I heard, or rather didn't hear. The upper river was eerily quiet and long stretches of the southern shore were returning to nature.

Five years later, my wife Susan and I finally returned to Newcastle to live and work. As the months went by, I sensed a more subtle change, in the attitudes of Tynesiders towards their river. I suspected we were collectively turning our backs on it, prompted no doubt by the fact that far fewer people worked on or beside the Tyne in its traditional industries. It also seemed to me that this process wasn't solely physical. We'd begun to take it – her – for granted. As my dad once wrote: 'Stuck in a traffic jam on the Swing Bridge or at the foot of Pilgrim Street, we never pause to think that she's at the bottom of it all. Without her we'd be lost; indeed we wouldn't be here.'

I felt this was more than a pity, and wondered how a playwright and screenwriter like me might affect these perceptions, even in a small way. So I came up with a plan: put simply, to find ways to celebrate the river and its effect on our culture. With this in mind I tentatively approached the Port of Tyne with an idea – a job application, basically – to become their writer in residence. The Port's chief executive Andrew Moffat instantly agreed, and I must here thank him for that and his part in what's followed. I set to work, with a little trepidation. Often writers in residence work in self-contained institutions like hospitals, schools or prisons, but here I was taking on not just the body responsible for safe movement on the river and the handling of much of its trade, but also by implication the Tyne itself, as well as the communities lining its shores. How could I do justice to all of that? One obvious way of starting was to encourage people to write about the river and its meaning in the lives of themselves and their families and publish it (eventually on a specially dedicated adjunct of the Port's own website: go to www.portoftyne.co.uk and follow the link to 'Writer In Residence'). People responded in significant numbers – some living far away from their native Tyneside – with pieces of writing that were sometimes funny, often moving and always vivid. A selection appears in these pages, peppering and enriching the narrative. I then went to work myself, interviewing a dozen people whose lives revolve around the river in interesting and surprising ways. With evocative photo portraits by David Tiernan, these were published by the Port in the slim volume, *Tyne People*.

I then had an idea for something rather fatter: a book examining in much more detail what was happening, or indeed not happening, along the river. Since I became the Port's writer in residence, I've almost lost count of the people who've told me, 'Oh, the river's dead now, isn't it?' I know what my instinctive reply is to that – indeed I've made it many times – but I wanted in the end to test it, and finally establish whether, as Mark Twain remarked after reading his own obituary, reports of its demise are premature. The nature of my response – this book – represents a return to journalistic roots. Half a lifetime ago, my first news editor on *The Journal* gave me two lessons I've never forgotten: first, if you want to find out what someone thinks about something, don't phone them up, go and see them, ideally on their home turf; second, if you want to get a feel for a place, get out of your car and walk it. Put another way, the best way of gauging the temperature is to feel the sun or indeed the rain on your face. So I set out to tell the stories of these riverside communities and the people, past and present, who have made their homes in them, a process I suppose of 'bearing witness' for untold numbers of Tynesiders whose lives have gone largely unrecorded. I began to understand that though a walk is very definitely rooted in the present, it also involves an examination of the past, and almost as inevitably, an imagination of the future. This Tyne walk therefore became a journey of both memory and hope, as well as a way for this particular Tynesider to get to know his river all over again.

This then was how *Tyne View* was born, but my earliest vision for the book was that it shouldn't be merely a procession of text, but an equal and artful juxtaposition of words with images. My invitation to Birtley, Charles and Christy to join me, and in the process hugely enrich my own work, had a further selfish motive behind it: I thought it would be rather lonely walking on my own, and I thank my collaborators for their engaging company as well as the quality of their contributions to our collective enterprise. Every morning we set out full of hope and curiosity, an expeditionary party like those of old (think Cook and Darwin), though in our case we weren't collecting fossils and botanical specimens, but facts, images, reflections, wise and funny remarks, fragments of life beside the water. The other difference of course is that we weren't travelling on water, but beside it; rather than being conveyed across oceans on the *Explorer* and the *Beagle*, but to our start and finish lines in a black cab belonging to the ever-obliging East Coast Taxis, driven by the hugely knowledgeable and equally sardonic Brian, though so obscure were some of the places we reached, even he had sometimes to consult his sat-nav. Each of the book's ten chapters follows a different day of our Tyne walk, recording the things we saw and heard en route and in follow-up interviews, the shorter 'On The Water' sections between the chapters giving contrasting water-borne perspectives, while the concluding coda, 'After', offers a resume of developments on the river in the year since July 2011 and some tentative general impressions and conclusions.

The morning I began my stint as the Port's writer in residence I came across a colour map of the working Tyne, dating from just before the First World War, detailing the many enterprises occupying the river frontage, the railway lines that served them and the communities that had sprung up to support them. Utterly beguiled, I sat and stared at it for an hour. I've since examined many other maps of the river, among them the first chart of its mouth assembled for the benefit of Elizabethan sailors, and another, drawn up 450 years later and viewed this time on computer, showing the position of the hundreds of sunken ships that litter the sea-bed in precisely the same area. In a way, this book represents a kind of mapping exercise too, not merely of a physical terrain, but also of the thoughts and feelings of the people we met along the way. Part-map, part-snapshot, part-testimony of the river at this moment in its long history, I like to think it might illuminate travellers at points in the future as well as the present. It certainly was a fascinating journey for my fellow cartographers and I, and I hope you enjoy its re-creation.

Michael Chaplin
Newcastle, July 2012

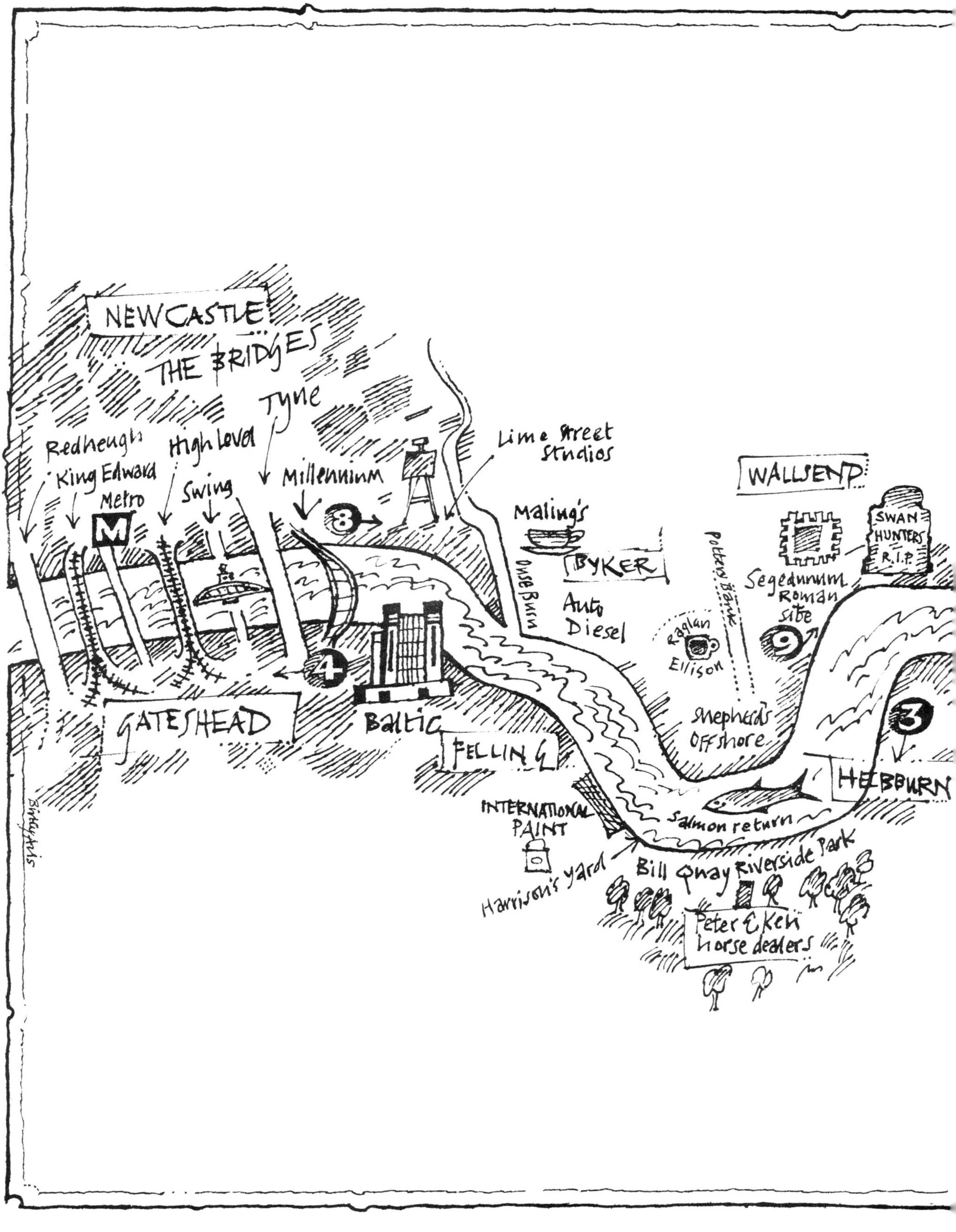
NEWCASTLE
THE BRIDGES
Tyne
Redheugh
High Level
King Edward
Metro
M
Swing
Millennium
8
Lime Street Studios
Maling's
Ouse Burn
BYKER
Auto Diesel
WALLSEND
Pottery Bank
SWAN HUNTERS R.I.P.
Segedunum Roman site
9
Raglan
Ellison
4
Baltic
GATESHEAD
FELLING
Shepherd's Offshore
3
HEBBURN
INTERNATIONAL PAINT
Salmon return
Harrison's yard
Bill Quay Riverside Park
Peter Eken horse dealers

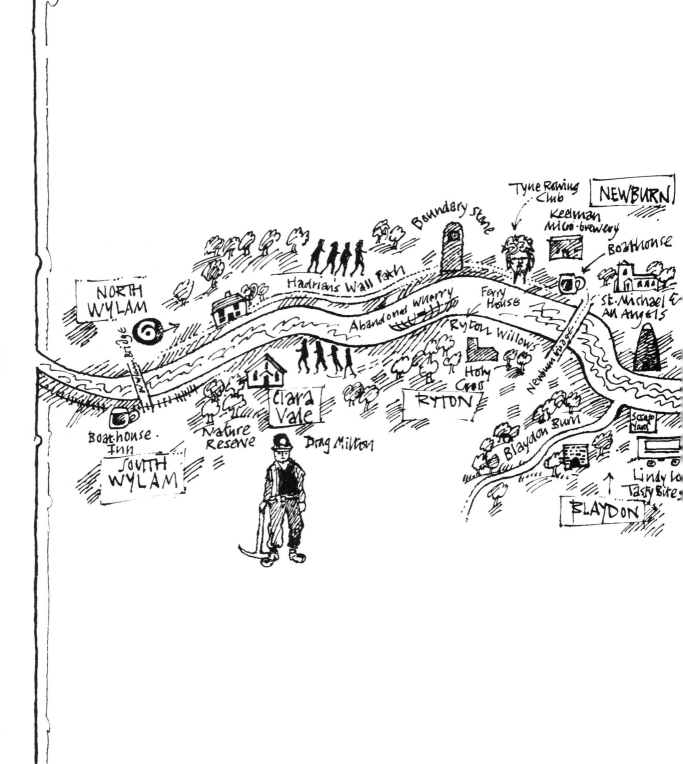

Adamsez
Abandoned rail bridge
Scotswood Bridge
ELSWICK
VICKERS ARMSTRONG
BAE SYSTEMS
Dingy Skipper Butterfly
THE BRIDGES
Redheugh
King Edward
M
7
Scotswood Road
Fiftypubs
Paradise Yard
Dunston Staiths
5
A1.
DUNSTON

DAY ONE

Costafine Town,
It's a fine town,
I'm coming home,
I feel so lonely,
I've been away too long

Costafine Town, Splinter

Our group of walkers stands at the end of the pier, waiting not for a show to begin, but a journey. We are slightly huddled together. It's unseasonably chilly, with strong onshore breezes: welcome to high summer on Tyneside. It is here that we learn our first fact, and hear our first story, of the Tyne Walk 2011, from pier watchman Mel Powles.

Fact: strictly speaking, the piers aren't piers, but breakwaters. Piers are defined as structures of iron or wood that stand on stilts. These structures rest on stone – three million tons of it. Another fact: at 5,317 feet, the south pier is substantially longer than the north, at 3,059. North Shields 0, South Shields 1.

Story: one bright morning during the Great War, a group of soldiers manning a coastal battery by the Collingwood Memorial a mile away on the other side of the river held an artillery exercise. They carefully sighted their gun, calibrated the correct range, lit the blue touch paper and retired. Mel points to the spot where the shell landed – a patch of repaired stonework on the north-western face of the south pier's lighthouse, a bijou version of its sister to the north. Fortunately, this instance of friendly fire caused no injury other than to the reputation of the Royal Artillery. For some reason I think about *Dad's Army* and what the battery commander's Captain Mainwaring might have put in his report. North Shields 1, South Shields 1.

We smile and then do what people do at the end of piers – burrow chins into coats and gaze out to sea. On the horizon to the south east are two tall, strange-looking structures on barges apparently approaching the Tyne. They will reappear in our walk several times over the following days and weeks. We pose for group photos and then start doing what we came for: walking the first part of the long parallelogram between here and the north pier, via Wylam Bridge. There are actually five walkers on this first day – artist Birtley Aris, photographer Charles Bell, poet Christy Ducker, Port of Tyne's chief executive Andrew Moffat, and I.

We walk about 25 yards before we stop. I pause to chat to a large man called Bob, whose massive thumbs are dexterously baiting line for plaice. He reports that fishing's been good these last few weeks. 'Caught a three pounder here last Sunday,' he says, licking his lips. 'By, lovely eating.' Other creatures nearby wouldn't disagree. 'I often see three seals at the river-mouth, fat with salmon.' As he spits out this last observation, it's clear Bob doesn't like seals, and one sight in particular rouses his ire – the creatures taking their rest, no doubt digesting their dinner, on the Black Middens, the notorious rocks near the north shore under the Collingwood Memorial.

Once another fisherman passed this way. One day in 1936, King George VI strolled along the pier in the company of South Shields' Mayor, Charles Henry Smith. The King remarked on the number of men fishing. Mr Mayor pointed out they'd mostly be unemployed, doing something useful with their empty days, and providing their families with fresh, nutritious food. King George ruminated, possibly even stammered as he replied:

'And… do they bring their own bait?'

'Oh aye, Your Majesty,' pronounced Charles Henry Smith, 'their lasses'll have made them up a few sandwiches before they left the house.'

The fact that this anecdote about the cultural disconnection between the central character in the film *The King's Speech* and a son of the Tyne who always spoke with a gleam in his eye was told to me by the latter's grandson, a former Reyrolle's fitter who now alternates between flourishing careers as a consultant in organisational change and legendary pantomime dame, might indicate the serendipitous richness to be found when you go for a walk along a river bank.

Meanwhile my companions are hearing another story from pier watchman Mel: that somewhere beneath our feet a time capsule was buried when the pier was being built. It seems no one is sure exactly where or what it contains, though there is a suspicion that the pier is the last resting place for a teddy bear. We also hear that the Tynemouth pier has its own hidden memento of Victorian childhood, but that is another story, for another day.

The man charged with the intimidating task of designing the piers was a typical eminent Victorian: James Walker was a Scottish engineer responsible for projects as diverse as London's Greenland Dock, the Bishops Rock Lighthouse, Vauxhall Bridge, and the Birmingham Canal; he even had a hand in the building of the Liverpool and Manchester Railway, where he crossed swords with Tyneside's own George Stephenson. In 1859 he was appointed to supervise the building of the piers by the Tyne Improvement Commission (forerunners of the Port of Tyne), but three years later fell out with the bewhiskered commissioners over money, and his contract wasn't renewed. Five years later his piers were wrecked by a great storm – it's said one engineer subsequently took his own life in despair – and it was then

decided their foundations should be deepened and their straight lines turned into sinuous curves. This was harder to achieve than it sounds; it actually took another 28 years to finish the job, with the help of teams of courageous divers, steam cranes manoeuvred into position along specially built railways and hundreds of hard-drinking navvies. But they finally finished the job, and the piers have welcomed travellers into the Tyne ever since.

As we amble along the south pier, I recall the day I started work as the Port's writer in residence and gazed at a document which bleakly sets out why the piers were built, compiled by one Horatio A Adamson, a member of the Tynemouth Volunteer Life Brigade: a list of the 114 ships lost, grounded or damaged at the mouth of the river between 1867 and 1887. Before the piers were built, ships entering or leaving the river had to negotiate a hazardous sand bar – during spring tides it was possible for the intrepid to wade across it at low water – and cope with tricky winds from the north east and south east, especially dangerous during the days of sail. The resulting tragedies were commonplace, captured for all time by local painters like JW Carmichael and John Scott – a glance at one of their angry seascapes is enough to induce a shiver. One entry from Adamson's register will suffice to tell the story: '21 April 1872 – The Brig *Gleaner* of Amble, in coming in, had one of the men at the wheel killed and the mate was washed overboard and drowned. Five of the crew were saved by the *Tom Perry* Lifeboat. Two of the crew of the *Northumberland* Lifeboat, John Wheatley and Jas. Watson, were washed out of her and drowned.'

The provision of lifeboats at the mouth of the Tyne has its roots in a terrible spectacle: in March 1789 a crowd on the beach watched the collier brig *Adventure* break up on the Herd Sands 300 yards away with the loss of all hands. A committee of local worthies, including a coal-owner (and someone we'll meet again soon) called Nicholas Fairles, established a rescue service with the boat *Original*, over the design of which two men, the wonderfully-named Richard Greathead and Willie Wouldhave, fought for the credit. Another disaster, this time in 1849, in which 20 men from the lifeboat *Providence* were lost while trying to rescue the crew of the brig *Betsy*, affected South Shields even more deeply, as all the victims were local Tyne pilots, who left behind 18 destitute widows and 46 children. The tragedy touched the nation; Queen Victoria sent a personal donation of 100 guineas to the appeal fund.

But rescue services didn't end there: like its sister service in Tynemouth, the South Shields Volunteer Life Brigade has for almost 150 years gone to the aid of mariners without using boats. Inside its curiously gabled, clapboarded and mustard-coloured watch-house standing guard at the base of the south pier, there are many stories with happier endings. Flicking on the lights of a long room, Secretary Tom Fennelly tells tales of epic derring-do on countless stormy nights since the Brigade was established in 1866. On the walls of this hidden museum are name boards of wrecked ships – the *Huntsman*, *Blenheim*, *Impulse*, *Olaf Kyrre*, the *Thomas and Elizabeth*; the fair faces of naively-painted figureheads from the *Ploughboy*, the *Blossom* and the Norwegian barque *Salween*; early examples of breeches buoys and other land-based rescue equipment as if designed by Heath Robinson; and ghostly photographs of mighty sailing ships stranded on the Haven beach a few yards away.

And then we come to Sid Clavery's knot collection.

By all accounts, Sid was 'a cantankerous old sod' who worked as a rigger in the Middle Dock a mile upstream and actually lived in his place of work, the riggers' loft. In response to a challenge issued in a pub, he set to and made 'the biggest collection of bends, knots, splices and fancy rope work in the world'. On two display boards are hitches, splices, bell ropes, stop and slip knots – pieces of handiwork so intricate that this ex-Boy Scout, who could never quite remember where the rabbit went after he came up through the hole, can only gaze in wonder. In fact we all stand and stare at for minutes on end; Christy seems particularly fascinated. Maybe it's the rich language of the names of the knots. I'm especially taken by the 'blood bight knot' and 'monkey's fist'. The knots are all made with condenser cord used in the steam engines of *HMS Edinburgh*, a warship repaired in the Middle Dock in 1941. In an apparently rare burst of generosity, Sid presented his collection to the Brigade in 1954 and they've jealously guarded it ever since, despite repeated expressions of interest from the National Maritime Museum.

Up the Norwegian cedar steps of a circular staircase, we find ourselves in the look-out, with windows offering a 360 degree view of sea, river, cliffs and port. I pick up a pair of massive and rather ancient binoculars and look out to sea: a few white horses prance but there'll be no wrecks today. But I give silent thanks to generations of brave men (and now women) over the last 200 years who have gone out into the night, in the teeth of howling winds and angry seas, to bring succour to people of whom they knew nothing except that they needed help.

The binoculars reveal something else: the strange structures we saw on the horizon an hour earlier have moved closer and are composed of immense Meccano-like constructions precariously perched on barges. We'll soon see them closer up.

Next to the Brigade building is a brick building pockmarked by bullet-holes put there by Nazi planes during the Second World War. This is the original Harbour Master's Office – now found near the Fish Quay at North Shields – but now, mostly, an Italian restaurant. Above it is the eyrie of Mel and the other watchmen, where they keep a keen eye on their beloved pier and try to keep their minds off the aroma of lasagne drifting up from below.

lighthouse
at Herd groyne

The first mile of our odyssey completed, we shake hands with Mel. In many ways this former shipyard boilermaker represents a template for the many dozens of Tynesiders we'll meet over the coming days: open, warm and friendly, with an easy smile, curious about we're doing, eager to share his knowledge of his part of the Tyne and his deep feelings for it. We will meet him again, and hear more of his story, on another day, on another pier…

We walk along the little beach of the Herd Sands, which retired Port of Tyne typist Dorothy Tweddell used to visit as a child every summer on trips from Ryton, always punctuated with fish and chips on the beach in the cool of evening, and watch other children, from Villareal Special School in Consett, being towed on inflatables behind a jet-ski and whooping with pleasure. Another kind of a cry tops this, the distinctive *kree-err* of the common tern, diving for fish disturbed by the motor a little further out.

One of the Tyne's most distinctive structures faces us: the rust-red lighthouse at the point of the Herd Groyne, built in 1882 to prevent sand from its beach silting up the river channels. I've lived with this charming building most of my life, in 2-D: 40 years ago my mother and father bought a landscape of the river mouth in which the lighthouse is both chief feature and point of perspective. It was painted by the artist John Peace, whose work I admire so much; not for the first time, nor the last, I must say that we'll come to John anon – when we reach his Lemington home.

Loitering under the lighthouse is a nautically bearded man. Now retired, Duncan Stephenson worked on the river for more than 50 years. He got his start on the last day of 1956, working on a tug with a Stuart Turner engine ('Never forgotten it – we had it singing like a sewing machine'), but soon graduated to the family business in which his father, grandfather, brother and cousins already laboured. He became a foy boatman.

This is an ancient trade, but unlike many other crafts on the river, it still survives. No one has yet found a better way of getting a ship's mooring lines to the shore than tossing them to men in a small boat who then convey them to the jetty. Duncan takes us up the riverside path to the foy boatmen's watch-house – think of a slightly bigger version of a London cabbies' shelter – which was built in 1933 but remains in use. He leans against the railing, grey water slapping the shore eight feet below him, and tells a foy boatman's tale.

'In the old days, the trade used to be unlicensed, and very competitive. When the foy men saw a ship appearing off the piers, they used to race each other, sculling down-river to reach the ship first. Once they got the job, they'd hook onto the stern and hitch a ride back upstream.'

If this sounds hazardous – rather similar to mates of mine who used to get a lift up Matthew Bank on their bikes by grabbing the rail on the open platform of old yellow Newcastle buses – the next stage of the docking operation knocked that into a cocked hat: manoeuvring the tiny boat between the rock of the immensely bigger ship and the hard place of the jetty as they moved closer together. Accidents could and did happen, but Duncan is still here, full of beans in fact, but stumped when I ask about the derivation of 'foy'. I tell him that a place where I used to live bore the motto *Garde Ta Foy*, which means 'keep the faith'. Maybe the foy boatmen were once recognised as people in whom you could place your trust.

Duncan points to a small estate of luxury homes – a ubiquitous development up and down the industrial Tyne – where once stood the British-Mexican (and then the Anglo-American) oil terminal.

'During the war, I used to hang about here because US Navy officers were regular visitors and I cadged spearmint gum and Hershey chocolate bars off them.'

His hand waves in another direction – to the remains of an old jetty he then used to swim off. It was years later when he discovered there'd been a sewage outfall nearby, but like many others who told us of their swimming exploits in the mucky Tyne of old, rosy-cheeked Duncan looks well on it, and buttonholes Andrew, giving him the Stephenson strategy for building trade on the river. The chief executive of the Port of Tyne listens carefully. The rest of us walk on.

The jetty Duncan and his pals used to dive off actually belonged to the Tyne pilots, another ancient, family-based river trade. The jetty was put here for a reason: it's just a hundred steps up to the Lawe Top (Lawe is Scots for hill), the few streets overlooking the river mouth where pilots and their families lived for 200 years. It was here that John Marshall grew up.

Like Duncan Stephenson, John's entire life is bound up with the Tyne. The river is almost part of his DNA. Both grandfathers were pilots, as were his dad, three uncles, and a cousin. In fact John's family – an intertwining of two Scots families, the Marshalls and the Duncans, were working as pilots – guiding ships in and out of the river – as far back as the mid-18th century. And they all lived on the Lawe Top, a vantage point that allowed them to see ships far in the offing.

'I first went out with my dad when I was about eight or nine. There was really no question what I was going to do. The trade had been passed on from generation to generation for centuries, and there seemed to be no reason why that should change.'

But change it did, especially for John. When the Miners' Strike of 1984-85 decimated the Tyne's trade in coal, John was forced to look for work elsewhere and found it in the Arabian Gulf, ironically not far from the home of the Tigris boatmen who were brought to the Tyne by the Romans 2,000 years ago, before coming home to ply his trade in fast-changing home waters once more.

A pilot has to be master of many things: handling the ship, often in difficult weather (when, as John says, 'the seagulls are going backwards'); negotiating the tides, channels and currents of the river; and the diplomacy of working with skippers from all over the world who entrust their ship to his guidance. A degree of nerve is required too – as I've seen myself – for transferring from pilot cutter to ship involves a somewhat hair-raising jump onto a rope-ladder as the two vessels are moving side by side, often in heavy seas.

'You have to be adept at reading people as well as the conditions, but it's often easier berthing a supertanker than taking a little ship into a narrow dock. Often you'd finish a job and feel the tension drain out of you.'

As the 90s progressed, the river's coal trade died. On 20 March 1998, John piloted the last collier to take coal from the Tyne, the *Lord Citrine* – he picked a piece from the deck as a souvenir and uses it every New Year's Eve as his first-foot gift – and then quite remarkably piloted the very first ship to bring coal *into* the Tyne, the *Antonie Oldendorff* on 18 June 2004. This trade – to fuel the power stations of Yorkshire – has grown ever since.

Now retired from pilotage, John's long family link with the Tyne has been severed. Neither of his children has become river pilots. Indeed John wryly remembers the time his daughter asked him a question that would have been unthinkable a generation before: 'What is coal, Dad?'

'Things change. Some industries die and others come along to take their place. The river will always be an important part of Tyneside. This is my place, my life. I often think of all those still mornings I'd bring a ship between the piers into the Tyne, the Cheviot Hills far in the distance. What a privilege it was!'

We clatter back down the steps, pausing to take in the curious shape of the Lawe Top beacon of 1832, and make our way past the Marine School, now part of South Tyneside College, a place with such a reputation for training sailors it attracts students from all over the world.

Ahead of us once stood the yard of the shipbuilders and repairers Rennoldson's, but we turn west and make our way along the incongruously named Wapping Street, heart of South Shields' historic boatbuilding trade – all those local pilots, fishermen and foy men needed craft that were well-made but inexpensive.

Along this narrow cul-de-sac are a series of wooden sheds, blackened with many applications of creosote. A door to one of them hangs open, and being a nosy type, I poke my head inside and shout out a hello.

A friendly voice calls back, 'Howay in then!'

So I step inside, and what greets my eye is the nearest to an Aladdin's Cave that Tyneside can offer – and the most interesting collection of clutter I've seen in many a long year.

A long, slightly dim interior, perhaps 60 feet long by 30 feet wide. The roof works on one side of the shed, but doesn't on the other: strips of plastic sheeting lift in the breeze – working over there in the rain, the chances are you'd get wet. On the opposite wall is a tool shed, though to describe it thus is like calling the Louvre a large building – there must an implement in there for every conceivable task for a craftsman working with wood, metal and engine. Above it, on a wide balcony, is a wood store, and machines for cutting, turning, planing and shaping timber, as well as a very satisfying pile of shavings and dust. Here are two tons of oak from Gracethwaite Sawmills by Lake Windermere, and a stack of mahogany from Devon. Elsewhere there are coils of rope, piles of driftwood, and a stove that's lit with a few handfuls of oak shavings. It has a tiny hand-made oven attached that's just the perfect size for baked potatoes – apart from good eating, there's nothing like a hot tatie for warming the hands on a winter's day by the river.

On the other side of the century-old shed, under the flapping plastic, running from the small street door to a pair of metal gates, is a gently sloping slipway, in which nestles a boat, and inside it is the man who bid us enter, a man with an open, guileless face. His name is Fred Crowell, the last repairer of wooden boats between Amble and Hull. He holds a strip of oak, and whorls of steam rise gently up from the small machine that's slowly bending the wood into the curved shape of the interior of the boat.

The *George Elmy* is a Liverpool-class lifeboat built in the Isle of Wight in 1949 and assigned to work out of Seaham Harbour. One winter's night in 1962 its crew of five took it out into a storm to look for a missing fishing coble, but on its return to harbour it was engulfed by a massive wave and capsized, with the loss of all hands, drowned within a few yards of the shore. The boat was recovered for use by several generations of fishermen before being spotted by a Seaham man at a Holyhead marine auction and subsequently bought by the East Durham Heritage Trust to grace the entrance to Seaham Marina. Fred has the job of restoring it – it'll take him the best part of a year – and tells its story while getting on with his work (unlike President Ford, he can walk and chew gum at the same time), moving nimbly around the shell of the interior. When this is commented on, Fred smiles: 'Aye, boatbuilders have to have feet like budgies.'

But his work is soon interrupted under interrogation from his guests. Fred patiently explains the detail of his craft: the clenching of a copper

CALOR GAS

Crancroff
boatyard

nail with a 'roved rivet' – the one he makes is sitting on the desk as I write; caulking the seams of the hull with twisted strands of cotton to prevent leaks; placing those strips of oak in opposing 'double diagonal' directions, which means lighter wood can be used, making the boat easier to handle. We note water lapping under the metal gates in front of the bow of the *George Elmy* and Fred starts explaining the tidal cycle to Christy with bits of wood representing the moon, the earth and the sun, which brings us neatly to the issue of what happens when a really high tide comes calling at Fred's shed.

'Sometimes it gets that high it's nearly enough to float me boat! But I know it's coming of course and I move all me equipment upstairs. This is a pain, but sometimes the sea offers a reward. One morning I came in and found a 12 by 12", 44-foot-long piece of pitch pine bumping against the river gate. I brought it inside and used the lot. Nothing's ever thrown away here.'

In the hour we're with him this is the only obvious thing Fred has to say, but he produces a final surprise. I've already come to sense that this is a man who can make anything – everything from beautiful gardens to gate-posts for the National Trust – a theory confirmed when Fred learns that Christy is a poet. 'You're a poet?' asks Fred, slight awe in his voice. He hurries into the tool-room and emerges with a file of papers, which he thrusts into Christy's hands: the poems he's written about the various boats he's repaired.

'I'm working on a boat often for a year or so and I get to know her intimately. So when it's time to let go, it's really hard. I get this ache inside. Writing something about that boat is a way of dealing with me feelings.' He smiles ruefully. 'Daft, isn't it?'

His attention is caught by the sight of Birtley sitting on a stool at the stern of the *George Elmy*, executing a rapid but quite exquisite watercolour of its sinuous curves, and the captivating interior of Fred's shed. The man himself leans over Birtley's shoulder, shaking his head in quiet wonder.

There's something touching about the sight of one master craftsman admiring the work of another.

It's time to drag ourselves away; we've a journey to make. Fred tells us to call again. Maybe we'll get a hot tatie next time.

Once there were twelve firms on the Tyne repairing wooden boats – Fred served his time with Robson's – but now he's the last, though his matchless skills are being passed on, in another way.

Next door is another blackened wooden shed, this time belonging to the North East Maritime Trust, a charity set up in 2005. Another lifeboat is under repair here – the *Henry Frederick Swan*, a former RNLI Lifeboat at Tynemouth – this time not by an individual but a cheerful crew of volunteers, many retired from careers in the maritime or engineering trades. The Trust's treasurer, former ship's master Tim West, walks us around the boat, built in 1917, in service till 1947, then used by many generations of Sea Scouts on the rivers Aln and Tyne and now being restored with the help of a £6,000 grant from the Port of Tyne's Community Fund.

There's a cheery air of camaraderie in this space as about a dozen men of a certain age work on the *Swan*, the Whitburn salmon boat *Spring Tide* and various fishing cobles. It's also home to the handsome little foy boat *Joan*, which happens to have been built in this very shed in 1920. The Trust has 135 members and a hard core of about 15 who work on the boats, including a boilermaker, carpenter, drayman, and marine engineer. Tim himself is a retired ship's master, who first came to the Tyne in 1960 – he remembers that such was the density of shipping, he had to climb over three other ships to reach the quay – and never quite left. The men are largely self-taught, finding lateral ways to circumvent problems, like the prohibitive cost of buying iron bolts and other metalwork: they bought a forge and taught each other to use it.

'None of us has boat-building experience but we're all fascinated by it. We learn by trial and error, and when we get really stuck we go next door and watch Fred. In return he comes in here to use our loo!'

A useful reminder on a long walk. We use the facilities and go.

⚓ TRADITION

Crowell's Boatyard, South Shields

It's what you make of it. Take it
or leave it a scatter of planks,
a leoparding wreck. Take it
you'll sweat yourself purple trying
to steam mahogany into ribs,
flare the frame like a giant's holding
of breath. Prepare to hop for miles
on feet that must be *budgie-like*.

If you're to clinch it, free from harm,
heel at the gaps with cotton caulk
before you deck it in flash
and gloss for the day you launch it –
back on the Tyne, *The George Elmy*,
your craft that weighs ten ton yet floats.

⚓

Fifty yards upstream, where Wapping Lane opens out into a small square, there's a street sign that makes us scratch our heads: it turns out 'Comical Corner' is a reference not to a meeting place for local wags, but to the first bend of the river nearby where the awkwardness of the river currents caused steering difficulties for incoming sailing ships. Further on, we encounter a call centre where the phones no longer ring and our second estate of up-market riverside homes, bisected by what was a dock and is now I suppose a superior water feature: the remnants of Brigham and Cowan's ship repair yard, founded in 1874 and finally closed in 1982. Something else of this Victorian enterprise survives not far away – the Brigham and Cowan Social Club, where old workmates gather together to reminisce and sup (allegedly) the cheapest beer on the Tyne.

Out on the river, a Tyne ferry leaves its station on the north shore and sets a diagonal course for its pontoon on the south. The proliferation of bridges and tunnels over the last 150 years has gradually reduced the number of Tyne ferries between Ryton and the sea from some 30 to this one survivor. At one time North and South Shields actually had three of their own: the Whitehill point ferry, the so-called Horse-and-Cart, and the 'Halfpenny Dodger', which landed at Comical Corner. They survive in the fond memories of many of the folk of both Shields.

The Halfpenny Dodger was popular for obvious reasons – it was cheap, and consequently used by itinerant French onion men and Cullercoats fish-wives with baskets of caller-herring they hoped to empty south of the river. The Horse and Cart ferry was popular with drinkers who capitalised on the different licensing hours in North and South Shields. They'd evacuate the Northumberland Arms, a last consolation for departing sailors, descend to the 10pm ferry, arriving at the south side where another 20 minutes' drinking time was to be had in the Ferry Inn at the top of the gangway. This ritual is maintained by one Paul Younger, mining engineer and pro-vice chancellor at Newcastle University, who once a year leads his pals on a pub crawl of the two Shields linked by the ferry, where the group entertains fellow passengers with song, and punctuated by a curry on Ocean Road, an event known as the Trans-Tyne Tipple. Glynis Barrie has her own reason for remembering the ferry, which once connected home and work: 'I lived at the top of Borough Bank in North Shields but worked in South Shields. I used to leave the house at 8.25am, run down the bank for the 8.30am ferry, and the skipper would shout, 'OK, she's on board – lift the drawbridge, we can gan now!'

The surviving ferry is operated by Nexus (meaning 'link' in Greek), carrying half a million passengers a year on the *Spirit of the Tyne* and *Pride of the Tyne*, the last boat built at Swan Hunter's in 1992. More than once I heard the same story about her: all the scrap metal left lying around the site was used on the *Pride*, including armour plating left over from the building of warships. This story may be comforting to travellers, but it isn't the favourite of ferry-master Ken Whitfield.

'Crossing from north to south one quiet evening, a dolphin came alongside and swam in front of us, criss-crossing the bow. All the passengers went to look. Like a dream it was.'

Just up the bank from the ferry landing is a new building largely of glass that juts out towards the river on a piece of land that once offered an open vista of water, sky and North Shields. This is the 'BT Centre of Excellence', attracted here by South Tyneside Council in return for the contracting-out to BT of various management services. Some have praised the council for bringing jobs to the town, but the building is by no means universally popular. Bob Stott, management consultant, pantomime dame and grandson of the Mayor who baffled George VI, dislikes it: 'The council has robbed the people of South Shields of one of the town's great glories – a wonderful view of its river, and for what? Another call centre. What poverty of imagination!'

A little way upstream are two solidly mid-Victorian stone buildings, the Customs House and the Tyne Port Health Authority, standing in front of a row of buildings of similar vintage in the curiously named street, Mill Dam. This small area has many associations with sea-farers, the earliest being the possibility that a branch of the Tyne estuary once branched south east to the sea, leaving the rest of what became South Shields as an island. Hereabouts sailors lodged, fed, drank, were hired and occasionally rioted: in 1930 there were disturbances involving local men affected by the world slump, and Yemeni sailors who had settled in the town. This community still flourishes: it was for this reason that Mohammed Ali came to Shields in 1977 to have his marriage blessed in the newly-established mosque (I know because I was there…).

Since I became the Port's writer in residence, I've come to regard South Tyneside as the one borough of Tyneside's quartet that most strongly identifies itself with river and sea. I suppose this is partly because it has six miles of coast and three miles of river-bank, partly to the feeling that it's the borough with the most distinctive character. In many ways it's a place apart, as Janis Blower would testify. She's what they call in Shields a 'skuet-ender', brought up near a row of fishing huts once used for curing fish ('skuet' being an ancient word, possibly even Norse, for this trade). Not that she ever cured any fish herself, though both her father and brother went to sea with a famous Tyneside company called Stag Lines, which was why their house was painted in their colours. Not that this was an inward-looking community: Janis's family had neighbours from Norway, Greece, Spain and Germany, and Shields developed its own community of Shetlanders as well as Yemenis.

When Janis went to work, she stayed in touch with the culture of the river and sea as a reporter for the town's paper, the *Shields Gazette* (it once bore the sub-title *& Shipping Telegraph)* and nearly 40 years later she's still there, having done just about every job in its newsroom, including a long-running column called *On The Waterfront* (between ads for merchant navy uniforms and ships' butchers) and most interesting of all, a heavily-used feature called *Readers' Requests*.

'Families of sailors would write in, asking for the whereabouts of ships their husband, son or boyfriend were on and we'd check with Lloyd's of London to find out its last and next port of call.'

Why these men kept their families in the dark about where they were, let alone what they were doing, can only be imagined. Janis smiles. 'I couldn't really say.'

Perhaps one of the roots of the strong attachment so-called 'Sand-dancers' have to their town lies in the fact that until recently a good proportion of its men spent their working lives away at sea. The feeling of loss and longing this created is reflected perfectly in Splinter's Top 20 hit of the early 70s quoted at the top of this chapter, a ballad of praise to 'Costafine Town', the area of Shields around Commercial Road: 'I feel so lonely, I've been away too long.' (Have a listen on YouTube: there's a guitar contribution from George Harrison, who signed Splinter to his Dark Horse label.)

Alan Mulvain was one of these many seamen. He used to hang about the Mill Dam, at first as a would-be sailor. He served his apprenticeship as a shipwright repairing colliers at Dowson's yard at Tyne Dock in the early 50s, but came from a seafaring family and in his teens became desperate to join his father and four brothers at sea.

'Every lunch-time I'd cycle down to the Seamen's Pool at Mill Dam and every day they'd say, there's nothing for you, lad. The Pool Office was down a side street, the union office next door. But at last I went down one day and the man said there was a job on a ship on the Thames but I had to be down there that day and I had to get me release from Dowson's. Then I had to get to Newcastle to catch a train to London and make my way to Tilbury. I'd never been to London and no idea where Tilbury was. I jumped in a taxi. The taxi was going along and the driver asked where I was going and when I told him he stopped his cab and asked me how much money I had. When I told him he slung me out. I'd no idea how I was going to get to my ship, but a copper was passing and he told me where to get a train to Tilbury.

So I got to the ship and got the job and my book was stamped November 5th 1953. I tell you, I never forgot that Guy Fawkes night.'

Over the next 13 years Alan sailed all over the world in many ships, taking in all kinds of sights and experiences, getting a first-hand look at a rapidly changing world: the growth of the Cold War, China's Cultural Revolution, the evils of apartheid in South Africa and the slow dismemberment of the British Empire. He experienced a fair bit of weather and might have had the occasional drink. But it was only in the last few years that these memories re-surfaced and Alan started getting up in the darkness of sleepless nights to write them down in nearly illegible long-hand. The end result is *Chippy Swinging The Lamp*, published in secret by his family – the reason why he came ashore all those years ago – and presented to him one recent Christmas.

'Me, an author! I tell you, I was amazed, and very touched. The best Christmas present I ever had.'

There are far fewer mariners based in Shields now, the result of the gradual withering of the British merchant fleet over the last 40 years, but there is a fine monument by the Mill Dam to their endeavour and courage. We stand by it, paying our own tribute, then remember that though we've barely walked three miles, we're starving. We head for the Customs House nearby. No declarations are made here now, no charges levied, except in the bar and the box office, for the Customs House is now the town's arts and entertainment centre, run by local boy and pantomime legend ('Tommy' to Bob Stott's 'Dame Dotty') Ray Spencer, who once fished for sprats off the quay here and whose upstairs office faces upstream, overlooking a vast empty site bounded by a high wall: once the Middle Dock, a place where ships were repaired for two centuries. This was where Ray's dad worked virtually his entire adult life; also where a 16-year-old local lad called Fred Newman went to work as a junior cost clerk and errand boy on 13 September 1965.

At that time the Middle Dock and Engineering Company was a family business run by the President of the Rugby Football Union, Sir Lawrence Edwards, with the help of a bowler-hatted Scot called Willie McMinnagle. It was less than 50 years ago, but Fred's memories summon up another age, almost a different planet.

'The entrance to the dock's offices was lined with wood panelling and marble. A uniformed commissionaire used to hang about there, a chap called Jack Brown who'd been injured in a yard accident and given this light job. I was in there once and heard a bell ring – Jack disappeared for five minutes, as it turned out to put coal on Sir Lawrie's fire. That was one of his jobs, along with filling the old boy's fountain pen.'

Thus the yard enshrined the British class system, but it did have its advantages for junior employees. Sir Lawrie's son-in-law was on the board of the Shields Commercial Building Society, which was how the young Fred Newman got his precious first mortgage.

In those days the Middle Dock served all kinds of shipping – tankers, sugar boats, Palm Line banana boats and the tail end of the whaling fleet. It had four docks and two quays and it wasn't uncommon for ten ships to be worked on at once.

'The yard didn't actually employ an estimator to price up jobs. Owners just booked in their ships without bothering to go to tender. The British fleet was still flourishing and it was a cash-rich business, but I don't reckon there was much investment. The yard had its own launch and every day it would go up and down the Tyne and someone would fill in a ledger with a note of all the ships at all the berths. The river was that busy, it took quite a while,' says Fred.

During these years Ray Spencer's dad worked at the Middle Dock as a caulker-burner – indeed most of the men on the Biddick Hall Estate where he lived were river folk. Many of his childhood memories relate to the yard as a source of bounty.

'Dad was always bringing stuff home. When ships came in for repair the galley would be emptied and he'd appear with all these cans of food without labels – we didn't know what was in them till we opened them. We used to chop sticks with this great big flensing knife from a Salvesen whaler. Once he brought me a whale's tooth he'd found. Things we used in the house like toasting forks and pokers were made in the yards and during the power cuts of the 70s Dad brought home carbon lamps with fantastically bright lights. He took his bait in an old gas mask bag he'd used in the Home Guard and he'd come home with it filled with wooden chocks we burned in winter.' Ray laughs. 'No wonder they went bust!'

It seems incredible in retrospect, but only 20 years separate the years of plenty when Fred Newman was a 'snotty-nosed kid' at the Middle Dock and they were turning away work, and its eventual closure in 1986, after mounting losses, numerous changes of ownership and innumerable rounds of 'crisis talks'. In the 30 years between 1970 and 2000, the Tyne and its industries were hit by a perfect storm. The loss of the British merchant fleet and then growing international competition in ship-repair and ship–building were first to sweep up the river. The shockingly rapid closure of the coal industry, and the loss of its historic trade on the Tyne, represented a second wave of despoliation. But before we get overly sentimental about what is in any case a historical fact, Ray Spencer offers another perspective:

'By the time he finished, Dad had gone deaf from the incredible noise of the yard and dodgy knees from 40 years of kneeling on the job. He also had industrial white finger. He retired at 57 and was dead at 62.'

Despite this, there are obvious regrets. Ray points to the fact that young people come all over the world to take courses at the Marine School, but they have more difficulty recruiting locally, though he has high hopes for the popularity of a new course for cruise ships, which need hairdressers and entertainers from the *X-Factor* generation as well as engineers and navigators. Another loss, he believes, is the sense of satisfaction that came from using hard-won skills to make difficult things.

'I remember standing in front of the Customs House the evening the *Ark Royal* left for the last time. An old man with a Union Jack on his shoulder pointed to a section of rail on the ship and said, 'I made that.'

'This is still a place with pride and social cohesion. It's just we lack focal points for it. When Westoe Colliery produced a million tons a year for the first time there was a sense of communal satisfaction. The same when ships left the river.'

Ray falls silent, then brightens again and points, physically and meta-phorically, to the enduring success of Nissan and its car terminal upstream – our designated end point today. We'd better get on our way there.

For the first time we're forced to detour away from the river, following the long perimeter wall of the Middle Dock, passing the carcass of the Commercial Hotel, where many of its employees once drank, and make our way towards a riverside enterprise that still survives. McNulty's constructs and refurbishes structures for the offshore energy industries. After a safety talk – we put on hats, boots and high visibility jackets – Sasha Keyworth shows us around their current workload: an accommodation module for the Talisman Auk oilfield and a sub-station for wind farms off the Lincolnshire coast. As if on cue, the 150-foot tall rusting structures we saw earlier – rig top-sides from the Indefatigable Field in the southern North Sea – make their stately way upstream on barges, with sea-weed still attached.

We climb an apparently endless temporary stairway, and look out over the river. At the eastern end of the yard is a crumbling white house, once the home of the Dock Master and family, now rather resembling Anthony Perkins' house in *Psycho*. Nearby there are huge tent structures for blasting steel structures before painting; under them live a family of foxes, who patrol the yard when everyone else goes home. Kestrels nest high in the modules, much as they would in a cathedral spire – there must be plenty of rodent food down below. Kittiwakes nest here too, but to see their nests we leave the yard and make our way to the other side of a vast brick engine shop, now rented for storage. Something stops us in our tracks: an impressive metal plaque set into a brick wall in memory of the war-dead workers of John Readhead Ltd, the shipyard that occupied the McNulty's site until the mid-80s. We stand and stare – Charles taking an inevitable photograph – as it also seems like a memorial to the 600 ships Readhead's built in its 100-year history. Most remarkably, in that time no less than 87 vessels – tramp steamers, the labourers of the oceans – were built for another family firm, Edward Hain of St Ives, Cornwall, all of their names beginning with the Cornish prefix *Tre-*, a reminder of how personal ties once sustained business relationships.

Past the Readhead engine shop is a pair of vast rusting gates, usually left slightly ajar, leading to one of my favourite spots on the river – a disused slipway that over time has become a flotsam beach. Charlie takes photos, Birtley likewise (he might sketch the scene at home later), Christy ruminates, while I scribble in my notebook and take in the view of Tyne Dock, our next destination. Above us, the window ledges of the engine shop house kittiwake nests and in front, the slipway affords a wonderful view upriver. Over the years it's also become a slightly treacherous playground for generations of children. Here, more than 60 years ago, former Port of Tyne cleaner Norma Spink came in a new white dress her mother had bought her for a special family event – she slipped out of the house while her parents were getting ready – and watched a group of children playing on steps at the water's edge. You may already sense what's coming next – and you're right. Into the water went Norma in her spotless dress, she howled in terror – not being able to swim – and some boys had to rescue her. She was still crying when she arrived home after a miserable trudge home, but that, as she ruefully remembers now, was only the beginning…

Up the road, we don another set of hard hats, yellow jackets and pit-yacker boots and are taken into the care of security man David Lee as we enter the eastern end of the Port of Tyne's vast 300-acre Tyne Dock site, crossing an area of once-contaminated land now reclaimed and known for some reason in these parts as Hill 60. On our right is a low, nondescript building which contains a rather remarkable story – uplifting and optimistic too, after the sad tale of the rapid death of the Middle Dock.

Ford Aerospace makes precision components for aircraft, helicopters in particular. In difficult economic times, it's basking in the relative security of a £9 million contract to supply Westland Helicopters for the next three years. Ninety-five people work on this site, 56 on another. So far, so good – but what elevates this hi-tech enterprise in this age of globalisation is the strength of its commitment to the local community.

The family firm is run by Geoff Ford, a dapper man with neat grey hair, and was set up by his grandfather in 1910 after he lost the ends of two fingers at work, was sacked by his employers, and decided to set up on his own. Originally a general engineering company, Ford's developed a brass corrugated steam joint called the Taylor's ring, then in the early 80s the company diversified into the aerospace industry. Most of the manufacturing is done in a spotless workshop by large computerised machines, but there's also a manual machine shop for small batches. If the edge of a disused coal dock seems an unlikely setting for a high-technology company, it makes perfect sense to Geoff Ford.

'I'm a Sand-dancer and proud of it. We're deeply aware of our responsibility to South Tyneside, the smallest metropolitan authority in the country. Every day 45,000 people leave the borough to work and only 15,000 come in. We have to change that, for the sake of the rich pool of talent here.'

As an example he points to young Callum Loftus, who recently won the Robert Ford Memorial Prize for Business Studies at South Tyneside College and was promptly snapped up to start an engineering apprentice-ship. The company currently has seven apprentices, including four adults who've taken a pay cut to learn new skills. With the support of South Tyneside College, the company is also creating the Ford Aerospace Engineering Academy to help prevent the loss of the legendary engineering skills of Tyneside.

BELOW
Port of Tyne security man David Lee.

'Young people need to be enthused about manufacturing because I truly believe that's where our future must lie, and if we do that I'm sure we have an excellent future,' says Geoff.

With this determination to invest in people as well as technology – the company also operates a profit-sharing scheme – Ford Aerospace is a growing enterprise that sets an impeccable example. It's early days yet, but Geoff Ford has already laid a claim to the title, Hero of the Tyne Walk 2011.

On the way out there's another human touch that makes me smile. The company has found an answer to the problem of how to store the small and fragile aluminium components they make for helicopters: they stack them in egg boxes.

We cross a road towards the water, and the entrance to a dock. A pilot cutter awaits a call from an incoming ship and a rather less elegant Port vessel is tied up: the *Clearwater* buzzes up and down the river collecting driftwood, 80 per cent of it recycled. A foy boat is having its wiring repaired and a fishing coble is being rebuilt. Out in the river the bed is being lowered to accommodate bigger vessels at Riverside Quay upstream. The vessel *Cork Sand* is moored, having her hold emptied of hundreds of tons of dredged material into a fleet of Caterpillar lorries, which then dump the spoil no more than a hundred yards away. Land is being reclaimed from water here, with 700,000 cubic metres of Tyne mud. This is the end of Tyne Dock, and standing gazing at the expanse of earth, I feel compelled to burst spontaneously into verse:

> *The summer season at Tyne Dock*
> *Lifted my boyhood in a crane*
> *Above the shaggy mining town*
> *Above the slaghills and the rocks*
> *Above the middens in back lanes*
> *And wooden hen-huts falling down*

Most of my life ago, I had a teacher at Sandyford Road Junior School called Miss Charters, a bird-like woman with a voice like a tiny bell, which often rang out poems she loved. *Tyne Dock* by Francis Scarfe was a favourite of hers – I suspect she may have come from South Shields – and mine. There was something about its language that was familiar and its air of melancholy that wasn't. It also connected with a regular family outing. Every so often I'd go with my parents to visit their friends Jack and Mary Maddison in South Shields and I always loved sitting on the top deck of the Newcastle bus and passing through what Catherine Cookson called 'the five great slime-filled' Tyne Dock arches – part of an intricate system of rail lines bringing coal to the 59-acre Dock – and catching glimpses of the secret world inside.

Tyne Dock was opened by the Tyne Improvement Commission in 1859 and had an immediate impact, with the later building of Dunston Staithes and Wallsend's Northumberland Dock, on the growth of coal exports from the Tyne over the next 40 years from four to twelve million tons a year, powering Thames power stations, European gas-works, Indian mills and American railways. Coaling stations for ships throughout the oceans of the world were fed with Newcastle coal; 'West Hartley coal' was as familiar a term to foreign buyers as 'Wallsend Main' was to a householder in Penge. This great trading edifice was entirely dependent on the speed of the Tyne staiths; but the Tyne Dock system, whereby wagons were fed through a dizzying system of gravity-fed lines and loops to the drops where the colliers waited, transcended efficiency: it was a thing of beauty that beguiled generations, small boys especially.

The actor Ron Cook spent his early years within sight and sound of the Dock in the early fifties until his dad got a job in a Midlands car plant and they moved to Coventry. He desperately missed the sea and the river, but it was another loss that kept him awake at night: he missed the familiar, comforting clank and bump of the coal wagons as they rolled down towards the water. Robert Forster, known to his friends as Bertie, was also brought up nearby and remembers cycling into the dock with sandwiches for his dad, who after skippering a Tyne tug became Lock Master at the Dock, wearing an imposing black uniform with a cap from a marine outfitter's in Portsmouth. The dock gates, with leather ball on a pole to indicate to incoming ships whether they were open or shut, were quite a responsibility: they were designed and built by Robert Stephenson, with hydraulics from Lord Armstrong.

Bertie regularly visited the Dock for another reason: nearby was the dock where iron ore was unloaded onto wagons bound for the steel works at Consett nine miles away, and his Uncle Stan often took him for a ride in the cab of his mighty 9-F steam loco, stained red with iron dust. Bertie remembers the long climb and the exhaustion of the firemen, often old men who'd failed to make it as drivers, whose job was to feed the insatiable beast with coal. At the end of the long haul, they'd slake their thirst with bottles of Newcastle Brown.

In time, both exports of coal and imports of iron came to an abrupt end, and Tyne Dock received no more vessels; apart from anything else, it was too small for the new generation of bulk carriers. So the Port have done what made business sense – filling in the Dock, making room for new developments, but in a decidedly clever way: by taking spoil displaced by the building of the new Tyne Tunnel and pumping it directly into the Dock. First, however, they had to think about its inhabitants, and arranged for the marine life to be carefully gathered up and released into the river. For the record, here's what was lurking in Tyne Dock:

- 413 shore crab
- 3 lobster
- 11 cod
- 487 pollack
- 95 eel

- 12 common goby
- 6 herring
- 3 plaice
- 2 long-spined sea scorpion
- 1 viviparous blenny

That single little blenny sounds insignificant by the way, but it's remarkable in two ways: the female fish is a parent on a heroic scale – it gives birth to between 3,000-4,400 live young; used by scientists to detect and measure toxins, the blenny's presence is also a sign the river is healthy – a fishy equivalent of the kingfisher.

So the fish at Tyne Dock are gone, and the small boys are gone, but there's still coal nearby – lots of it – though it's not leaving the Tyne, but entering it. Passing mountains of silvery cubes and rusting scrap (of which more later), we gaze at three immense cranes at the waterside and a system of conveyors leading to a three-quarter-mile-long coal dump with nine different bays. These facilities were built in 2004 after the port signed a ten-year agreement with Drax power stations in South Yorkshire, six years after the old plant for the export of coal was dismantled and sold to the New Zealand port of Nelson. Each bay holds cargoes from different ships, to keep separate coal with varying sulphur levels. This is a valuable business for the Port, but also, in the view of the river's history, rich in irony.

As we contemplate the Cheviot Hill of coal, I tell my companions about the *MV Miho Pracat* and coal train 6H93. A few months earlier, I went on board the former and rode in the cab of the latter to find out more about this new trade, and the huge journeys that make it possible. On this particular one there had first been other trains, to bring coal from the Kuznetsk Basin in south west Siberia, home of the biggest coal deposits in the world, to the port of Ust-Luga near St Petersburg, where 58,000 tons were loaded on board the Croatian ship skippered by a genial chain-smoker called Davor Mojsic, who piloted it across an ice-strewn Baltic and intemperate North Sea to the Tyne. Almost 1,400 tons of this cargo were then loaded on board a GB Railfreight train composed of 21 wagons and powered by locomotive 66712, glamorously named *Peterborough Signalbox*, for the last leg of an epic journey. I went with it – and not simply because I've always loved trains.

At the start of the 120-mile journey, I sat beside driver Mark Harrison in a cab that positively throbbed with the din from the vast V10 engine behind us. We pulled slowly up the climb from the dock to join the coastal route from Newcastle to Middlesbrough at Brockley Whins, slipped through Heworth and Felling and then joined the main East Coast route at the end of the King Edward Bridge in Gateshead. From there we rattled south, crossing the Durham Viaduct, the pit village of Ferryhill, where I spent the first few years of my life (and learnt to love steam locos), Darlington and York, and then turned in a giant loop to the Drax cooling towers – the warm ponds at their base allegedly home to huge eels – and followed a giant circle towards the bunkers. Trains were ahead of us and behind us from the ports of Hull, Immingham and Redcar as well as Tyne Dock. Finally the train entered a long shed and one by one the wagons were emptied of their cargo, Siberian coal dropping into underground bunkers and then sent to a crushing mill, where a steel ball crushed the dusty coal into fine particles. This was then blown into one of six giant generating burners.

Finally I learnt a strange and beguiling fact: the coal that's taken 12 days

to reach its destination is usually vapourised before the train that's brought it on the final leg has even left the Drax site.

This reversal of the Tyne's historic trade may seem incomprehensible to many, especially the bringing of coal halfway around the world to a place that still has huge reserves underground, but it's an indisputable fact that a port can't create an industry, it can only service it, and this Port is doing well out of these imports. In 2011 more than two million tons of foreign coal were handled, and that's not taking into account the further import of almost a million tons of bio-fuels (wood pellets to you and me, mostly from the USA), which also make their way to Drax, via a new store at the Tyne Dock site.

Many times during our walk we met people who claimed they rarely saw ships on the Tyne nowadays. This may be true, up to a point, but the statement lacks context. The majority of the Tyne's river traffic is concentrated in the last mile of its journey to the sea, nearly all in the last three miles. This is because the ships are immensely bigger than they were in Tyne Dock's heyday. In July 2011, the biggest ship ever to enter the Tyne, the 750-foot long *Alam Penting*, docked at the newly deepened Riverside Quay, carrying 75,000 tons of coal from New Orleans: this was getting on for a hundred times the size of a cargo of a classic Tyne collier of 1900.

It's late afternoon, and proud Port chief executive Andrew Moffat and cheery security man David Lee lead the slightly weary walkers past rows of Hitachi excavators made in Hebburn to the last facility on their site; last but certainly not least – the Nissan terminal.

On three berths of varying sizes, a team of local drivers move around half a million vehicles a year from a vast car park and up ramps and onto an endless procession of slab-shaped car carriers. These members of a fleet prefixed *City of-* may not be the pinnacle of the naval architect's art, but they're certainly ubiquitous on the river, often to be seen anchored off Tynemouth, waiting for a berth and taking a break in their constant shuttle between the Tyne and the Continent.

This evening the six decks of the *City of Lutece*, registered in Valetta, is being loaded with 600 Jukes and Qashqais. Its bigger sisters, the so-called 'mother ships', hold six times as many. We climb the ramp onto the stern, vehicles whizzing past, and watch the operation for a few minutes. Two Ukrainian crewmen greet us – their fellows are mostly from Syria and the Lebanon – but given that they can't speak English and we can't speak Ukrainian, conversation is limited. In any case it's too noisy. But when I ask how they like Newcastle, one smiles and makes an international swigging gesture with his elbow. How he manages a drink, I'm not sure – the boat's barely in port for six hours, and then it's off again to another car park in an unknown city by the sea. What a strange life…

We make the final leg of our day's journey along a system of metal walkways called Dolphin No 1 towards the mouth of the River Don. On our left is the Nissan terminal, where vast quantities of Scandinavian timber used to season on Jarrow Slake – before being used to prop up seams in the region's pits – and local children, including Catherine Cookson, jumped from log to log in a perilous game they called 'jumping the piano'. A dunking in the black water, or mud, of the Slake wasn't the only risk they ran; watchmen used to patrol the ponds from floating sheds. Nearby a solitary vessel was once moored; on this hospital ship sailors who arrived on the Tyne with some noisome disease recovered – or died. It was only reachable by boat.

Standing on Bollard No 63, looking up the Don and across to Bede's World, I make the last observation of the day in my notebook: the melancholy calls of redshank and curlew.

Below our feet, great slabs of grey stone are piled in a breakwater almost as impressive as the one we saw at the end of the pier. But these great stones are cut in neat right angles; indeed it turns out they've been recycled: the remains of those famous railway arches are still performing a service not far from Tyne Dock.

Which makes me think again of the poem, and its writer. Francis Scarfe was a South Shields boy orphaned by a small tragedy at sea, a bright lad who finished his inter-war education at Cambridge and the Sorbonne, became a Parisian literary figure who wrote surrealist poetry and drank with the movement's foremost figures. But the man who later had a good war and became a revered teacher of literature never forgot the small town of his birth. Indeed he remained haunted by its unique atmosphere, as the last verse of his most famous poem makes clear:

> *The boyish season is still there*
> *For clapping hands and leaping feet*
> *Across the slagheaps and the dunes*
> *And still it breaks into my care*
> *Though I will never find the street*
> *Nor find the old impulsive tune*
> *Nor ever lose that child's despair.*

A minibus approaches. It's 7pm. The first day of our Tyne Walk is ended.

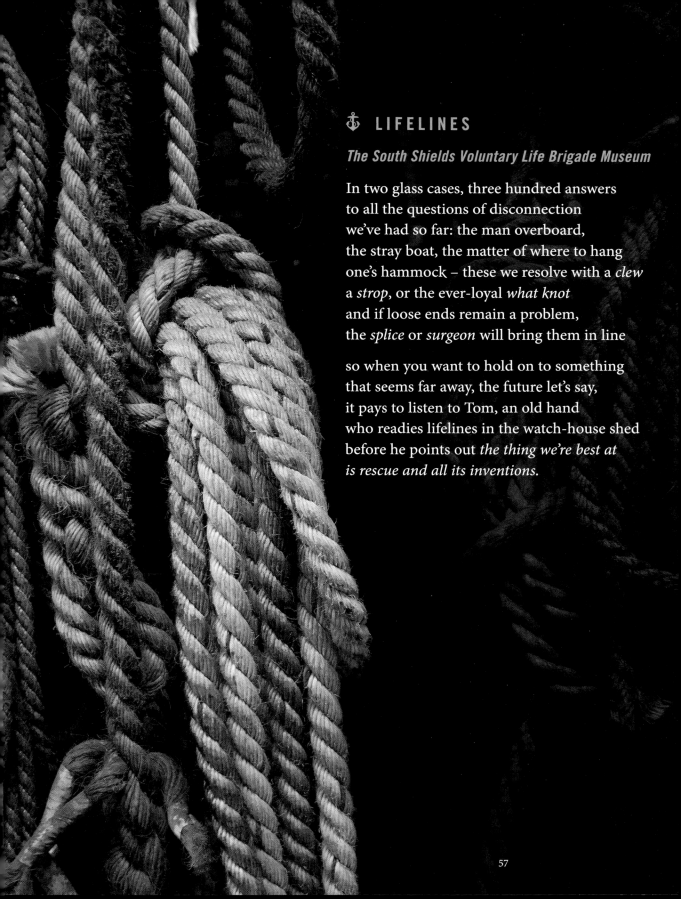

⚓ LIFELINES

The South Shields Voluntary Life Brigade Museum

In two glass cases, three hundred answers
to all the questions of disconnection
we've had so far: the man overboard,
the stray boat, the matter of where to hang
one's hammock – these we resolve with a *clew*
a *strop*, or the ever-loyal *what knot*
and if loose ends remain a problem,
the *splice* or *surgeon* will bring them in line

so when you want to hold on to something
that seems far away, the future let's say,
it pays to listen to Tom, an old hand
who readies lifelines in the watch-house shed
before he points out *the thing we're best at*
is rescue and all its inventions.

Three men are sitting in the wheelhouse of a fishing boat as it gently rolls on an incoming tide, sipping brown liquid and telling tall tales about a mysterious creature of the sea.

It reminded me of one of my favourite scenes in the movies, when a fisherman called Quint tells his shipmates the story of the *USS Indianapolis* and the terrible fate that met its shipwrecked crew.

But this isn't Cape Cod but the mouth of the Tyne, we're drinking tea rather than whisky, and I'm not in a remake of *Jaws*. The speaker with the grizzled grey beard may bear a passing resemblance to Robert Shaw, but he's a veteran fisherman from South Shields called Derek Heselton. And we're not chewing over the great white shark, but another mythic beast – the salmon.

The story Derek tells is one of the great recent successes of the river. Indeed the science writer and Northumberland fisherman Matt Ridley describes it as 'the most striking example of the natural regeneration of an ecosystem in Europe in the last 50 years'. It began when Derek and his marra Brian Jordan were boys and just beginning their long careers as salmon hunters of the Tyne.

Derek and Brian went to school together in Shields, and as both families had maritime histories, there wasn't much doubt about where they might find their living. In 50 years they haven't strayed far from home.

'We got our first licences to net salmon near the mouth of the river in 1964. The river was busy with shipping of all kinds, but it was filthy too. You wouldn't believe what we had to fish in,' says Brian.

Those were literally the darkest days for water quality on the Tyne. Before riverside industry really got going, salmon were so plentiful and cheap that according to wood engraver Thomas Bewick, the indentures of some Newcastle apprentices solemnly swore that they wouldn't be fed its pink flesh more than twice a week. In the 1930s the river was still clean enough for King George V to fish for salmon in it, but the Second World War and unchecked pollution from sewage and industrial waste made its banks – never mind its boats – a less than desirable place to linger. In 1959, no salmon or sea trout were caught on the Tyne, but time, a vast investment in drainage and sewage infrastructure and, it has to be said, the decline of the river's heavy industries have wrought a remarkable turnaround. The Tyne is now officially the best river for salmon in England and Wales,

OPPOSITE AND OVERLEAF
Salmon hunters Brian
Jordan and Derek Heselton.

and enjoyed a record-breaking season in 2011, with a total *declared* catch of precisely 5,663. Each fish caught has a value of more than £4,000 to the local community through the jobs it creates, Derek's and Brian's included.

'We pull beautiful fish from this water, as big as 20 to 30 pounds. We do get a bit of stick sometimes from the anglers further up, but given the thousands and thousands of fish on the river every year, I say there's more than enough for everyone,' says Brian on the deck of their boat, the *Nicola Joanne*, named after both their daughters. The two men share pretty much everything.

They fish just outside the Tyne at two places off South Shields – Pier Berth and Gun Berth, fixing their 'T-nets' (they do what it says on the tin), which are made by Brian and designed to lead even the canniest salmon into the deadest of dead ends.

'The berths have been used for centuries and there's a reason for that. The salmon seem to like their playgrounds,' says Derek.

The pair hold one of only four highly regulated licences issued by the Environment Agency for the right to fish off the Tyne. The season is short, from 1 June to 31 August, the demand for their catch is high. Often their salmon are sold by their factor in North Shields before they've even been brought ashore. Most of them end up on dinner plates on the Continent, though Derek and Brian have been known to eat wild salmon themselves, once when they managed to persuade a seal inside their net to drop its catch.

'Seals are very aggressive when you're both after the same fish,' says Brian. 'Their claws are wicked and they don't have those teeth for sucking soup, but this one dropped a fish. It had bitten the head off, but we took the rest home and it was beautiful.'

But it's not the eating, nor the financial rewards, that have kept these two as salmon hunters all these years.

'It gets a hold of you. It's such a primitive, instinctive thing in all of us, and the first day of the season, the first catch, there's an incredible feeling of excitement. You can forget St James's Park!'

The morning I went out in the *Nicola Joanne* was out of season and the net had been laid inside the pier to catch fish so radio tags could be attached to them to gather information on their extraordinary life-cycle. Juvenile fish over-winter off Iceland, the adults even further, off Greenland, but it seemed they hadn't come home quite yet. The only fish we caught in four hours were two stubby and decidedly unprepossessing lumpsuckers.

I ask if they made good eating. 'Only if you like a mouthful of cotton wool,' says Derek.

With that, Brian disappears below to refresh the drinks, Earl Grey this time, and Derek tells another story – of the morning their previous boat was mown down by a steel-hulled trawler and they both nearly drowned in the waters that have sustained them for nearly 50 years.

'I've had a different outlook ever since. Live life to the full. Another glass of wine? Why not? We could have been dead. That's why we can't wait to get out here. I mean, look at it.'

I did. A bulk carrier slipped between the piers, the spring sun played on gently shifting waves.

'Beautiful,' murmured the hunter-gatherer.

CHIPS HOT DOGS
¼ POUNDERS

DAY TWO

Hebburn, I'm in Hebburn,
And my heart beats so that I can hardly speak…
Anon, after Irving Berlin

We're standing a few yards from a collection of stones that were dressed and assembled to make a monastery the best part of 1,500 years ago. The church whose construction followed has been a beacon of peace, learning and contemplation for most of the centuries since. Here, one of the greatest Northerners who ever lived spent his time as a scholar and thinker. St Paul's Church, Jarrow, which stands near the intersection of the Tyne and one of its tributaries, was the home of the Venerable Bede and generations of monks until the Vikings came raiding up the river with less peaceful thoughts on their minds.

We turn and look eastwards and gaze at a different landscape: the Nissan car terminal, with row upon row of cars built at the huge plant down the A19. Not so long ago this was the dreary, muddy waste of Jarrow Slake, or as the local folk called it, 'the Slacks'. Here, on the far side of the muddy River Don, other acts of violence once took place that disfigured our more recent history, and here to tell the terrible story of William Jobling is the writer, songsmith, poet and 'Jarra lad', Tom Kelly.

Nearby, a woman stands under a huge cherry tree, gathering fruit.

It is the summer of 1832, a bitter time along the Tyne as thousands of miners are on strike in the long struggle for better wages and reduced working hours. They are particularly set on shortening shifts for boys, and ending the iniquity of the 'tommy shop', the system by which miners' families are obliged to buy the necessities of life at inflated prices from shops owned by the coal-owners. The strike has been lengthy and bitter, with violence on both sides, despite the entreaties of the miners' leader Thomas Hepburn to his men to keep the peace. The owners have drafted in blacklegs to keep the pits going, while many strikers and their families have been evicted from cottages owned by their employers. Recently there was a pitched battle in North Shields between strikers and militia, during which a constable shot and killed a local miners' leader who was trying to calm the crowd; the guilty man was given a lenient six-month sentence. Both banks of the Tyne are waiting for a spark to blow the powder keg.

OPPOSITE
Textile artist Ali Rhind and helpers create adornments for Bede's World.

On 11 June, two months after the strike began, William Jobling and Ralph Armstrong, two colliers at Jarrow's Alfred pit, a colliery with an appalling safety record, go drinking in Turner's pub on the proceeds of a shilling Jobling has begged on the highway. Their tanks full but pockets empty, they return to the road between Shields and Jarrow and stop another horseman: Nicholas Fairles, a 71-year-old coal-owner and magistrate. This is a man evidently not without human feeling – he'd been one of the movers behind the provision of South Shields' first lifeboat. But there is little kindness on display on the lonely road that June day: Fairles indignantly refuses to put his hand in his pocket, at which point Jobling turns away, but his friend Armstrong drags Fairles from his horse and attacks him with a stone and stick, leaving him on the ground with serious head injuries. Unfortunately for the two fleeing pitmen, the assault is witnessed by other passers-by. Two hours after the attack, Jobling is arrested on South Shields sands, where the Whitsun horse racing is taking place. Ralph Armstrong is never found, or indeed seen again. Later there is speculation that he returned to his first calling of the sea, or may even have emigrated to Australia. Will Jobling is left to face the music on his own.

BELOW
Tom Kelly plus walker with notebook.

Justice was both swift and harsh. Jobling was identified by Fairles but the dying man, who'd once employed Jobling's wife Isabella in his house, agreed that he'd taken no part in the assault ('I never milested you,' the pitman muttered), but ten days later he was tried for murder at Durham Assizes and conducted his own defence. The proceedings were over in four hours, the jury barely taking 15 minutes to reach their verdict. Jobling was sentenced to hang, his body to be covered in pitch and suspended in chains from a gibbet erected on Jarrow Slake a short walk from the scene of the attack. The judge made it clear that he intended this to be a warning to his fellow miners in their 'illegal proceedings'. I remember an apposite phrase from my school-boy history, to describe the death by firing squad of Admiral Byng, who had overseen the loss of Minorca to the French during the Seven Years War. He was executed, commented Voltaire, 'to encourage the others'. Many have seen Jobling's death as judicial murder.

It seems the episode had the desired effect. After Jobling's body was conveyed to Jarrow, escorted by a troop of Hussars and two companies of infantrymen, and hung in his gibbet a short distance from Isabella's cottage, crowds came to see the broken and defiled body. Perhaps they were 'encouraged': the strike petered out, the miners' union was broken, Tommy Hepburn was forced to sell tea from door to door until the suffering of his starving family forced him to beg for work at Felling Colliery, which he was given on condition he had no further dealings with the union. The pitmen's basic aims weren't achieved for another 40 years.

Ancient history, you might say. But the fate of William Jobling is a story that just won't die. The composer Will Todd recently wrote an opera about it, and on the desk in front of me as I write is a starkly powerful representation of Jobling in his gibbet: a maquette of a much larger sculpture made for an exhibition at Jarrow's Bede Gallery in the early 70s by South Shields-born artist Laurie Wheatley (he made his living building film sets). I have it because Laurie gave it to my father – there's an inscription on the base – in thanks for the inspiration given him by an essay Sid wrote about the story. I recovered it from a drawer in my parents' house where it had lain for 40 years, my dad's wish to have it on display firmly quashed by my mother. 'It always gave me the creeps,' she told me the other day. I understand – it's strong meat. But then so is the story, as Tom Kelly remembers: 'Folk memory of Will Jobling survived even into the 1950s, when I was a little 'un living not far away. Old people used to talk about the hanging man on the Slacks. When you misbehaved you were threatened with him. Will Jobling'll come and get you! It was a pretty terrifying image, I can tell you.'

My dad got it right in the title of that essay about the mythic power of the tale: *Jobling Speaks*. As he wrote, 'Still in my mind, Jobling walks; bars, cross-bars and collars, stirrups struck off, face moving towards me, he comes through the mist, milky and tenuous which so often swirls over the slake, moving over the black waters to walk the oily shore, the old road and the low hidden bridge where it all began. In my dream he is a colossus, black, the tattered clothes flying. Slowly the blind face turns. Muffled comes a voice: 'Who deals justice now? Is it still iron – iron for them?'

As we turn away from that low hidden bridge, the cherry-gatherer, who answers my greeting in an East European language, toddles off carrying two heavy plastic bags – and we walk along the bank of the Don towards the Tyne, passing a redshank calling from its perch on the handle of a beached supermarket trolley and a white plastic chair that speaks of someone's attachment to this curious place. I get a sense that in the town whose riverside boundary we're about to explore, history hangs heavy, as well as the search for justice that didn't end with the death of Jobling. Not that this history is entirely malign. There's a story that when Jobling's body was finally cut down by his friends in the dead of night, it was buried, gibbet and all, in the consecrated ground of St Paul's. In this exquisite, blunt-towered Saxon church, there are various treasures, including something described as Bede's chair, (which almost certainly isn't) and, embedded high in a wall, a tiny Romanesque window composed of a mosaic of the oldest window glass in Europe. But above all there's a pervasive sense that on this spot the remarkable Bede once lived and died, prayed and above all thought. To get a clearer sense of the man, we walk across what Tom Kelly and his pals used to call 'Charlie's park' (after its keeper), skirt around the elegantly bijou Jarrow Hall and enter one of my favourite museums on Tyneside, Bede's World. Stopping to say hello to textile artist Ali Rhind, whose workshop group are making nine acoustic wall hangings based on shards of medieval glass excavated from the site, we wander its rooms, learning a great deal about the man and his times also. But it's only when we walk around the serene little farm on a promontory jutting out into the Tyne (designed to evoke the appearance and atmosphere of a mediaeval settlement) that the impact of it all really settles in the mind. Consider the following:

The name Jarrow is derived from 'Gyrwe', the Anglo-Saxon for 'place of the marsh dwellers'.

Bede is most famous for writing the very first history of the English-speaking people, but also wrote texts on the early Church, epigrams, hymns and the art of poetic metre.

This historian and scholar was also a scientist who carried out pioneering work on natural phenomena like lunar and solar cycles, eclipses and tides, all observed from the banks of the Tyne.

He was a man driven by the thirst for knowledge – 'no one in this life is so wise that his learning cannot be increased' – and by the powerful need to communicate.

The Jarrow monastery created matchless treasures, like the Franks Casket, a fabulously decorated box made of whalebone, and the Codex Amiatinus, a Bible written out and illustrated by the monks – but nothing so beautiful as some of Bede's thoughts.

As we climb a mound that offers a fine view out over the Tyne and watch the breeze ruffling the water and a tug nudging the car-carrier *Nordic Ace* through a 180-degree turn towards a berth at the car terminal, the piers just visible in the distance, I remember the words Bede wrote that have quietly haunted me ever since I first came across them: a man's life, he said, is like the brief flight of a sparrow from one end to the other of a lighted hall where a king is feasting with his men one cold winter's night.

As we turn away – our party of walkers today includes Jake Campbell, a young poet from South Shields – I remember one last thing about Bede that makes its mark on this scribbler. To write all those books, he first had to make the quills. He even had to make his own ink.

Our plan today is to trace the riverside boundaries of the twin towns of Jarrow and Hebburn; to get a sense of how and why they developed, and what makes each different and distinctive from the other. The first aim is immediately blunted, and not for the last time today; we have to skirt inland around a Shell oil terminal. Visitors are also discouraged from entering the next section of river frontage, but we take a peek anyway, looking over the custard-yellow sand dunes of the Cemex sand and gravel depot; at a dock the company's aggregate carrier *Sand Heron* is tied up. This was once the site of the Mercantile Dry Dock, where the 15-year-old Tom Kelly got his first job as a clerk in the beguilingly-named Time Office. Like many other yards up and down the Tyne, the Mercantile was a casualty of the slump of the 1980s, but in its heyday drew its workers from both sides of the river. Their daily journeys cross-Tyne were made easy by a feature of the river that until today I've never explored: the Tyne Pedestrian Tunnel, just a short walk upstream. There's another reason why I'm intrigued by it: it was opened three weeks after I was born in July 1951.

We descend the deepest – and slowest – escalator I've ever travelled; at 200 feet deep the longest in the world when it was installed and the UK's first purpose built pedestrian tunnel. There are two 900-feet-long inter-linked tunnels: one for northward travellers, the other southbound. The walls are lined with green and yellow tiles, the floor paved with stone flags.

The halfway point is marked with the words *County of Durham* on one side and *County of Northumberland* on the other. This morning it's more or less deserted – we meet one solitary walker coming the other way – but in its heyday, when hundreds of workers needed to get to the other side of the river for work, the tunnel was always busy, as retired Port of Tyne surveyor Don Graham remembers.

'I went through the tunnel very soon after it was opened. I was riding the first bike I ever had – it was a great adventure – but I wasn't the only one. The tunnel was absolutely chocker! Very few people had cars back then.'

Similar memories are being aired nearby at Dunn Street School, where children are interviewing older Tynesiders about the tunnel for a project to commemorate the 60th anniversary of its opening. Ken Findlay recalls that many people living in Jarrow actually worked on the north side of the river, chiefly Swan Hunter's for the men and Haggie's Rope Works for the women. Dorothy from East Howdon used to come the other way, to go shopping in Jarrow with her mother because it was cheaper. She remembers straddling the mid-point so that one foot was in Durham and the other in Northumberland. 'It was something I always did, but to be honest, I used to find the tunnel a little bit scary,' she says.

I know what she means. Tunnels are intimidating places, especially tunnels under a river. It's hard to forget the weight of all that water pressing down, and riding that slow escalator back to the sunshine, accompanied by the eeriest of creaks, easy to sense the ghosts of travellers past. But I do recommend a visit to the Tyne Pedestrian Tunnel, one of the hidden wonders of the riverside.

We move on through Jarrow town centre, passing a defunct Burton's tailors and the more modest JK Clothing (School Wear and Alteration Service, Fashion Wear and Vertical Tanning), then a pub called the Jarrow Crusader, and pass up the opportunity for a pint to picnic in the sunshine on a patch of grass. Charlie uses my penknife to bisect a Mars Bar and pays for his taste for chocolate by slicing his finger instead. We should have gone to the pub.

One first aid session later, we return to the riverside, and the chemical works operated by Rohm and Haas, the American-based multi-national, where they make 'biocides' (germ-killers, basically), used in cosmetics, shampoos, paint preservatives and water treatment. It's a big site, occupying about half a mile of river frontage, but production is so automated now-adays, the company employs just 56 people. I'm rather shocked by the figure, especially when I consider the size of the workforce at the enterprise that preceded Rohm and Haas, which took over the site in the mid-50s: once upon a time, 10,000 people worked here.

⚓ OUT OF SIGHT

If I ever get to the Taj Mahal,
or land on the moon, or phone my sister
right from the top of Burj Khalifa,
I know I'll feel like I do down here, cheating

nature, breathing tightly, wondering how
the human hand can be so slight
yet bring about marvels. Eighty-five feet
below high water, anything's possible

even a walk from shore to shore in air
that's engineered to be here. This tunnel
hums with neon light against the awful
press of soil, the trillion weight of Tyne

moving so close I think I might hear
the tides heave, the silt creep, a faint tectonics
grumbling away below the echoic
manoeuvres of ships which skim past my head

while the escalators pomp out a tune
to mark the tunnel's sixtieth birthday
under the river, its sunken beauty
party to few but the seals' ovations.

A clue to the nature of that business lies in the name of a large building on the Rohm and Haas site: the so-called Berengaria Shed, named after the ship of the same name that once passed this way. The ocean liner *RMS Berengaria* is notable in maritime history for various reasons: built in 1912 for the Hamburg America Line with the original name *Imperator*, it was at 51,000 tons for a time the biggest passenger ship in the world; it later became the flagship of the Cunard Line, and also featured in the F Scott Fitzgerald novel *The Beautiful and the Damned*; and when it was finally broken up, it marked the death throes of the company that within a century made and almost broke the town of Jarrow: Palmers.

Like many great industrial enterprises of the Victorian age, it was the life-work of a charismatic titan, the son of a South Shields whaling captain called Charles Mark Palmer. In 1851 he opened the yard that bore the family name. He was 29 and Jarrow was a pit village with a population of about 1,000 people. The following year he launched a ship with a revolutionary design and an immense impact on the fortunes, in no particular order, of himself, the town of Jarrow, the Tyne and the great Northern coalfield. The *John Bowes* was the first iron screw collier to be built; it revolutionised the way coal was carried. The ship could be loaded within four hours, travel to London in 48 and return to the Tyne within 24. Before this, two average-sized collier brigs would take more than a month to complete the same work. Palmer introduced two other innovations: he was one of the first to realise the value of Cleveland ironstone, which was smelted in blast furnaces at Jarrow from 1860, and also developed the use of rolled rather than forged armour plate. As a result, many of the ships he built were for the Royal Navy. As I write I'm looking at a photo of a rather amazing painting by a man called H Elrington Gibb: a representation, as if at anchor at the Scapa Flow naval base in Orkney, of the 43 Navy ships built at Palmers during the Great War. In its 80-year history, the yard built a total of 1,000 vessels, precisely one a month.

This was only possible because Jarrow grew from a pit village to a town, and Palmer oversaw its growth: he built schools and hospitals as well as a Mechanics Institute and Reading Room, became the town's Mayor and its Liberal MP, before becoming a baronet. He is also, indirectly, the reason for Tom Kelly's existence.

'My mam's family were Cumiskeys, originally from Clunbar in County Galway and my dad's family were from Kilkenny. They came here in the late 19th century because Palmer was desperate for labour and he advertised in Ireland. It might have helped his cause that as a prominent Liberal, he supported Irish home rule. So the men came here to work for him, working in shifts and staying in lodging houses where the beds were always warm; then the families followed and a community based around St Bede's church was established, with its pubs, school, close terraces and strong sense of Irish-Catholic identity. I remember my mother telling me that Gaelic was spoken in my great-grandparents' house. In the 1920s the IRA blew up the old bridge over the Don on the road to South Shields.

'Jarrow has been called "Little Ireland", as a third of the population had an Irish connection. The street where I lived was called Hope Street. Now that's a laugh.'

In essence, Palmer's Jarrow became a company town, a status that offered many benefits in times of plenty – certainly while the paternalistic Palmer was alive – but significant perils when the century turned and the economic tide went out. After Palmers was closed in 1933 by the cartel National Shipbuilders' Securities, an embargo was placed on shipbuilding in the town for 40 years. The poverty that resulted from 75 per cent unemployment led to the epic Jarrow Crusade that in the ironic words of Jarrow-born writer Alan Plater in his epic play *Close The Coalhouse Door*, 'stirred the conscience of the nation', but resulted in little help from the Government. Another phrase stuck: 'The Town That Was Murdered', the title of a justifiably angry book by a Jarrow MP several generations after Palmer, Ellen Wilkinson.

'What finally saved Jarrow was a little German with a funny 'tache,' says Tom Kelly, 'but the Second World War only postponed the end of ship-building in Jarrow. It stopped altogether in the mid-80s, and my dad, who had lost two toes in an accident at Palmers Hebburn, had to look for labouring work elsewhere.'

I'm keen to get a sense of who the employers of Jarrow are nowadays. They're certainly less visible than they were in the days of Charles Mark Palmer, but after following a false trail along a section of riverside path that fizzles out at the dead end of an iron fence – a middle-aged guy having a quiet smoke tells us it's the eastern boundary of the old Palmers Hebburn yard, bought from the firm established by another Victorian engineering giant, Robert Stephenson – we stumble across TEDCO on a thoroughfare whose name hints at the past: Rolling Mill Road.

I already knew about TEDCO – an acronym, standing for Tyneside Economic Development Company – because some people working there had read something about the walk and invited us to drop by. That was our plan, but then we got lost in the maze of winding 'ways' and buddleia bushes of the Viking Industrial Park. We're hot and thirsty and footsore, and greet a distant sign announcing TEDCO with the relief of desert pilgrims glimpsing an oasis. But no mirage here: within a few minutes, we're slumped in the air-conditioned cool of its reception area, being plied with drinks and chocolate cake by the welcoming Janice Stott (wife of Bob). After a few minutes, my brain cools enough to start asking the elementary question: what happens at TEDCO?

The short answer is, lots of stuff. TEDCO houses the workshops and offices – the language of the business park prefers the neutral word 'units' – of more than 100 enterprises. The majority of these businesses offer services, everything from plumbing to internet selling, bouncy castles to 'surface replication techniques', but it's encouraging to note from the clients' list Janice puts into my hand that a few at least are manufacturing things. There are two steel fabricators and a company specialising in paper coatings, as well as a firm of precision engineers. But it almost goes without saying that what there isn't is another Charles Mark Palmer.

But there is another acronym floating in the ether here, found in every regional development strategy document of the last 30 years: SME, which stands for 'small and medium enterprise'. TEDCO is full of SME's, most of them employing a workforce that could be counted on the fingers of two hands. There are many similar places up and down the Tyne – we'll come across many more in the days ahead – and we begin to understand that they've replaced, at least to some extent, the great monolithic employers of the past, whose employees could be counted in the thousands. Replaced in many cases in a literal sense too: many of these business parks and small industrial estates occupy land where the great Victorian ventures once sprang up; TEDCO, for instance, lies at the eastern edge of Palmers Jarrow works. Even the biggest employers on the Tyne nowadays, like the Port itself, have fewer than a thousand people on their books, and they are small in number. So TEDCO, you might say, is the future.

Still unable to walk along the waterside, we return to the dreary main road up the hill, its most romantic aspect being a name that suggests a previous use – Wagonway Road – and pass quietly and unannounced from Jarrow into Hebburn. Our guide here is to be Ron French, son of the town, retired ship's engineer and historian of shipbuilding on the Tyne, who immediately points to a feature on the westward horizon that offers a clue to its past and present: the impossibly tall and slender spire of St Andrew's Church: a good place to begin our exploration.

Two years after Charles Mark Palmer opened his yard downriver in Jarrow, a young Scot called Andrew Leslie arrived on the Tyne from Aberdeen. The son of crofters who had been cleared off their lands in Shetland, he wanted to open a shipyard of his own and thought the Tyne offered better opportunities. He brought a few trusted men with him, and when the little yard that bore his name began to flourish, he went back to his home city for more workers, constructing a community to house them on the hillside above the works. Like Palmer in Jarrow, he built schools, a Mechanics' Institute and St Andrew's Presbyterian church, which still stands as a statement of social as well as religious identity. We're here, it seems to say, and as you can see, we build things. In time, the monocultural nature of this community gave rise to a name similar to the 'Little Ireland' of Jarrow: Little Aberdeen.

A hundred years later, in Leslie's centenary year of 1952, certain things began to click in the brain of the young Ron French – the significance of certain things in his home town: surnames; street names like Bon Accord Street (Bon Accord being the motto of Aberdeen); pub names like the Caledonian; the now-defunct Hebburn Argyle FC, who played at Campbell Park; the pipes and drums of the Hebburn Pipe Band; the ancient curling ponds his father talked about; the Orange Lodge (still surviving) on the corner of Victoria and Station Roads. This town, he realised, was made by the Scots, the reason one street had always been known by the hitherto inexplicable nickname of 'Oatmeal Terrace'.

I wonder why this hadn't always been obvious to Ron, but the answer lies in the fact that in the early 20th century the monoculture of Victorian times began to change. In time, the thrifty Aberdonian Presbyterians prospered and moved away from the yard, educating their children in the process. Thus Hawthorn Leslie's – a merger of the Hebburn yard with the company that had made their boilers, the locomotive makers Hawthorn's of St Peter's over the river – had to find new workers, so in time Little Aberdeen became another Little Ireland – and once a year Ron French had to run a very particular kind of gauntlet.

'On St Patrick's Day, the Catholic schools gave their pupils the day off, and in the afternoon they'd ambush us Protestant lads on our way home from school on the railway bridge by the Catholic Church. They'd challenge you by saying, 'Green peas or barley?' – meaning Catholic or Protestant? Of course, they knew you were Protestant – you were on your way home from school – so they whacked you with balls of string with stones inside which they twirled around on the ends of string. The strange thing is that for the rest of the year these lads were your pals. You played football together. It was a ritual, a game. No lasting harm done.'

Tom Kelly remembers his family's tales of similar rituals in Jarrow. The corresponding challenge there was 'English, Irish or Scots English?' – or the abbreviated 'EIS?' – but there too, give or take the odd march or damaged bridge, the separate existence of Orange Lodge and Iona Club, sectarianism failed to poison community relations in the way it continues to do on Clydeside. Maybe a third, if small, ethnic influx had a positive effect.

The third of Hebburn's big employers of the 20th century, along with Hawthorn Leslie's and Palmers of Hebburn, was Reyrolle's, the makers of switch-gear for electric power stations. The French engineer Alphonse Reyrolle came to Hebburn in 1901 to open a workshop in partnership with a local accountant called Norbert Merz, whose brother Charles was, helpfully, consulting engineer for the Newcastle upon Tyne Electricity Supply Co. Ltd. The new enterprise had just 54 employees, some of them Reyrolle's countrymen, but, riding the immense wave of domestic electrification, eventually supported a workforce of 12,000 people, including Ron French's dad. Allegedly few of them were Catholics, certainly among the gaffers. According to the stories I heard, Reyrolle's was dominated by Freemasonry.

More positively, there's a nice story about Alphonse touring his plant one day and stopping to watch a young apprentice filing a piece of metal. After a moment the patriarch intervened and told the lad he'd paid for the whole of the file: 'You're only using the middle of it.' The tone was fatherly, the intervention decisive. Alphonse took his jacket and showed his most junior employee how it should be done. On such infinitesimally small details, I suppose, mighty industrial empires are built.

An apprentice from a later era was management consultant and part-time pantomime dame Bob Stott: 'When I started in 1962 I wasn't to know that I would end up being responsible for the training and development of 50 apprentices and 30 graduates every year. I loved Reyrolle. It was a family, and a brilliant training ground for me as an engineer, a manager and leader. If you were Reyrolle trained, you were one of the best.'

Ron French didn't follow his dad into Reyrolle's, but went to Hawthorn Leslie's as an office boy. We walk down Ellison Street to the yard entrance. Sadly, thieves have recently ripped out the beautiful tiled water fountain provided by Leslie for his thirsty workers (a typically paternalistic touch), but Ron's memories are stirred nonetheless.

'In the morning if you weren't sharp inside these gates you got locked out and lost 15 minutes' pay. Shipyard managers weren't noted for their generosity. I remember in 1952 they brought out a book celebrating the yard's centenary. All the workers got a copy, which we thought was a nice gesture, but then we got our pay at the end of the week and found they'd deducted half a crown to pay for it.

'I have a memory of the workforce walking down the hill in the morning with their caps on one side, the 'Beatty angle' it was called, after the British commander at the Battle of Jutland in 1916, who was married to an American heiress and therefore rather dismissive of naval convention. The managing director was Sir Herbert Babington Robin Rowell, who'd been a flying ace in World War I. I saw him in the corridors of power when I was a junior clerk, but despite his name, he was no mug. He'd worked in every workshop in the yard before he took over.'

Probably the most famous ship built at Hawthorn Leslie's will always be associated with another unconventional sailor, Lord Louis Mountbatten. The ship was the *HMS Kelly*, built at the yard before World War II and then substantially rebuilt after it was torpedoed by enemy action off the Dutch coast. When it was put under tow by *HMS Bulldog,* the master asked Mountbatten where he wanted his ship to be taken, and got an immediate reply: Hebburn. He had spent time in the town, watching his ship literally taking shape, and been impressed by the quality of the workmanship. Huge crowds turned out along the Tyne to see her return, with a gash in a flank the size of a double-decker bus, her surviving crew standing to attention along both rails. As a nine-year-old boy, Ron French stood outside the gates of Hebburn Cemetery watching Mountbatten lead a procession of gun carriages carrying coffins of the 27 sailors killed in the attack. A year later, on 23 May 1941, the rebuilt destroyer was sunk by dive bombers in the Battle of Crete, with the loss of a further nine officers and 121 men. I go to look at the Kelly Memorial in the town's cemetery.

I run my eyes down the long list of the sailors who died in these attacks. There's something moving about the names, possibly the prosaic ranks, or even the profusion of initials: Leading Signalman A Amos, Boy First Class EWF Bethell, Leading Stoker V Gough. I wonder what young Bethell's mam called him – was it Ernie, or Eddie, or Eric?

In classic British fashion, the sad story of a ship that went to the bottom of the Med was refashioned and fictionalised to make a powerful piece of war propaganda: the film *In Which We Serve,* in which Noel Coward played the role of an iron-jawed naval commander with less than total conviction. He intoned the film's powerful first words: 'This is the story of a ship.' Some scenes were shot at Hawthorn Leslie's, so the yard's workers had the distinction of appearing in a film that was a big hit on both sides of the Atlantic and nominated for an Oscar for best picture of 1942 (it lost out to *Casablanca*).

A generation later, another film crew came to the Tyne, to make a BBC documentary about a musical version of the *Kelly* story, written by Alan Price and our guide to Jarrow, Tom Kelly. Tom remembers going to London for a screening of the film and meeting Mountbatten. The old boy was drinking Pimm's and dressed in the full regalia of an Admiral of the Fleet. Tom was rather over-awed: 'I remember thinking, this man was the last Viceroy of India! He was a friend of Charlie Chaplin! But he liked the film: in his elegant upper-class drawl, he said, "Won't be a dry eye in the house, will there?"'

Two years after this meeting, Mountbatten himself died at sea, when the Provisional IRA blew up his fishing boat on a summer's day in a ravishingly pretty bay off the coast of County Sligo.

The story of *HMS Kelly* will always have the power to move. The memory of the yard that built it however is fading. Indeed, the three biggest employers of Ron French's youth have all more or less gone: Hawthorn Leslie's, Palmer's Hebburn, and Reyrolle's (though the German conglomerate Siemens still operate a remnant here of the company they took over in 2005).

The reasons why the Tyne's shipbuilding and repair base folded within a generation are many and various, as well as hotly disputed, and will be spoken about often in these pages. Everyone along the river, it seems, has an opinion, and Ron French has his, typically succinct:

'When I started at Hawthorn Leslie's there were said to be 28 unions governing all the trades; the yards the Germans rebuilt after the war had just three.'

After a day in which we've largely been kept away from the riverside by wire fences and 'Trespassers Will Be Prosecuted' signs, it's a relief to walk down Cavalier View towards the water. On our left is one of those small estates of new houses that have colonised much former industrial land by the Tyne, in front of us a gate that marks the demarcation between the old Palmer's and Hawthorn Leslie yards. A car slowly passes us and then turns and parks. A man in his early sixties gets out and walks towards a section of brick wall with a thicket of buddleia and willow scrub on the other side.

Being nosey I wander over and engage John Welsh in conversation. It turns out that he was born nearby in Mons Avenue (various local streets bear the names of First World War battles) but left Hebburn 25 years ago. It was in Palmer's yard in Hebburn that he learned his trade as an electrician. He lives in Yorkshire now.

'I'm up to see my sick mother, but whenever I come back I'm always drawn to this place, to the river and where my working life began. The yard had three docks and used to repair dry cargo vessels and oilers and often there were three ships tied up along the quays waiting to get into a dock.'

On the walk I heard other stories about Palmer's. One day I got an email from a woman called Marion Scaife in Bermuda about her husband, who also served his time in Palmer's in the 1950s – and a high-heeled shoe.

'Once the heel of my brand new patent leather stiletto shoe broke off. My husband took the shoe to work to drill out the screw. That particular day he was working on the *Caltex Wellington* that was in Palmer's for repair. As the ship was getting ready to sail there was a rush to get the job finished. In the haste my husband left behind his haversack with my shoe inside. He managed to contact the ship's engineer and when the ship next docked this man was kind enough to mail my shoe back to Hebburn. We often wonder where the *Caltex Wellington* is now and often joke about 'the Wellington which went to sea with the shoe'.

On a bench overlooking the river, we came across a man sunning himself. It turned out Kevin Blair had also graduated from the Palmer's Hebburn finishing school for working men, in his case as a fitter. These were the days – in the mid-60s – when the fire equipment consisted of squeezy bottles filled with water, but the tale of Kevin's I liked best was a fishy one.

'I hadn't been there long when a ship came into one of the dry docks for repair. Once it got in, the dock door closed and the water was emptied out. As it cleared, I saw men running to climb the ladders down into the bottom of the deck. I asked this chap what they were doing and he told me to wait. I looked down and saw lots of fish jumping around – they'd swum into the

dock and got themselves trapped. The men were going around collecting the fish – cod, salmon, the lot – using fish-gaffs they'd made from soldering irons. As far as I can remember, they didn't take the fish home to eat, but to the local fish shop to boost their wages. It was a kind of perk of the job – and a regular sight.'

Indeed it was – all around the Tyne, ex-shipyarders tell me about the dry dock fishing trade. Working beside the river offered bounty in other forms, as Kevin remembers from other jobs:

'When I worked at Smith's in North Shields, some of the lads used to go rabbiting on the site. There were traps all over the place. And when the sprat boat came in, the mackerel followed it into the river. At bait time, lads dropped lines into the river and caught loads which they sold to the Chinese crews of ships tied up nearby.'

Hunting wasn't the only sport enjoyed in the yards. Kevin, who first got to know Palmer's Hebburn as a boy sharing his uncle's bait in the cab of his crane, remembers the yard's apprentices playing football in the empty dock-bottom: 'One day as we were playing, someone started letting in the water from the river and there was mad scramble up the ladders and out.'

There is though another story about the yard, and we've yet to hear the end of it. Palmer's Hebburn is still in business, now operated, after a bewilderingly complicated ownership history over the last 40 years, by A&P, and while we're walking the Tyne, the yard is nearing the completion of a quite extraordinary contract: building two sections for a new aircraft carrier for the Royal Navy. Finance director Graham Littledyke shows us these massive structures, more than 4,000 tons of British steel, one section of the flight deck, being finished off on a newly rebuilt quay before being loaded onto a giant barge, the *AMT Commander* of Liverpool, for a trip up the east coast to Rosyth, where they'll be assembled with other sections being built at other yards around Britain. In other words, this is Lego writ large, but when the barge finally left the Tyne, crowds of people gathered along its banks to hail this latest product of the river's engineering skills.

This £50 million contract represents a new direction for A&P, since the yard's principal business over its recent history has been ship repair and ship conversion (lengthening or indeed shortening vessels), but recent contracts building subsea structures for oil exploration encouraged A&P to bid for more construction work. That decision seems to have been vindicated, especially in view of the slowing of repair business brought on by the credit crunch. The yard has won another order from the Navy for a second pair of sections for another aircraft carrier, which has allowed A&P to invest

OPPOSITE
Former Palmer's
apprentice John Welsh.

85

in the yard. The Glasgow-built cranes at the dry dock and riverside have been recently refitted and repainted to extend their life, and there are rows of IMG Panel Line welding machines in the massive fabrication shed. This space is awesomely quiet; the only work going on is a bit of maintenance painting. The floor is covered with feathers from the shed's resident pigeons, but even they respect the cathedral-like silence. The atmosphere somehow seems ominous.

There's one other thing we notice: there are signs everywhere in Romanian. Much of the steelwork for the aircraft-carrier was fashioned by Eastern European hands. This and one or two other observations raise questions in my mind, and some weeks later I return late one chilly afternoon to have them answered, by a man we met on our first visit – Fred Newman, the 'snotty-nosed kid' who started his career on the river as junior clerk at South Shields' Middle Dock in 1965, who over the years that followed rose through the ranks to become managing director of A&P. He's now executive director ('pre-retirement title', he smiles), with specific responsibility for the aircraft carrier contracts.

He embarks on a lengthy account of his career, which frequently intersects with the history of the yard where we're now sitting. It's such a complex story sometimes even he gets lost, but there is no confusion about its end-point: A&P is the last surviving ship repair yard on the Tyne.

'Once upon a time, there were loads, I worked in most of them, but this one is the last one standing', he says.

I ask a short question back, conscious it may not get a short answer. 'How has it happened?' For a few seconds, I'm not sure it'll get *any* answer. Fred sits, looking at the floor, and sighs, and speaks.

'Not easy to say. Lots of things come into my mind, like the fact that at one point, a company that was a forerunner of this one, A&P Appledore, created a consultancy in the early 70s that won contracts to set up yards all over the world, in the Far East, for example, that subsequently competed with us. Ironic – you might say they created a monster, which then destroyed the Tyne.

'But that's not the real reason. Back when I started, the British maritime fleet was massive; British ships were repaired in British yards. Then the owners disappeared and the fleet disappeared, and I mean disappeared. It seemed to happen very quickly. '

I remember something Ron French told me: during the Falklands War in 1982, Margaret Thatcher's Government struggled to find 50 suitable ships to support the Task Force sent to win the islands back from Argentina. A similar exercise during the first Gulf War of 1991 produced only eight British vessels; 140 foreign-flag ships were chartered to plug the gap. Globalisation, and its intensive drive to force down costs, hit merchant shipping early. Fred Newman agrees.

'The Tyne yards were suddenly faced with much more competition. Big jobs started going to Poland and Finland, for instance, where they had cheaper labour and cheaper steel. Now it's China. These lower costs have made our decline almost inevitable. As a result we became much more dependent upon the Government and the Royal Navy, the contract for the aircraft carrier sections being the latest example.'

Here Fred's voice drops: he has some worrying news. Work on the second carrier was due to start in 2012, but because of the Coalition's spending cuts, has now been put back to January 2013. This delay has serious implications for the yard. 'What we need is a major refit or a piece of ship surgery, but the market's depressed because of the credit crunch and the recession that's followed. We need to find a sizeable job to tide us over the next year.'

If they don't, the implication is obvious, for the yard's 124 blue-collar employees, 81 other staff, 22 apprentices, contract staff averaging 500 per year, even the Romanian steel-workers, hired to plug the skills gap created by the industrial downturn of the last 30 years.

'We've tried everything, we really have. In my experience the old owners tended to take the money and run but from the mid-80s onwards we've reinvested money in the business and in the last three years we've had more investment than in the previous 30. The problem is that the work just doesn't seem to be there. I'm not sure what we're going to do.'

Fred's voice drops lower. He seems sad, resigned almost. But he brightens when I mention Kevin Blair's story about fishing in the deep dock a few yards from where we're sitting. He remembers an old mate of his, Dave Rawlings, who once had his picture taken cradling a salmon he'd caught in the dock bottom.

We shake hands and he starts switching off the lights. Outside the tide is going out, the sky darkening, the remains of the sunset lightening the vista upriver. The yard is quiet, no clang of steel. Somewhere a man whistles. The tune is cheerful, he's obviously going home. I stand on the dock and look at the water.

The walk of our second day, through the differing but parallel towns of Jarrow and Hebburn, has been suffused with history. Just reflect: the Venerable Bede, William Jobling, the Jarrow Marchers and 'Wee Ellen' Wilkinson; IRA bombings and Orange Lodges; Lord Louis Mountbatten, the men who built *HMS Kelly* and the other men who died in her; and all the other men and women who travelled from other places to find a future on the south bank of the Tyne, and their descendants of today, who quite

Going into the
Dock Bottom?
Remember!!

Is your Boarding Card in
the Card Rack? If not, go
and do it NOW!!

It could save your life.

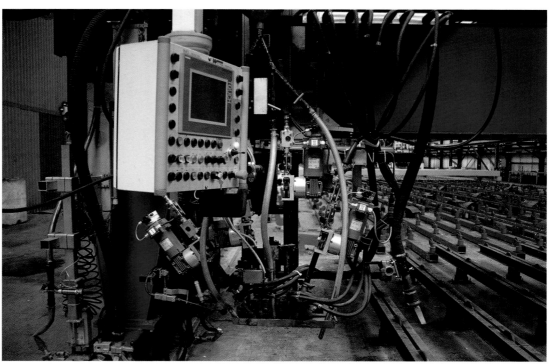

naturally wonder – and worry – what kind of future they and their children might have in this place.

At the end of the day I feel rather full of this history. Not for the first time, or the last, I have a sense that on this Tyne walk it's easy to be overwhelmed by it, to the extent that it's difficult to concentrate on the present, let alone the future. As we wait for Brian to take us home in his East Coast taxi, I remember two quotes from this second day on the hoof.

First, from the writer of *Robinson Crusoe*, Daniel Defoe, who passed this way in 1727: 'They build ships here to perfection, a great many, I mean as to strength and firmness and to bear the sea… '

Second, from Ron French, Hebburn boy, Hawthorn Leslie fitter and turner, ship's engineer and shipyard historian, when I ask him about the future of the river. His answer is brief and to the point. 'Ferry trips, that's basically it'.

Settling into my seat for the journey home, I reflect: well, he should know. But it seems irredeemably bleak. Being an irredeemable optimist – happy fool, some might say – I can't quite accept it. Then I remember Paul Younger.

Paul is another product of Hebburn, from a later generation, the child of a family that united its Protestant and Catholic communities. He grew up in Ann Street, at number 64, which, he likes to recall, was the last house in the terrace before the river. Hardly surprisingly, he loves the Tyne and its people, and is a great advocate for their interconnected future.

Close by 64 Ann Street were the remains of a ballast hill, a mound of sand and gravel originally tipped onto the bank from the holds of colliers in the 19th century to make way for Tyne coal. Safe disposal of such 'waste' – often containing flints from the bed of the Thames – didn't come along until much later, thankfully for Paul and his mates.

'We played on the ballast hills and loved these flints. We didn't know what they were and where they came from, but were fascinated by their rounded knobbly bits and razor-sharp edges. Most of all we loved the fact you could bash them on the pavement and make sparks.'

The flints weren't the only wonder of these hills, many of which have now been cleared from the Tyne's banks. They also became the home of many non-native species of plants that germinated from seeds carried in ships' holds. Consider the beauty of the names of these other flourishing 'immigrants' to the Tyne: hedgerow cranesbill, hoary cress, field eryngo, spotted medick, wild teasel, rough dog's tail and tall melilot. Somehow they escaped the attentions of generations of boys with swishing sticks, like Paul.

'From exploring the ballast hills and the quarries of Hebburn, I got my interest in geology and from the Tyne as a whole I got my fascination for geography. We used to cross the river on the old mid-Tyne ferry and the ferrymen used to let us sit on the roof and ring the bell.'

Paul did well at school and vividly remembers his mother and father intoning the same mantra to him: 'No bloody pit, no bloody shipyard'. He went instead to Newcastle University to study geology and then civil and mining engineering, and it was in pursuit of the latter that he went underground for the first time, to the undersea coal-face at Westoe Colliery in South Shields. It was a kind of epiphany.

'We went five miles out. I thought it was brilliant. It added another dimension to my imagination. I thought it was the nearest I'd ever get to space travel. Mind, I was glad I didn't have to do the digging!'

He booms with laughter. With his large frame and warm Geordie accent, Paul doesn't come over as your average university professor, let alone pro-vice chancellor (engagement), but his roots grow deep and are carefully nurtured. An American girlfriend in his university days might have played a part in that.

'She was from a rich Florida family but she loved Newcastle. Once I took her home to meet my mam and dad. We took the Metro to Wallsend and then the old ferry to Hebburn. There was so much going on – cranes turning and lifting, little boats, rivet guns, buzzers going – she said to me, you're so lucky to have grown up surrounded by all this. She was right.

'It's a dramatic landscape. It cleans itself twice a day, but you can still taste and smell the past. It hurts me to see what's happened in the last 30 years, but I passionately believe in the Tyne's prospects. Where we once built ships, I think we'll soon be building turbines for offshore wind technology. But that's just the start for the river and Tyneside as a whole,' he says.

Paul has another industrial ace up his sleeve, but that's for another day, when we plod along the shore opposite Hebburn's iconic 180-foot-high spire. But before we go, we should record that the building at its base is about to be home for a traditional Tyneside industry that unlike shipbuilding has managed to survive.

St Andrew's Presbyterian church seems destined to become the head-quarters of the Jarrow Brewery.

You know I came close to meltdown
but let's not talk about that now
it's summer and you can rest yourself
in my open arms by the Don

just shy of the mainstream, and forgive
my wobbles, my ad hoc splint,
while I show you my favourite view
of silt and seed. Each day's a gift

when so much time's been spent, working
airports, security, weddings,
odd crime scenes. It's true, I envy
job-for-life, screwdown seating,

the sort you get on Tyne ferries,
but only because it's sturdy:
the Tyne itself I find too sly,
its big gob makes me edgy

so I'll stay put right here, on the fringe
mudflats where every dawn brings
the crabman on his redshank legs,
the grass, and the pylons' singing.

Tales of the Tyne recorded in the cabin of the Port of Tyne survey vessel *Lynceus* on a journey from Tyne Dock to Newcastle Quayside and back, Wednesday 14 December. Doing most of the talking were Harbour Master Mike Nicholson, Port hydrographer Phil Lynch and coxswain Jeff Burns.

PHIL: We've been dredging off Riverside Quay here at Tyne Dock so we can handle fully-laden Panamax (large ships that can navigate the Panama Canal) at the lowest of tides – ten metres deep in the channels and 13 metres at the quay. We get two types of deposits – sand blown in from the sea and Pennine peat and mud coming downriver.

MIKE: Then there's the foreign objects – cars, safes, old cannons and cannon balls. Off Swan Hunter's, a dredger once came up with an anchor off the *Mauretania*, and foreign coins are always being found – sailors coming ashore used to toss them overboard.

PHIL: I once saw these tubes sticking out of the sea wall at Jarrow Slake. Turned out they were ancient depth charges. We had to get the Royal Navy lads from Rosyth to deal with them.

MIKE (ON APPROACHING WALKER): Just coming up to where the Walker bone-yard used to be. Everybody knows about it, everybody used to smell it! They boiled up animal bones for glue.

MC: We even used to smell it in Jesmond. (Derisive laughter from the Harbour Master.) When it appeared, we knew the wind must be from the south east.

PHIL: The worst smell I ever encountered was inside a derelict Co-op depot in Teams, where they used to salt animal skins. When they abandoned it, they didn't take their stock with them…

MIKE: A shipping agent once went on board a ship tied up at Walker. There seemed no one on board – it was like the *Marie Celeste*. Then he found the crew lined up on the rail on the river side, with their binoculars out – watching a very energetic courting couple in Hebburn.

PHIL: Back in the 80s, I was doing some surveying work here in a boat and we tied up on the Walker shore to eat our sandwiches. The tide was going out, and when we tried to move, we found we couldn't – we'd moored unknowingly, and very neatly, above the skeleton of an abandoned Tyne wherry [wooden barge] and the falling tide had dropped us right inside. We couldn't move. We just had to wait until the tide came up again.

Look – (he points) – you can still see the timbers.

MIKE: This here is the Tyne Main turning circle – they excavated the bank on the south side to widen the river and make it possible to turn ships around.

PHIL: I once saw something in the river here. I thought it was a body and pulled it out. Turned out to be an inflatable woman.

MIKE: Did you give her the kiss of life?

PHIL: Didn't a Jaguar once go into the river on the south side near here?

MIKE: And another time a JCB digger from an aggregate yard, put there by a disgruntled ex-employee. When we got to the Jag, the front end was still sticking up. One of the lads jumped on the bonnet, wound down the window, and took the tax disc.

PHIL (ON APPROACHING THE QUAYSIDE): When I started working for the Port of Tyne in 1979, the head office was in Bewick Street by the Central Station. It was quite Dickensian. Uniformed stewards used to bring you tea and coffee and everyone was Mr This and Mr That. The furniture was dark mahogany and there were these beautiful tables specially made for looking at charts. The directors often had furniture made by the Port's carpenters, things like gun cabinets! Meanwhile I was always being told off for having long hair…

MIKE: You had hair?

PHIL: We worked a five and a half day week. Monday to Friday you had to wear a suit, but on the Saturday morning you were allowed to appear in a sports jacket. (Today Phil is wearing jumper, jeans and Crocs.)

Mike goes with some officials from Newcastle City Council to inspect the Quay, and Phil and I gaze at the Millennium Bridge nearby and the framework of piles and fenders in the water below (soon to be removed) where seals are often seen patrolling an unofficial salmon run. It turns out Phil has seen seals even further upriver – he once saw one at Newburn. This prompts me to ask: what's the strangest thing you've ever seen on the Tyne? He's not long in answering.

PHIL: In the early years on the job, we had a bitterly cold winter. It was so cold there was ice on the river. One day I was working high up, above the bridges, and there were actually ice floes coming downstream. I got on with my work, and then I looked upstream. This ice floe was coming down and it seemed to have something on it. As it got closer I saw it was a dog, it must have got stranded on this piece of ice that broke away. Then I saw it was a greyhound and it was sitting down. As it passed the boat, I realised it was dead, frozen to the ice. Surreal. I'll never forget it.

Mike returns and the *Lynceus* turns for Tyne Dock. A couple of miles downstream we pass the abandoned Russian ice-breaker *Ice Maiden*, soon to be sold for scrap.

MIKE: In the old days of Communism, each Russian ship had a commissar on board to prevent the crew fraternising with decadent Geordies in North Shields. They never managed to stop one sort of fraternisation. I often saw ladies of the night staggering along the quay in the early morning after a night on board. I don't think they were discussing permanent revolution.
MC: I heard a similar story elsewhere: in the early 1950s there was a ship in Jarrow's Mercantile Dock on which work was finished. Suddenly it was ordered out to sea by its owners and a dozen female guests had to be disembarked mid-stream by the pilot cutter.

A glimpse of the Fish Quay prompts a conversation about the bounty sometimes provided by the river.

PHIL: I remember a container full of poinsettia plants went into the water and people pulled them out and took them home to dry out. I never heard of one that survived. And didn't someone once steal a consignment of Coca-Cola concentrate and the police had to put out a warning? The stuff was lethal.
JEFF: I can top that. A container full of wheels of Edam cheese once went in the water. The foy boats came back so full of them, they nearly capsized. For weeks after, everyone on the Tyne was eating Edam cheese. If you went into a pub and asked for a cheese toastie, you knew what you'd get – these great wheels of funny-looking cheese sat on the bar…

We're still laughing as we dock.

Tiger in the tank: engine room of Port of Tyne pilot cutter *Collingwood*.

DAY THREE

The big ships sail up, the big ships sail down, a great northern river
Funnels of red, funnels of black, banded with yellow and silver
Bringing in cargoes of oil and wood, taking home girders of steel and pig iron
All coloured faces, flags from all places, high from the stern-posts are flying

Great Northern River, Graeme Miles

As we amble down Ellison Street at the start of today's walk from Hebburn to Gateshead, I tilt my face towards the morning sun. It's already warm. We've actually had a day off, due to Thursday's heavy rain, and might therefore be accused of being fair-weather walkers, but then so are many others, and one of the pleasures of our ramble are the chance encounters with Tynesiders out for a stroll in the sun, walking their dogs or just catching the breeze.

As it turns out, day three will be a day of trees – as well as tugs and horses and cakes and tins of paint – and green will be its predominant colour, so let's begin it with a story about one tree in particular.

One of the good people I work with at the Port of Tyne is assistant marketing and communications manager Lisa Donohoe, who grew up not far from the river. When she was six years old, she helped her dad replant a small tree that was growing too big for their little garden. They carefully dug it up, brought it to a patch of waste ground by the Tyne just to the west of Hebburn, and there chose a spot for it. The waste ground is now part of Riverside Park, a place where Lisa and her family used to sledge at times when the predominant riverside colour was white; she remembers the terrifying thrill of speeding downhill towards the water. Lisa still visits the park, and always goes to look at 'her' tree; it's grown, obviously, in the 25 years since it took root here. Where once Lisa could enfold the trunk in her little hands, now she can barely embrace it with her adult arms, her fingers now barely touching.

There's something about this little tale that's touching, perhaps because it reminds me of a song, the apparently simple but rather epic air in Northumbrian dialect, *Sair Fyeld Hinny*, in which an old man addresses a gnarled oak tree that's much older than him but still retains its vigour. You're still growing, he laments, while all I face is death. If this sounds rather morbid, especially on a sunny Friday morning, all I'd say in reply is that it's impossible, for me anyway, to walk through a wood, or stroll by a river, without reflecting on the fragility of human life.

OPPOSITE
Remains of RB Harrison's shipyard, Bill Quay.

101

Down Ellison Road, we pass an estate of new detached houses. In front of one, a slogan on a van announces: 'Irresistible – As Seen on *Britain's Got Talent*, Local Girl Trio – Party Yourself Into Shape With Zumba Fitness'. Beyond it, at the bottom of the road, the old Mid-Tyne ferry used to tie up. During launches at the Walker Naval Yard opposite, people used to congregate on its pontoon to get a good view. They also used to get their feet wet, from the post-launch wave that swept across the river. During the supertanker era, this wave turned into a mini-tsunami and it wasn't uncommon for the wet patch to reach the thigh.

No launches today, but I remember the claim by Ron French: you're only a proper river-sider if born within sight of the shipyard cranes and within smell of the Walker bone-yard. Well, the cranes are still there – some of them – but the smell's gone, though somehow it's retained a mythic quality. Maybe it's time to address the issue head on, or nose on, even though it means breaking the book format, briefly crossing the Tyne to pay a meta-phorical visit to the Walker ferry landing, and just up the hill, opposite the Neptune Yard, the long-gone but still potent bone-yard.

To guide us is a man we find sitting on a bench on the new pontoon at Riverside Park, Kevin Blair, who once watched salmon being gaffed in a dry dock bottom at Palmers of Hebburn almost 50 years ago, but also remem-bers a certain local aroma – and how one day it changed his daily routine.

'I once came down that lane at the end of the day to get the ferry home to Hebburn. As I passed the bone-yard there was the usual smell that made your belly heave. I saw this huge skip full of bones – they'd boil them up to make glue – and men from the yard sitting on the edge of it eating their bait. My stomach heaved. At that moment I decided I was going to drive me car to work in future. I couldn't face the stink any longer.'

But that wasn't the only ferry peril to be faced back then.

'When the ferry was docking, men used to jump from it onto the shore to get a quick getaway, but before I started driving I saw a few who missed! I tell you I never fancied falling in that stuff back then. Of course, it's so much cleaner now.'

As if on cue, out in the river there's the splash of an itinerant salmon. There are humbler creatures lower down. In the mud below where we're sitting, the falling tide has revealed a neat row of tyres. Christy asks if they're there by accident and I say no, and smile at a memory. I tell my companions the story: a friend and I were walking the last stretch of the Hadrian's Wall walk from Bowness to Wallsend one Sunday morning a few years ago when we saw a rather bizarre sight: a man on his knees in the thick, cloying mud of another low tide, digging with his hands in the mud. We stopped to watch. It became evident he was searching inside a giant tractor tyre, then dropping his discoveries in a bucket. After a while he plodged through the clarts back to the shore, wearing nothing but a pair of underpants, literally covered in Tyne mud. The bucket was full of crabs, which he was going to sell to fishermen. The tyres had been placed in the mud deliberately. Every few days the cheery, filthy man harvested his crop of crabs – they liked to colonise the inside of the tyres. Up and down the river we saw lots of these crab farms. A new industry of the Tyne!

On the opposite bank the hulk of a ship squats in sullen silence, its peeling blue paint a shabby counterpoint to a pristine sky. The icebreaker *Ice Maiden*, built in the Ukraine in 1992 as the *Paadeberg*, once supplied scientific bases deep in the Antarctic, before being gutted in the USA and then towed into the Tyne to be given a £30 million upgrade and conversion at A&P. The owners then went bust, work stopped, and she was moved to the north bank while teams of lawyers and accountants tried to work out her future. They didn't get too far: she's been acquired by a Tyneside scrapyard, and will soon be broken up.

A little way upriver is a ship with a longer sea-life. Under the shadow of two big yellow cranes that have survived from the Vickers Armstrong days, the *Fugro Saltire* of Bergen, an offshore construction and survey vessel, is moored at Shepherd's yard, winding piping on board from one giant bobbin to another.

Kevin Blair adjusts his wraparound shades and contemplates them.

'Ships ain't what they used to be,' he says mildly. 'Most of them are just boxes.'

Despite this, since arthritis enforced an early retirement from the yards in 1987, Kevin has made it his business – passion is a more fitting word – to keep a unique photographic record of ships entering and leaving the river. Keeping in touch with shipping movements via Marine Band radio, the small man with a camera has become a familiar sight to sailors visiting the Tyne. Including historical scenes (for example, the growing ribs of the *Mauretania* at Swan Hunters on 4 April 1905), the immaculately catalogued Blair archive now numbers 40,000 photos and growing. He's building a new collection: a photo and postcard record of all naval ships built on the Tyne. When asked the inevitable question – why? – Kevin smiles, shakes his head and says he doesn't really know. His fascination for ships is obvious; I'd guess their connection to his own family history might be another reason.

Kevin's dad was another incomer: a sailor on *HMS Penelope*, which once sailed up the river for repair at Hawthorn Leslie's, he then met a girl – and stayed. In time his son worked at the yard himself, as well as at Palmer's Hebburn and Smith's repair yard at North Shields. Asked for his memories of a working life on the Tyne, Kevin offers a perspective that manages to be both vivid and rigorously unsentimental. He's not alone in that. In our experience, ex-shipyard workers don't do misty-eyed nostalgia.

'Once you were accepted, the crack was brilliant. I mostly liked the job for the company, and the feeling of working together, building this thing. But God, the conditions could be terrible. The cold, the wind, the rain. I mostly worked on engines. It was very dirty work. Every time I worked with cast iron I used to get these terrible nose bleeds – the dust interfered with me tubes. This was before hard hats came in – for years all I had for protection was a woolly hat.'

In his time at Hawthorn Leslie in the late 40s, Ron French recalls the worker's hat of choice was the so-called 'Geordie umbrella' (the flat cap); the use of gloves was rare and if men were issued with a pair for a particular job they had to return them once the work was complete.

'I vividly remember getting a steel speck in my eye while operating a grinder and the first aid man declaring he couldn't extract it with his magnet, due to the eyeball having skinned over. So I had to make my way to the eye hospital in Newcastle and I was given a large wad of cotton wool to hold over the injured eye, plus a pass-out note for the gateman! I went under my own steam and expense, climbing the steep bank up to the Newcastle road and catching a Northern bus and ended up lying on a pristine white sheeted hospital table, boots, cap et al. After the skinned-over section of the pupil was scraped away, the magnet and tweezers did their job and I was free to dash back to work! I had to be there at knocking-off time to collect my time card and hand it in at the Time Office on the way out and prove that I'd actually been in that day. That's how it was back then.'

Now I want a story from Kevin – any story. He stops to think. Kevin's face suddenly warms into a big grin.

'In the late 60s, not long after we won the World Cup, the German Navy ship *Scharnhorst* – like the famous battleship from the Second World War – came into Palmers for repair and me and me workmates used to have contests with the crew – games of football, boxing matches, who could drink the most.'

I ask who won them.

'Well, the Geordies certainly didn't lose that last one.'

A middle-aged man in Lycra on a flash racing bike stops for a natter – he and Kevin are old workmates. Every day the cyclist ranges far and wide, clocking up the miles, but Keelman's Way, the cycling route along the south bank of the Tyne from Gateshead to South Shields (I recommend it), is his favourite ride.

As we move away, the conversation between Kevin and his mate falters, and my last glimpse captures two of them, looking across the water into the middle distance: the default position of many who loiter by the water.

Heading west through the Riverside Park, we encounter an £150,000 art-work, Flash@Hebburn, the work of Leeds artist Charles Quick, consisting of 12 eight-metre-tall columns, that nightly runs through different light sequences suggesting the town's industrial history. Given that we passed in the middle of a sunny day, all it suggested to me – forgive me if this sounds like a *Daily Mail* hatchet job on 'crackpot councils' – were the lights at the end of an airport runway. Rather more eloquent was the solitary white plastic chair, just like its twin by the River Don, placed on the grassy slope nearby: a point of solitary and unpretentious contemplation.

We move on, passing the site of an old alkali works, the Tharsis Copper Works, and a long abandoned foreshore once the property of the Newcastle Shipbuilding Company. This rather grand-sounding enterprise is probably one of the least successful in the city's history: before it closed in 1921 it managed to build just two ships. Further along are the rotting remains of the Pelaw Main coal staith, to which a network of rail lines brought the product of various local collieries, including Hebburn, where Humphrey Davy tested his miners' safety lamp (but according to many, not before Geordie Stephenson tried out his a few miles away at Killingworth).

At last we're required to climb away from the riverside, as the path skirts a rocky foreshore and behind it, a 60-foot cliff. Halfway up, I stop to catch my breath, turn and look downriver. From this vantage point, there's a clear view of the land now occupied by Shepherd Offshore and Wellstream, another energy services company. This was once the site of the Walker Naval Yard, established by Armstrong-Whitworth in 1912 to build the kind of warships no longer possible at their old yard at Elswick; basically battle-ships had become too big to squeeze past a fully-open Swing Bridge. The slipways at the new yard were cunningly positioned to take advantage of the bend of the river at Walker, which meant that ships as long as 1,000 feet could safely be launched upstream towards the bank where I'm now stand-ing. I wonder if the cliff we've been climbing might actually be man-made. Was it blasted away to make even more leeway for these ships? It later turns out that my hunch is correct…

There are shouts from my fellow walkers ahead; aspersions are being cast on my fitness. The path finally enters woodland, that surprising but increasingly common urban landscape. A succession of those familiar colonisers of former industrial land – rose bay willowherb, black knapweed, toadflax and tansy (what names!) – have combined with various grasses over the last 40 years to produce ground that now supports trees, not just the hardy willow, but also hawthorn, field maple and cherry. There are rumours that orchids lurk in the depth of this wood, along with less pleasing urban detritus. I don't find any, but there are lots of perky cowslips, and rather too many footpaths. Making for an appointment for which we're already late, we're suddenly lost – in Bill Quay.

Then we see a pair of unpretentious iron gates set between high hedges, beyond them a car, garage, and a flight of beguiling steps leading down to a house set on its own surrounded by trees. We open the gate…

The house is single, substantial, Edwardian; the garden verdant, idiosyncratic and in places crazily vertical. Knowing our place, we knock at the tradesman's entrance at the back, and the current owners welcome us inside the immaculate kitchen – a Welsh dresser is brimful of tea-sets – to hear the story of the house's first. The telling of the tale is helped down by tea, salmon sandwiches and a table bearing the feather-light burden of three cakes. We learn much about the estimable character of our hostess, Margaret Wear, when she laughs and tells us she didn't bake them herself – they were ordered up from her sister. But by, they were good…

Because our mouths are full, there are no questions forthcoming, so Alan Wear starts the tale, and then Margaret takes it over, and for the next hour or so, an invisible baton is passed between them as the life and times of RB Harrison Ltd are recounted over a gradually diminishing jam sponge.

Once upon a time there was a man called Robert Bell Harrison. Not much is known about his background, but around the turn of the 20th century he took it into his head to go into the ship repair business. He bought a little yard on a bend of the river at Bill Quay that had been established by a man

BELOW
The river narrows at Bill Quay and International Paint.

called William Boutland in 1820. Robert Harrison apparently didn't know much about ships or how to build them, but had the good sense to hire a man who did, a shipwright from over the river at St Anthony's called Philip Brown. On a bend of the river, they rebuilt the yard, with two slipways, a fitting shop and a little quay with steam winches to service them all.

We've come to think of shipyards as massive enterprises with thousands of workers – and there were once a few of those – but there were also many more smaller enterprises, bijou yards, you might say, especially near its mouth and along the upper river towards Newcastle and Gateshead. They built and repaired smaller vessels, and often carefully constructed a particular niche in the trade. In time the niche carved out by Harrison's and its small workforce (never numbering more than 100) was the servicing of tugs. Overseeing it all was the genial and polite Robert Harrison, who was the opposite of an absentee owner: he lived quite literally over the shop, taking on the significant task of building a house on that Bill Quay cliff in 1910, then having steps cut into it to make a short if slightly arduous journey to and from work. He ran the yard, through depressions and two world wars, until he finally sold out before dying in 1953.

Many of the Harrison's workers lived locally – in the early days the foremen and their families lived in the bucolically-named White Cottage and Rose Cottage – and together with the workers at an another small shipyard slightly upstream, Wood Skinner's, they sustained the small nearby community of Bill Quay, its shops and pubs. There were three pubs on the way up the hill to Pelaw station: the Albion, the Cricketers and the Wardley Inn, which were only known to local people as, respectively, the Bottom Bar, the Middle Bar and the Top Bar.

After Robert Harrison's death, the yard was sold first to France Fenwick as a base for their fleet of Tyne tugs, then sold on to the multi-national Lonrho before being run in its dying days by a local businessman called George Cruttwell.

Cut to 1979 and Alan and Margaret Wear are looking for a new home. Together they run a busy upholstery and flooring business and have four growing children. They need a substantial home at a reasonable price, hopefully a place with character. This is what brings them to the Harrison house, but it's in a bad way: empty for some time, thieves have stripped out many original features and vandals have done their worst. At the bottom of the garden they find the remnants of Mr Harrison's piano. But there's something about the house and its setting, particularly its amazing view downriver, that the couple can't ignore. They swallow hard and buy it.

In time Alan and Margaret became part of the Harrison's family. They and their children were woken every morning by the yard coming to life. They made friends with its workers, bought their meat at Sharp's the butchers (who once upon a time grazed their sheep in the Wesleyan chapel garden), and took a drink in the Albion by the yard gates, which was then run by Jimmy Copeland, who swore like a trooper, and his wife, Doris, who didn't – she was a genteel Christian. The bar had an open fire with a small rug in front, explains Alan, and two rows of yellow lines. 'If you crossed them, Jimmy would bellow, don't park your arse in front of that fire!' When Alan called into the yard for a natter, he was often given a job to do and got his hands dirty. Many times, he recalls with a laugh, he helped haul a boat in its cradle up the slipways. When grandchildren came along and visited the house, Margaret would take them to the front door, hoist them in her arms and they'd wave to the yard's crane driver, Bobby, whose little cab was high above the water but level with the house. Bobby would always wave back. The children have grown up, but haven't forgotten the man in the crane.

Harrison's limped through the 80s, that terrible decade for Tyneside industry. There was less demand for tugs on the river, and the fleet was cut back. The yard diversified into fishing boats, but then they began to be laid up, so the yard began working on yachts. They even repaired an ocean-going schooner that once belonged to Kaiser Wilhelm of Germany. By now the workforce was down to no more than 20, but in the early 90s they were finally paid off and RB Harrison Ltd finally died. Sharp's butcher's shop has also gone, and sadly the Albion has joined the long list of riverside pubs where the last pint has been drawn. But there's a real sense in which the little yard still lives on, in the pretty tree-fringed house above it. People often knock on its back door as we did, mostly former employees or their descendants, often people from far away. Alan and Margaret Wear have become unofficial but enthusiastic custodians of the Harrison's story.

At their kitchen table the tea things are pushed aside and some photos tumble onto the cloth. Given to the Wears 30 years ago by a foreman at the yard, who had been given them in turn by a previous manager, they provide a snapshot of life in one of the Tyne's smallest enterprises. One in particular catches my eye: a group of men on the Harrison quay gazing at the camera in the 1930s, most wearing labouring clothes, but at the end of the row a man with white hair and moustache stares at the camera, with a watch chain hanging from his waistcoat pocket: the picture of an Edwardian gentleman – Robert Harrison. At the back a small black cat, the yard cat obviously, perches precariously on a bald man's shoulder.

'After we moved in and the yard closed, we fed the shipyard cats. There were a few of them, to keep the mice and rats down, I suppose. Mind, they were pretty feral – they wouldn't come into the house. We put their food at the back door. Then gradually, they stopped coming,' says Margaret.

In front of the bald man in the photo is a boy, obviously an apprentice. This turns out to be Alan's much older brother-in-law, the late Peter Kenny,

who worked at Harrison's for two years before going to sea. One of his duties was to climb up the steps to the gaffer's house and then run to Bill Quay's shops for the housekeeper's messages. He was universally known around the yard as 'the boy'.

(A few months later I return to the house with another visitor – Ronnie Soden, who served his time as a marine fitter at Harrison's in the early 50s. Once he ran messages too, going to the side door of the Middle Bar to place bets for his workmates, on one unforgettable occasion carrying £200 for a single, spectacular punt. At bait time on sunny days he'd take the yard's foy boat out on the still waters of the Tyne and skull down to Pelaw staith and back. Other times he'd accompany the yard manager Sidney Armstrong – a bit of a martinet who always wore a 'dutt' (bowler hat) – on trips in the yard launch *Halcyon* up and down the river. The crack is good that afternoon too, but as Ronnie remarks, 'I wish I'd had a camera then. I wasn't that interested in what was going on or the stories the men told, but now I'm 77 I've got bags of curiosity. Life's the wrong way round, isn't it?')

Back on the sunny summer's day, the walkers explore the house and gardens restored over 30 years by our hosts. In the immaculate front room is a painting Margaret's working on, a copy of TM Hemy's famous picture of the *Mauretania* leaving the Tyne in 1907, now hanging in Newcastle's Discovery Museum. Outside we inspect Mr Harrison's meat store, which he had built into the hillside (the hooks were still hanging when the Wears first moved in), later used as an air raid shelter. There are other objects in the garden from the yard – an old anvil and several heavy rusting chains. Harrison planted many trees in his virgin garden. 'He obviously loved nuts, because there are plenty of them and we enjoy their fruit,' says Alan. 'He was a nice man apparently, people spoke well of him.'

The garden is a fine and private place. Periodically the trees planted by Robert Harrison have to be pruned so Alan and Margaret can enjoy that amazing view. 'I don't know what I'd do if I couldn't see the Naval Yard cranes every morning,' says Margaret.

The Wears walk down the hill with us to look at the remains of the yard. We squeeze through a gap in the old gates. The sheds and offices have gone. The site has been colonised by a riot of brambles, the inevitable rosebay willowherb and willow scrub now growing to maturity. The walls of the electrical house are covered in graffiti, the floor littered with empty spray paint and lager cans. It's the same in the winding house. The remnants of two slipways are still evident as well as concrete pillars built as bases for cranes.

There are five fishermen ranged along the quay, including the amiable, bare-chested Simon, who's drinking Foster's and sunbathing. He welcomes the chance to talk.

OPPOSITE
Alan and Margaret Wear (above), and Margaret's depiction of the *Mauretania* leaving the Tyne.

111

PREVIOUS PAGE
Dead and alive: remains of
Harrison's Yard, Bill Quay,
in foreground with Simon
fishing and 'chilling',
and behind, Offshore
Technology Park, Walker.

'I'm just chillin'. It's one of the best fishing spots on the river. I once caught a three and a half pound cod here, but today it's just eels and crabs. You get no bother – nae nutters, though we have to keep the teeny toe rags away 'cos they light fires and cause bother'. Simon praises the graffiti – 'it's decorative' – and confides that Harrison's provides other bounty besides fish. 'At low tide I collect bits of scrap. It stops your fishing gear getting snagged as well as giving you a bit pocket money'. He pops another can and offers it around; we thank Simon and move on, leaving him to his chilling in the sunshine.

But let's not leave the Harrison's story just yet.

In the autumn of 2009, not long after starting work as the Port's writer in residence, I spent a month in northern California at an artists' retreat, working on a project that's quite literally another story. With a group of poets and painters, I lived in a ranch-house overlooking a quiet valley with giant trees and a population of coyotes. In the evenings the fog would roll in from the distant Pacific, slowly creep up the valley and silently envelop the house. In the mornings it would make the journey in reverse so that by 10 the sun would be out and the Pacific again visible, the deepest blue I've ever seen.

In that month I took one day off to travel the 50 miles with a friend into one of my favourite cities, San Francisco. In the morning I wandered the wacky shops and cafes of the old hippy district of Haight-Ashbury, my phone going mental with texts from friends recording the progress of Newcastle's away fixture at Sheffield United (we won), and in the evening went to a gig by the band *The Tiger Lilies*. In the afternoon, I wandered the considerable waterside of the city and there encountered a sight that brought me up short: a small vessel called the *Eppleton Hall*. The name was obviously familiar, even to a non-Wearsider. Further investigation proved me right: here, on the west coast of the USA, was a vessel built on the Tyne but which also laboured on the Wear.

The story…

The *Eppleton Hall* (known on Tyneside as 'the *Eppy*') is the last remaining example of a Tyne paddle tug. She was built by Hepple's of South Shields in 1914 for the Lambton and Hetton Collieries and named after the Lambton family home near Penshaw. She was designed to tow colliers to and from Tyne Dock, but after coal nationalisation in 1948, was bought by the tug-owners France Fenwick (which shortly afterwards bought Harrison's) and moved into service on the Wear until 1964, before ending its active life at Seaham Harbour. She was sold for scrap in 1967, and left on a mud bank in Dunston where a fire destroyed her interior and deck: a sad end for the little workhorse. Then entering the tale came the intriguingly named Karl Kortum, director of the San Francisco Maritime Museum. He decided a Tyne paddle tug was just what his museum needed, so he bought it and had it painstakingly restored at – you guessed it – Harrison's yard in Bill Quay. And a good job they made of it too, as the little ship had to chug halfway round the world – across the Atlantic Ocean, through the Panama Canal, under the Golden Gate Bridge and all – to reach its last resting place.

So, as the old hippy anthem goes, if you're going to San Francisco – go and see a little piece of the Tyne's maritime heritage.

We say a fond farewell to the Wears as they return to South Bank, Bill Quay. Another old song springs to mind: Peggy Lee's sublime *The Folks Who Live On the Hill.*

Down the hill towards the river, roofer Jimmy Donaldson is pottering about in his workshop next to his house in Hoyson Villas. This one has another wondrous view of the river, this time upstream. 'It's a lovely spot and I can't think of living anywhere else, despite the eyesore down the hill,' says Jimmy, the last a reference to a car graveyard (specifically for VW's) colonising an old paintworks. Charles is drawn to the crazy shapes made by the little mountains of ancient Beetles and Polos before a gadgy politely moves us on – some of the walls are unsafe. A smaller scrapyard nearby excites my pleasure, for parked in a corner is an ancient white van, its flanks emblazoned with the words *Live Theatre*, once used to transport the sets and props of plays touring the halls and working-men's clubs of the North East, a few of mine included. Many times, in places like Shildon, Ferryhill and Wallsend, I helped with the 'get-in' and get-out' alongside actors and technicians who became good friends as a result of our play-making. I have a little Proustian moment peering through the yard gates, aided not by the aroma of 'petite madeleine' cakes, but the sight of that rusting Bedford van.

Out on the river a canoe holding two men and a rod moves slowly upstream. Peter Hill is looking for his supper. Our conversation echoes over the water. His amiable accent is plainly Welsh, so I ask the obvious question. 'How did I get to Bill Quay? How else? I met a beautiful woman'. They paddle on…

Fairfield Park nearby was once the home of the Wood Skinner Shipyard: they built gunboats on the surviving slipway. After the yard closed in 1925, the site was used for a new high-tech industry: the making of radar systems for ships, latterly by Marconi. When Marconi closed down here in the 1980s, the site was bought by the Livingston Group, the Teesside-based machine tool firm then diversifying into property. Fairfield is one of many similar estates up and down the river, offering workshop and office space to a wide range of businesses, but I'm here to talk to Livingston's former deputy chairman, who has his office here. He's in a unique position to talk about the recent past and future of the river, because after a career in politics and a thorough steeping in the issues of economic development, he's chair of the Port of Tyne and until recently deputy chair of the Government's regional growth fund. His name is Ian Wrigglesworth.

'One of the things people tend to forget is that industrial production needs far fewer people than it used to. Redcar had and hopefully will again have the biggest blast furnace in Europe. It employed 4,000 people, but just compare that to Armstrong's in Newcastle that once employed 25,000. In the machine tool industry there were enormous shops that don't exist any more because today they're run by computers, not manual workers, and to make them pay you've got to keep them going 24 hours a day, to pay the costs of the technology. This means that enterprises have to be increasingly specialised, like Rolls Royce on Scotswood Road. It only makes vehicle doors but makes them 24 hours a day, day after day – a concentration of clever machines in one place that cost millions and millions and never stop but don't need people. I exaggerate but you know what I mean – the days of the vast employers on one site are by and large over'.

Sir Ian has similarly trenchant views on the industrial retrenchment of the last 50 years; he had a close-up view of it.

'In my view it's a myth that we lost out to the Far East on cost; if we lost out it's because the capital investment just wasn't there. People blame the trade unions for the collapse of manufacturing industry but I think many industrial enterprises got the unions they deserved. Managements had rigid hierarchical structures and did things because they'd always done it. There was a lot of inertia but there's also been this continuing disdain in our culture for industry and trade.'

Despite this, he remains bullish about the region's prospects, and the Tyne in particular.

'No other city in Britain has been so involved in industrial development as Newcastle. It's staggering to me. It's been going on for 2,000 years and it all began with coal, which has had so much influence on our history and culture. Engineering came out of that. We inherit this legacy and can build on it. Being so close to Dogger Bank, the Tyne from the middle river down could be the Aberdeen of wind power, providing everything from construction and maintenance to accountancy and legals. That's the prize, but we have to be aware of stiff competition from the Tees and Humber as well as Holland and Germany, and we must act together as a region, and avoid petty politicking and squabbling.'

As we walk back to the gate, I ask Sir Ian about the economic prospects of where we're standing now, on the upper river. He sniffs the air.

'Well, there are businesses here and elsewhere and that's good. But you see we're surrounded by trees and greenery, and that's marvellous. Nothing to apologise for or feel bad about. Up here, I think the use of the river is mostly about leisure, people enjoying the tranquility of the riverside. I wish I had more time to enjoy it myself.'

We've barely walked 50 yards from an urban river scene – stacked VW auto wrecks – before Ian Wrigglesworth's final point seems immediately to be echoed: we hear the unmistakable sound of horses' hooves.

We turn a corner and see a boy leading a pony along a path, its front legs flicking outwards in a beguiling way, further on a triangular collection of sheds surrounded by a fence into which are set various gates. One is open and a softly smiling man by the name of Peter Pharoah stands with his hands on hips. I give my usual speech about the walk, and he stands aside, pointing the way into a dark doorway, from which a grating noise can be heard. In a little stable a young woman called Ruth Parker has her hands inside a horse's mouth. In fact she's filing the pony's teeth, having just extracted its so-called wolf teeth. Well, she would: Ruth is one of the very few equine dentists in the North. Christy notices instantly that she has beautifully manicured nails.

Nearby, Peter is grooming a young stallion, Murphy, not surprisingly from Ireland. He saw him on YouTube – the indispensable tool of the horse dealer – and was instantly smitten. It's easy to see why – a delicately striking combination of grey and white, Murphy has a pink mouth and nose, which Peter says need to be smothered in Factor 50 on hot days. I assume this is a joke, but it isn't. Murphy is a highly prized Blue Blagdon, and about to receive – or should that be serve? – 'his first lady friend', as Peter coyly puts it.

Peter Pharoah keeps 'heavy cobs' and the occasional trotting horse. A friend with the equally intriguing name of Ken Flax has the yard next to him. Today Peter is also breaking in a stallion which is naturally reluctant to leave his lady friend in the conjugal stable. 'He came here as wild as a hawk but he's calmed down a bit now,' he says, then turning to another horse, 'This one we call Horse With No Name because he came in dead as a dodo but we've got him going now.' There are 15-20 horses in the yards which Peter and his friends are training up before selling them on. This is a big thing in the local area; Peter reckons there are about 200 horses in the Felling area, tethered on various spare bits of land.

The stables were once Greys Buildings, a collection of houses, pubs and shops that served local industry ('It was a dirty old slum really,' says Peter), but all that remains is a kerb running down the hill. Peter was born and brought up not far away, and remains a Felling lad, though I notice he refers to the place as 'the Felling'. When I question this, he has an answer – he usually does: 'In the olden days there were woods all over here and they were cut down. So that's how it got the name – the place of the felling.'

His face is straight, but I wonder for a moment if I'm being gently had. Apparently not, as it turns out…

A stepping pony returns from a run and a little dog called Paddy – Ken found him at Appleby Horse Fair – barks out the fact. There are other animals on the site – including three lurchers, one of whom is called Raptor, described by Peter as a thief and a bully, as well as an albino fox that Peter glimpses regularly.

Ken used to train horses that were often sold for racing on legitimate tracks like York and Musselburgh – 'people knew they'd get good goers here' – but it should also be said that there's a current vogue for illegal road racing; races on motorways in the early morning sounds particularly hairy, but I guess that's the point. Peter accepts there's a stigma attached to his world, he thinks unfairly: 'People think we're villains but we're just people who love horses, and I tell you there's no one looks after them better than us here.' As evidence for that, we need to look no further than the presence of equine dentist Ruth. There are other rising costs – hay has doubled in price in recent years – and the problem of vandals. During a World Cup match in the summer of 2010, some evil spirit set one of Ken's stables alight, and despite desperate efforts to evacuate the horses, one of them died, a tragedy that deeply affected its owner, or as Peter graphically puts it: 'Ken lost his plug for a spell after that, but he's on the mend now.'

Peter stumps off to get some feed for two giggling lasses – the yard receives many visitors – while Charlie looks for images and Birtley draws a horse peering out of a stable. Rather inconveniently she keeps moving her head.

I suppose when it comes right down to it, Peter's yard qualifies as that acronym beloved of economic development experts – SME, small and medium-sized business. If so, it's an SME with a difference, as Peter makes clear.

'I don't make any money out of it. I've a lovely wife, who works very hard so I can do what I love to do. I had a job once, at Nissan, for about six months, but I hated it. One day I walked out and never went back.'

We take our leave. It's mid afternoon and there are a few miles to walk yet. Peter Pharoah and Ken Flax wave us off.

How many cracking people can you meet in a day's walk? As it turns out, we're not yet done.

To the people who claim this is *not women's work*,
I expect Ruth would say *take a seat. Think again*
when she's eyeball to chin with a Blue Blagdon horse
who's allowed her to rasp a steel file on his teeth
without flinching. At first, you might waver and think

this appears medieval, especially the blood
which has bangled Ruth's arms, but you'll notice a hush
in the stable as well, an acoustic of trust
as she goes about freeing the horse from his *hooks*
of enamel, a job she calls *floating*. Unfazed

by the risk that those hooves could so easily rise
in the air and descend with a crash, Ruth persists.
If she didn't, that kick to her face years ago
or the rivals who told her to quit would rear up
in her memory and bruise today's calm. At Bill Quay

she's unslept, having hiked overnight from Carlisle
to raise money for kids, but her focus remains
on the Blue, which suggests the old proverb is right
when it says the way someone approaches a horse
is the way they approach the whole business of life.

Horse people of Bill Quay: equine dentist Ruth Parker and trainer Peter Pharoah.

As we make the short way to the next river landmark, the dying clatter of horses' hooves makes my thoughts drift to a man called Robert Saint. Perhaps I should have mentioned him before now, for he was a Hebburn man, recently honoured long after his death with a plaque on his old home in Victoria Road East. A pitman who laboured in the notoriously gassy pit of his home town until it closed in 1932, he was also a talented musician. He was so moved by an explosion caused by firedamp that entombed 250 men at Gresford Colliery in North Wales in 1934 that he sat down and wrote an air for brass band named after the pit. In the 75 years this simple but profoundly moving melody has been played at countless Miners' Galas and funerals, and in time has become known as 'The Miners' Hymn'. Most recently it was sung at the conclusion of Lee Hall's marvellous play about the Ashington Group, *The Pitmen Painters*. Saint died a relatively young man of 50 from a toxic combination of heart disease, bronchitis and asthma, but not before he signed away his rights in *Gresford* to the National Union of Mineworkers for the benefit of Aged Miners' Homes in Durham. And why did the sound of Peter's horses make me think of this admirable man? After he left the pit and endured a few years of unemployment, Robert Saint became an inspector for the National Equine Defence League, and with his family set up an animal refuge in Hebburn, first in the back yard of his flat, and then on a farm at Hedworth, where horses could run free. By all accounts, his compassion for animals was first stirred by the condition of pit ponies he worked alongside at Hebburn Colliery. By way of tribute, I start humming the melancholic, sighing, falling notes of Robert Saint's masterpiece.

There's a history going back 250 years of chemical manufacture along the shore downstream of Gateshead. This tradition in turn spawned the making of paint that not only survives, but positively flourishes. In fact International Paint, with more than 1,000 workers, is the biggest private employer in the borough of Gateshead.

The site they occupy is roughly triangular and covers 47 hectares, with a river frontage stretching almost a quarter of a mile. The business was started in 1896 by two German immigrants, the brothers Holzapfel. Their first workshop was in Dun Cow Yard in the centre of Gateshead (the original wooden barrel they used there is displayed in IP's reception) and they moved to a zinc works on the riverside so that raw materials could be brought and finished goods taken out by boat. That ceased some years ago, and given this setting on the steep slope of a ballast hill, the works might have moved to an out-of-town site more convenient for container lorries – or even in the frequent pattern of a globalised world, closed down altogether, for IP long ago passed out of local control, being owned first by Courtauld's, and then bought in 1998 by the Dutch multi-national AkzoNobel. Neither of these things happened: International Paint is not only staying in Gateshead, but expanding.

We're given the tour by works manager Simon Harrison, a chemical engineer by trade. He tells us the plant makes various kinds of specialised paint – marine coatings, powder coatings for autos and fire protection coatings (a business that's grown significantly since 9/11). As we amble downhill, passing boards on which paint samples are hung out to dry and weather, avoiding the 40 fork-lift trucks that constantly whizz around the site, I ask the dumb question, how do you make paint?

'It's very simple, like making a cake. You mix dry materials with wet materials. The trick is how you do it'.

Bearing out Ian Wrigglesworth's remarks on modern industrial production, the polymer plant at IP runs 24 hours a day, seven days a week, but takes only 16 men to run it, four on each shift. The 120 people who work in manufacturing are outnumbered by 350-400 in research and development (the remainder of the workforce occupy marketing and office functions). More than £5 million has been spent recently on a research lab in fire protection and 50 new jobs have been created.

'This is an innovation-led business and I'm happy to say that Gateshead has the largest R&D concentration in the whole AkzoNobel worldwide business, which has 65,000 employees,' says Simon.

By way of example, one of the labs on the site, the so-called 'slime lab', won the Queen's Award For Industry in 2008 for its work on marine infestation. Following growing concern about the toxic elements in marine paint to deter the growth of marine organisms, IP developed a new product, a bio-paint called 'Inter-sleek 900', which is so smooth even the most tenacious of creatures can't settle on it.

As we walk east along a lane called Tyne Street, a public right of way till the 1980s (it even has its own Victorian postbox, sadly out of use), Simon tells a story about the remarkable properties of Inter-sleek 900: 'A ship sailed after being painted and then docked in a port that the captain knew very well. He switched off the engines in the usual place, but because of the smooth underside, the ship sailed way past its regular stopping point, and bumped into the quay.'

This suggests the reason why AkzoNobel, one of the Fortune Top 500 companies in the world, allowed International Paint to retain both its name and distinctive red propeller logo: they want to retain the company's brand leadership, especially in marine coatings, which Simon succinctly describes:

'We can paint a boat in its entirety with many different kinds of paint. Our competitors can't.'

We arrive at the east end of the site, known at the plant as 'the morgue', a reference to the regularity with which the bodies of unfortunate 'jumpers' from the bridges upstream are carried by currents and tides. More happily, workers on their breaks – and there are few today, inevitably gazing at the river – often see jumping salmon and from time to time seals catching them. IP has played its part in the river's clean-up – there are no discharges from the site into the river. It seems the right place to ask Simon for the secret of IP's success. He doesn't pause.

'The bedrock of the company and what we've achieved are the people here. They're loyal, sensible and very hard working'.

By way of example, we meet Richard Kelly, who has worked at IP for more than 40 years, mostly as a forklift driver. More remarkably, he is the fourth generation of his family to have worked here. Both

ABOVE
Local historian and last in long line of paint makers Richard Kelly.

his grandfather and great-grandfather worked for the brothers Holzapfel in their little shed in Dun Cow Lane. A single man with a literary turn of phrase ('I remember my first day like it was yesterday. It was a foggy morning and the mist was rising off the river, like something out of Charles Dickens'), Richard has both Scots and Irish blood but with an extra ingredient in the genetic cocktail: he has a bit of Danish from his granny's side. Also something of a historian of his native Felling, Richard can remember when Tyne Street was a real street; it had a Co-op, a butcher's, an abattoir – and a mortuary. He hopes to develop this interest when he retires in 2012.

'IP have been good and secure employers. There's a family feel to the place. In all this time, I've only been on strike once, in the late 70s, and that was over before it started. I live 20 minutes' walk from here and it's good to work locally. I'm sorry to be going but the arthritis has got to my hands and knees. My eyes aren't too clever either. I'm also sorry I'm the last family member to work here. Quite a thing, four generations, isn't it?'

In fact, the entire visit to International Paints has been quite a thing. It's marvellous to hear about a historic Tyneside enterprise that's been acquired by a foreign multi-national not to kill off the competition, but to develop its potential as a worldwide brand-leader. Marvellous too to hear that it's working – and that at the root of it is a skilled and committed Tyne workforce.

I feel like celebrating. We weave our way through the dozens of businesses on East Gateshead's trading estates, and return to the river at Friars

Goose marina. Hundreds of years ago, there was a monastery here; maybe the monks bred fowl. We make for the Elephant on the Tyne pub, and collapse on the terrace. Out on the water, the salmon are also celebrating with the odd triple salko, but two speedboats driven by two youths who evidently have masculinity issues drive them into the deeps. But nothing can spoil our mood – and yes, I'll come clean – alcohol is consumed in the summer sun of a Friday afternoon.

Out in the water, some of the boats from the marina are moored. My gaze settles on one, with the name *Canny 'Bairn*, and I wonder who the bairn is, and where he or she is now.

Time for a second pint?

After three days of sun, the glow is on our faces, but I feel something similar inside, despite the warning signs about contaminated soil at the edge of the final patch of riverside woodland and the noisy pecking of the demolition men at Spillers Mill on the north side. It strikes me the disturbance has emptied the little white tower built for local kittiwakes until I realise their breeding season is over and they must have gone to sea. The trees whose company we've had all day and shade we've enjoyed finally peter out. It strikes me that in thousands of years' time they will be compressed deep underground and slowly turn into coal.

Down a lane and a last collection of SME's – an aggregate yard, Honda Marine dealer, supplier of fancy goods and the inevitable scrapyard, we turn a corner and there it is – Tyneside's Xanadu, its mighty span of smiling bridges, every returning Geordie's vision of *hyem*.

Quite naturally, our pace slows: you can't hurry this bit.

Both quaysides are packed with folk: gangs of stags and hens limbering up for a weekend on the lash, more mellow *Guardian*-readers heading over the swooping Millennium Bridge for Gateshead's cathedrals of art and music, the Baltic and the Sage. Many have commented on the apparent fact that Newcastle-Gateshead now sells culture rather than coal – personally I believe the developments driven mostly by Gateshead Council weren't just strategic imperatives but both inspired and life-enhancing – but there is a more precise and ironic way of characterising this seismic shift, a curious fact I only discovered that very evening.

Everyone knows that the Baltic Centre for Contemporary Art was once a mill, but it didn't contain just any old grain. It used to store feed for pit ponies, beloved of Robert Saint and so many other pitmen.

It might have apparently passed into history, but you see, on a Tyne Walk, you can never quite escape the giant fact of coal.

It's the kind of invitation to get small boys excited – and grown men ecstatic.

'Do you fancy going for a ride up and down the Tyne in a tug? If you behave yourselves, you might even get a go driving.'

A few days later on a chilly autumn afternoon, we're waiting on Northumbrian Quay at North Shields, just downstream from a vast Ijmuiden ferry, watching an example of the tug-man's art as the coal carrier *Bogdan* of Valletta is shepherded out to sea by the tugs *Yarm Cross* and *Svitzer Lyndhurst*. As they pass, the *Svitzer Redbridge* appears, hovering to find a spot to take us on board. As we hop from foot to foot, with excitement rather than cold, we examine our pleasure craft for the afternoon.

It's a kind of push me-pull you vessel, without obvious aft and stern, a high glass-sided conning tower amidships, in which skipper Tommy Appleby stands, nudging his way to the quay. It is frankly not the most elegant craft we've seen on the river – it appears rather demeaningly on the website uglyships.com – but despite its looks is perfectly fitted for its task of persuading vastly bigger vessels to follow its lead. Having arrived on the Tyne in February 2011, it is also the latest in a very long list of more than 1,400 tugs, from the *Abeille* to the *Zeta*, that have laboured on the river in the last 170 years.

In 1816 Joseph Price of Gateshead bought three paddle steamers that had been used to establish, without success, a passenger service on the river. Two years later he began using them to tow sailing vessels in and out of the Tyne, with immediate benefits: larger vessels could now navigate the river up to Newcastle and delays due to adverse wind and weather were much reduced. As a result a typical Newcastle collier could manage 13 voyages a year to the Thames, instead of the previous eight. These early tugs were made of wood and clinker-built, with simple steam boilers (the *Eagle* for example had an engine made by James Watt) and side-mounted paddle wheels. These features gave them a shallow draught and superb manoeuvrability, essential in helping sailing ships overcome the very difficult conditions at the mouth of the river in the days before piers. Over time the wood would be replaced by iron and then by steel, as the building of tugs for the Tyne and many other rivers became a staple of the river's burgeoning shipbuilding industry. More than 100 firms built tugs between the 1820s and the 1990s, from JP Almond to T Young & Son, both of North Shields. The list includes a familiar name: the Wouldhave family, who were involved in the building of the first lifeboat at South Shields.

The *Redbridge* was built in Hull in 1995, since when it has worked various rivers, but its crew – Stephen Brown, Les Robertson and Tommy Appleby – are all from the Tyne. Down below we inspect the facilities. There are three bedrooms and the beds are all made up; once the crew goes onboard they're never entirely sure when they'll come off. As if to prove the point, a washing machine is spinning somewhere, but its paltry motor is drowned out by the deafening roar of the tug's engines. Up on the glass-sided bridge the air is slightly nippy and Tommy confirms that up here it's chilly in winter and boiling hot in the summer, so much so that a previous master used to grow tomatoes in it, the *Redbridge* thus becoming the only mobile greenhouse on the Tyne.

Going upriver we watch the car-carrier *Precious Ace* moving away from her berth at the Nissan car terminal at Tyne Dock. As the pilot goes on board, a gust of the offshore wind moves her towards the centre of the river, but the tugs in attendance nudge her gently back. This cannot be done without serious welly in the engine room below; the *Redbridge* has Finnish Wärtsilä engines equivalent to 4,300 horsepower and for those in the know, a Voith-Schneider propulsion system. Scoff at its size or shape if you like, but the big daddy on the Tyne is actually your modern tug.

When the first tugs began working the river, pioneering engineers were opening workshops, among them Robert Hawthorn at Forth Banks in 1817 and George Stephenson in South Street in 1823. Both were to concentrate on railway engines, a development fuelled by the need to get coal to market, as indeed was the demand for tugs. Fifteen vessels were used for towing on the Tyne by 1822; Hawthorn's engined four of them. Small firms sprang up along the river and many shipbuilders added engine shops to their yards to produce their own machinery, but in the longer term, Gateshead, South Shields and North Shields became the main centres for building tugs. By the 1860s there were a staggering 250 steam tugs on the Tyne as further demand from shipbuilders and ship-repairers for their services grew. Their hungry appetite for coal usually restricted operations to the river, but some tugs made longer trips out to sea to look for business, with coal piled on the decks until they were almost awash. Tyne tugs were also sold to other ports. An 1852 Admiralty survey of the tugs in London, Bristol and Liverpool showed that 40 were built on the Tyne. The list of tug-owners on the Tyne is almost as long as the tug-builders. There was healthy competition between them – though many shipbuilders operated their own vessels – but over time their numbers consolidated and now there is only one, Svitzer, which has 500 vessels in 40 countries, employing 4,500 principally in towage and salvage. They took over Tyne Towage, the last of the family-run tug businesses on the river, and now operate three tugs on the river, which also cover the Wear and the Blyth, as well as five more on the Tees.

As we approach Hebburn to inspect the swanky new Svitzer moorings just downstream of A&P, we hear from our skipper that we must have seen the *Redbridge* on the first day of our walk: it helped deliver those sections of obsolete rigs into the river for cutting-up at Swan's. Tommy Appleby has worked on tugs all his life. He was seven when he first sailed on one – his uncle and two brothers were in the trade – and 15 when he joined the *Bamburgh*. There was never much doubt what he was going to do with his life, he says.

I've come to appreciate that for every mariner met, there is a tale (or ten) to be heard. So I ask Tommy for his. He does not disappoint.

'I was once sailing in the Channel and a bird flopped on the deck. It was obviously knackered. We took it in the messroom and there it stayed for three days, taking drinks, bits of food from us as we ate, it even swayed with the movement of the boat. Then to top it all, when one of us started looking at a chart, it looked too.'

I know, I know, but Tommy had the grace to smile as we laughed. However, as the man said, strange things happen at sea.

Now it's Tommy's turn to laugh. He asks us if we'd like to have a go steering the *Redbridge* back to Northumbrian Quay, We form an orderly queue and he stands back to watch. We are all utterly hopeless.

It looks so easy: the control is the kind of rubber knob familiar to all those who played computer games in the 1980s, but its use defies logic, and we are soon… well, all at sea. As each of us veers towards this bank or that, Tommy has to step in to keep us on the straight and narrow with the deft use of one finger. For the record, in a poor field, Birtley comes last, his steering like the course of a drunken sailor after a night on bad beer. He seems more concerned with getting a photographic record of his exploits. 'Take my picture,' he beseeches Charlie, 'my brother's an engineer, he'll never believe this.'

Meanwhile I make a mental note to research the arcane history of 'tugs on Tyne'. I'm not hopeful, but someone points me in the direction of the website 'Tyne Tugs and Builders', which is full of riches both factual and photographic, and an example of the way in which the web has democratised the telling of local history. In the course of researching this book, I've encountered many non-professional historians who've made it their business to research and publish accounts of the particular elements of Tyne history that fascinate them, and it's time to pay them due respect. For one thing, this book would have been the poorer without them.

Once Tommy is back in charge, we're soon docking again at North Shields. I ask who ultimately owns the vessel; it turns out Svitzer is part of the huge shipping and transport concern Maersk. The Danes, it seems, are a people who have somehow managed to hold on to their marine infrastructure, and with it, its skills and traditions. I wonder what their secret is.

The crew will soon be going off duty. I ask Tommy what he does with his time off. He smiles.

He makes models of old tugboats.

DAY FOUR

It's cold up there in summer, like sittin' inside a fridge,
Still Aa wish Aa was on the Quayside, looking at the old Tyne Bridge...
...Ah'm comin' home, Newcastle, ye can keep ya London wine,
Aa'd walk the streets aal day an' aal neet for a bottle of the River Tyne...

I'm Coming Home, Newcastle, Busker

It is a wonderful thing, and actually rather an unusual thing, to drive a bridge.

This is for the obvious reason that by and large bridges don't move, but among Tyneside's many distinctions is a bridge that actually swings (and what's more, another that tilts or even possibly winks). And I was on the Swing Bridge the day it pirouetted majestically from its base deep down in the Tyne mud, not for its primary purpose of letting ships pass through, but to honour its presiding genius in the presence of his descendant and friends.

And let me tell you – we all had a ball, rather setting the tone for this fourth day of our Tyne walk, which started in bright sunshine and ended in heavy rain, but was nevertheless dominated by a sense of the playful, during which we were reminded time and again how much pleasure people enjoy on or beside rivers. And the man who built the Swing Bridge, Victorian inventor and entrepreneur par excellence though he was, probably had as much fun as anyone...

I should say straight away that despite being long dead William Armstrong played a significant role in my upbringing. I was brought up in a Jesmond house barely a hundred yards from the dene he presented to the people of his native Newcastle, and throughout childhood it was my playground. When I started going to Heaton Grammar School, perched above the dene, I joined Armstrong House (house colours marine blue, alongside the yellow of Collingwood, green of Grey and red of Stephenson), and my journeys there involved crossing the great iron bridge that he had flung over the Ouseburn. There was still road traffic on it then, but in later years a friend would sometimes cross Armstrong Bridge by walking along its parapet to impress the girls heading for Heaton High (he later became an RAF pilot). I also went dancing to the Junco Partners in the Armstrong's Banqueting Hall nearby.

The choices William Armstrong made for his city retreat and country hideaway at Cragside near Rothbury weren't accidental; wherever he lingered, there had to be running water. But this lifelong love affair had an intensely practical aspect: all his life he burned with the desire to channel

PREVIOUS PAGES
Schooner *James Leathard* slowly en route from Dunston to Tyne Dock for wholesale restoration.

water's elemental power – and the Swing Bridge was an ultimate expression of his success.

The roots of this fascination with water lay in the place of his birth and upbringing. William George Armstrong was born in 1810 within a good stone's throw of the Tyne in the tiny hamlet of Shield Field, once the mustering place for English soldiers setting out for battles against marauding Scots. The back garden of the family home in Pleasant Row tumbled down into the Pandon Dene, where little mills hummed, birds sang and the burn gurgled a song of its own. It would soon be bridged (hence New Bridge Street), filled in and occupied by workshops and factories to make a very different Shieldfield, but in Armstrong's youth, it was a beguiling place, as a contemporary writer made clear: 'The mass of apple-blossom and the teeming luxuriance of the foliage which covered the banks, the little summer-houses in the trim gardens, and the winding pathway from the town to the Shieldfield formed a picture of rare sylvan beauty.'

Reading that, you get an inkling of what with his vast wealth the man who due to his love of angling became known as 'the Kingfisher' tried to achieve in Jesmond Dene and Cragside towards the end of his life: recreate the paradise he had known at its beginning.

At school young William showed a passion for mechanics, but his self-made father had a plan for his son to study the law. But after he qualified and returned to Newcastle to practise as a solicitor, much of Armstrong's spare time was filled with ruminations about engines. His desk was covered in drawings rather than contracts: firstly for an 'improved waterwheel', the principles of which he sketched out while fishing one day, then for a hydraulic crane capable of lifting great weights with the single stroke of a piston. With the encouragement of men like Michael Faraday, inventor of the electrical motor, he conducted his own research and demonstrated the results to rapt audiences at his beloved Lit and Phil, the private library near what became Robert Stephenson's Central Station. In 1847 Armstrong finally took the plunge into a brave new world: he gave up the law and set up the firm WG Armstrong & Company along the banks of the Tyne at Elswick. The company soon began receiving orders for Armstrong's first great invention – the hydraulic crane that later gave its name to a celebrated pub among many on the Scotswood Road – from railway companies, shipyards and docks. Armstrong adapted the crane's operating principles to make hydraulic dock gates, and as ever strong-willed and fleet of foot, soon made his company compete in other fields of engineering, including building bridges and making ever-bigger guns for the battleships and destroyers of the world's navies. In 1850 Armstrong's yard employed 300 men, but within a dozen years the workforce had grown twelvefold; it carried on growing at a similar rate for the remainder of this extraordinary's man's life.

Not that the building of a great industrial empire was entirely without its problems. Ironically, one of Armstrong's biggest was caused by water, specifically his beloved Tyne and its bridging. The 18th century stone bridge at Newcastle with its nine arches made it difficult for Armstrong to get the products of his Elswick works downriver and out to sea, especially as the naval guns in which he specialised became ever greater. The solution was typical of both his engineering genius and political chutzpah: he persuaded the city authorities and the Tyne Improvement Commission (the forerunner of the Port of Tyne) to demolish the old bridge and build a new one, the sweetener being that Armstrong's would supply and install the ironwork and machinery, which was of course water-powered. Three masonry piers set into cast iron cylinders were sunk to a depth of 45 feet below low water and filled with concrete. The moving parts of the bridge, 281 feet long and weighing more than 1,450 tons, were designed to revolve through ninety degrees on the centre pier to allow ships to make passage 104 feet wide on either side. The controls were mounted in the cupola over the roadway and the machinery on the central pier. Power came from two hydraulic accumulators driven by steam pumps and the bridge first swung on 17 July 1876 to allow the *Europa* upriver to take on board at Elswick a gun for the Italian Government, at 104 tons the largest ever constructed. But Armstrong soon broke his own record; and of course the bridge gave him a gateway to the sea – the prelude to opening a shipyard at Elswick. Another story, for another day…

On our sunny Monday morning, we're greeted on the bridge by its custodian – strictly speaking, its maintenance fitter, a man with a name straight out of central casting. But Geordie Fenwick, with his mordant sense of humour, 'lazy eye' and deep reverence for another engineer with a Northumbrian name, turns out to be a singular man and a fine host. It's barely a few minutes before he's talking passionately about the water accumulator, one of Armstrong's earliest inventions, a simple but ingenious device that still powers the Swing Bridge.

'Basically, the accumulator's a cast-iron cylinder fitted with a plunger pumped up with water. Once the set position is reached, the motor cuts out and the 60-ton weight of the accumulator top then powers the engines. The plunger is slowly raised to draw in water, until the downward force of the weight is sufficient to force the water below into pipes at great pressure. It's this pressure that turns wheels on a circular track, which then turn the bridge.

'Actually, there are two accumulators. Armstrong was obviously a canny man because everywhere you look on this bridge, there are two of everything.'

Geordie then takes us to the motor room on the western side of the pontoon and demonstrates some working parts. Wheels turn, pistons pump.

The only significant change to the original design of Armstrong and his collaborator John F Ure, chief engineer of the Tyne Improvement Commission, is that the accumulators are now raised by electric rather than the original steam-driven pumps. But pretty much everything else is what he installed, and still working as well as it did 140 years ago. And the brass-work gleams – Geordie and his watchmen see to that. My friends are entranced. Charlie crouches to take close-ups of Victorian workmanship while Geordie ruminates.

'As an engineering man, you can't spend the time I have, getting to know the intricacies of how the bridge works, and not give the man credit. Every day I see the brilliance of his mind, as well as the skills of his people in the workings of the bridge. You just have to marvel at the workmanship. It's an honour to work with it every day,' says Geordie, who served his time at Swan Hunter.

It's estimated the bridge has swung well over 250,000 times: it had its busiest year in 1924, opening almost 20 times a day, but since the closing of Dunston staiths in 1980, and the subsequent closure of Stella power station, the bridge barely opens once a week nowadays, though it and the river crossing it carries continue to be manned and maintained by the Port of Tyne. Hence my excitement to be on the bridge when it did, standing in its control turret as bells rang, barriers descended and the traffic stopped, watching Geordie push and pull at various levers in a complicated sequence. Slowly, silently, gracefully, Armstrong's bridge began to swing in a 360-degree circle.

OPPOSITE
Swing Bridge maintenance fitter and custodian, Geordie Fenwick.

BELOW
Working parts on William Armstrong's masterpiece.

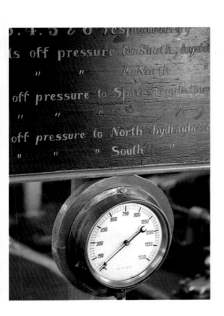

No driver tooted impatiently, pedestrians stared, even a train stopped on the King Edward Bridge as if in homage. There's something beguilingly graceful about this little bridge. Gradually, Geordie slowed its progress, but much to his embarrassment, it drifted past its stopping place. He blamed the chit-chat in the turret and the stickiness in its mechanism caused by lack of use and took the wisecracks from his guests well. One of them had a special reason to be here: Francis (aka Frankie) Armstrong farms near Bamburgh and is a descendant of the great man.

'To see it operating so well is not just a testament to its current keepers, but to my forebear who designed it. Lord Armstrong has left Newcastle an astonishing legacy and I'm very proud of that.'

Maintenance of the bridge can be difficult as well as costly; in the winter of 2010-11, the castings on pipes supplying the bridge's hydraulics burst and new parts had to be specially made by a firm supplying machinery for architectural monuments. The bridge was unable to open for a few months, but is now swinging as well as ever.

As we leave the motor room Geordie tells Christy that ships went up the Newcastle side and came down on the Gateshead side. There were different charges for passage, according to the contents of the ship's hold: a cargo of rags cost a farthing per ton while explosives were fifteen shillings. We return to Geordie's little office where his bait box sits on the desk. He's on duty on his own today, which inspires him to produce a photo of the bridge's staff from the 1930s; there are 19 of them, including the Bridge Master.

'See how efficient I am!' he bellows. 'Talk about multi-tasking!'

There's more laughter as Geordie escorts us off the premises. He points to a sewage outfall on the Newcastle bank and recalls that during a flash flood the previous winter he watched it disgorge a torrent containing brown furry mammals: Newcastle's population of rats had been caught napping.

Another more devastating flood passed this way on a Sunday in November 1771. Three days of heavy rain upstream created a torrent that undermined the old medieval bridge that stood like the original wooden Roman bridge (Pons Ælius) more or less on the site of the Swing Bridge. Like the ancient London Bridge, shops and houses clung to its structure, but after the flood carried away first the middle arch, then two more, six people lost their lives. More arches collapsed in the next few weeks – thus necessitating the building of the Georgian bridge that Armstrong had dismantled – but curiously one arch remains: under the Swing Bridge roadway at the Newcastle side.

The Great Flood of 1771 produced a legend I've never quite been able to prove or disprove. During the collapse of the bridge, a baby was said to have survived the falling masonry, its cradle carried downriver by the torrent. Some time later the cradle was found, according to different versions of the tale either on Jarrow Slake or at North Shields, and the finder took the bairn home where it was adopted by him and his wife before eventually being recovered by his true parents, a rich Newcastle merchant and his wife. Tom Hadaway, Shields fish merchant and playwright, once wrote a short play based on the story for Live Theatre, a hundred yards from the site of the bridge. It was, like all of Tom's work, matchless in its human understanding and tenderness. There's another story about the flood, of another writer, Dr Johnson's amanuensis, James Boswell. Staying with his brother in Newcastle on a journey from Scotland to London, he was held up by the wrecked bridge, but didn't take the situation lying down: he hired a pontoon onto which his coach was driven and ferried to Gateshead so he could complete his journey and record more aphorisms. A man who is tired of Tyneside and all that…

There's one more bridge story as we properly start our walk. Reaching the Gateshead side of the bridge, Geordie Fenwick points to an iron buttress into which the unfortunate Newcastle United player Kieron Dyer apparently once crashed his £120,000 sports car on the way home from an evidently lively evening on the party ship *Tuxedo Princess*. Geordie was there and relays the final score: Ferrari 0, Swing Bridge 1. Poor Kieron – canny player, but he missed more open goals than just about any Newcastle player I can remember. He was though exceptional at hitting bridges, as well as Lee Bowyer, of course…

Turning right into Pipewellgate, so named for the old wooden pipes that carried away Gateshead's waste water centuries ago, we encounter Graeme Rigby of the film and photography archive Amber. Over 40 years they've constructed a unique archive of life in the North East (and many other places) and in the process made many films about the Tyne. A film show for a rainy day? We make a date…

The first building on the road upstream is the restaurant *O de Vie*, splendidly housed in a station built in 1910 for the River Police, set up by the Admiralty under pressure from ship-owners whose cargoes were constantly being pilfered. To stem the crime wave (pun intended) the authorities hired 19 men good and true and provided them with six rowing boats, launched from the terrace where we now stand supping caffè latte. Next door is the Baja Beach Club, a tatty outpost of club culture that has outlived its 15 minutes (or less) of Quayside hip-dom. A peeling poster announces with unconvincing cool: 'Pimp My Shot'.

We turn back to look back at a side-view of the little bridge and down at the brown waters swirling underneath. Somewhere down there – when the river was wider and slower – the Roman Emperor Hadrian built the first bridge over the Tyne in 120 AD near the site of the second station on his new wall. At various times in the 19 centuries since, pieces of its original wooden foundations have come to the surface, most recently through the excavations of engineers. The wood is oak – more correctly, bog oak – dark of colour and very fine. I know this because I've held a piece in my hands, rubbing my fingers in wonder across its close-grained surfaces. Now it's time to tell you what it was: the surviving piece of Roman infrastructure had been fashioned into a casket given to a fine man called John Gillespie, a Scottish engineer who won the Port's golf tournament three times running. John worked his way up the ranks at the Tyne Improvement Commission and Port of Tyne before becoming the latter's chief engineer and then chief executive from 1973 to 1983. John has had a happier and longer retirement than one of his predecessors, a man named Gedye, who on his retirement travelled to Panama to help build its canal: one night, slung on a hammock between two palm trees, he was bitten by a vampire bat and died. Such things do not of course occur at Tyne Dock.

Coffee break over, we move on. Standing here you can't help but look up at the great smiling arch of the Tyne Bridge. I once wrote a little play about an encounter between two people for whom the bridge has a strong personal meaning. Running through their conversation was the awareness that this is a place where some people try, and sometimes succeed in, the taking of their lives. Retired Port of Tyne typist Dorothy Tweddell told me a story about this. She used to work in the recently demolished, unlovely office block near the Sage. Once she and her workmates saw someone climbing onto the arch and making their way to its highest point. This wasn't the first time they'd seen such a thing, and they did what they'd always done before – call the police. But this young man was different: he carried a small dog with him. The Inland Revenue workers were aghast, and so was the young man's girlfriend (or possibly ex) when she was brought by the police to 'help'. In this case, there was no gentle coaxing: she bellowed into the megaphone something to the effect that if he didn't bring her pooch back to safety, he'd be in big trouble.

Turning away into Pipewellgate, we see there are virtually no buildings on the riverside lane or the hillside above it far into the distance. In fact this is the emptiest stretch of Tyne bank we've walked along so far. The only features are early examples of Gateshead Council's admirable commitment to public art (culminating of course in the *Angel of the North*) and a plot of poppies blowing in the breeze. We pass the site of Joseph Price's glassworks

(one of the town's historic industries), a skeleton of an abandoned boat in the river mud by what used to be Brett's Oils, whose red neon sign reflected in the water at night always welcomed this homeward traveller on the King Edward Railway Bridge all the years I lived and worked in London. At the moment a coal train is rattling slowly across it, while a little Metro train scoots southwards and disappears into the side of Gateshead's cliff. There is, frankly, not that much to observe and write about.

Of course it wasn't always like this. I have a reproduction of a painting dating from 1935 by Edward M O'Rourke Dickey of this very bank, framed by the High Level and from the perspective of the Swing's central pontoon. In a vaguely Cubist style, it captures the jumble of red and purple roofs of workshops, mills and tenements tumbling down to the Tyne. At the top of the hill is the station where trains from the south terminated until Robert Stephenson finished his double-decker bridge in 1849, and around it the huge Greenesfield railway works sprang up. In the second half of the 19th century this was the town's biggest employer, employing 3,300 people. Back then there was plenty to write about, if rarely in the good news category; indeed one cataclysmic event excited the interest and pen of Victorian England's most famous novelist and journalist. This stretch of the Tyne was a place of fire as well as flood.

Just after midnight on Friday 6 October 1854, passers-by spotted a fire in a new mill on the Gateshead waterside by the old bridge, belonging to a firm of worsted tweed manufacturers. The fire was on an upper storey, so local people tried to salvage the stock lower down. But Wilson's used oil to treat the wool, and these barrels caught alight and the fire quickly spread. Within an hour, despite the efforts of the Newcastle and 'North British' fire engines, the fire was out of control; within two, the building was a complete wreck. The night's difficulties were just beginning.

Nearby was a seven-storey warehouse owned by a man called Charles Bertram, soundly built with 'a double fire-proof structure', used to store thousands of tons of sulphur, nitrate of soda and other combustibles. You'll guess what's coming next. The intense heat from the Wilson's mill fire caused the sulphur to ignite, melt and stream in a burning blue liquid from Bertram's windows. The military arrived with their fire engine, to no avail. By 3am, the entire warehouse was one body of flames 'most awfully magnificent', illuminating with a lurid purple light the river and its shipping, the High Level Bridge, the Castle, and the steeples of All Saints' and St Nicholas' Cathedral. The firestorm began to consume the whole of Gateshead's bankside; it could be seen 20 miles away, and streams of sightseers came to look, lining the bridges, quaysides, even the boats on the water.

Then, finally, the warehouse blew with the most tremendous explosion.

According to the editor of the popular periodical *Household Words*, Mr Charles Dickens:

'A prodigious quantity of burning material was thrown across the Tyne, and scores of people upon Newcastle Quayside were thrown down, and many of them rendered insensible by the shock. The mass of burning embers which flew from Gateshead set fire to the ships in the river, and passing over the quay, pitched upon the dense range of buildings used as offices and warehouses by the Newcastle merchants, which, in an incredibly short period became one mass of flames. The vapour from the burning sulphur came in dense masses across the river, causing numbers of people to fall down insensible; and in every direction the affrighted inhabitants of the lanes and alleys bordering the Quayside, Newcastle, and in the lower part of Gateshead, might be seen flying in every direction as before an earthquake.'

The force of this explosion was quite awe-inspiring: spectators on the High Level felt the new bridge shake; vessels on the river lifted as if lashed by a sudden storm; a huge granite block from the cart tramway outside the warehouse was flung 400 yards through the roof of the Grey Horse pub; an 18-pound rock fell into an opticians in Newcastle's Grey Street and when workmen discovered it the next morning it was still too hot to touch; gas lights in a Jarrow paper mill were blown out; miners in Monkwearmouth colliery 11 miles away, the deepest in the country, heard the explosion and came to the surface, anxious to know the cause; close to the explosion, the venerable St Mary's church was shattered to a wreck. The hands on the dial of its clock stood at ten minutes past three. Then the fires started in Newcastle…

Considering the disaster's scale, the death toll of 53 could have been much higher. The dead included the son of John Dobson, the architect who had recently remodeled Newcastle, and according to Dickens, 'Mr. Pattison, Town Councillor; Ensign Poynter, Corporal Armstrong and a private of the Cameronians; Mr. Charles Bertram (the warehouse owner); Mr. Davison Jr, miller; police constable Scott; Mr. Hamilton, hairdresser; Mr. Willis, skinner; and two women of Gateshead'. About 500 people were injured and 200 families lost their tenement homes, which in a later commentary in *Household Words*, Dickens the social reformer suggested was a kind of blessing, these cholera-ridden slums having created much greater misery in the past: 'We think the Newcastle fire not so much a calamity as the possession of any town council that allows pestilence to slaughter men from day to day, from year to year, from generation to generation, and opposes no check to its cruelty.'

It would be nice to think that the combination of the Great Fire of Newcastle and Gateshead and the fulminations of Charles Dickens brought an end to poverty and poor housing on these banks of the Tyne; in fact,

district were waiting to wave us off. En route, crossing the Redheugh Bridge, he was spotted, window down, sitting in the front seat, and dozens of car horns sounded the equivalent of a football chant. I had to laugh, and I did: it was like being part of a royal progress, or a motorcade (except there was no grassy knoll), or even Pope John Paul II's arrival in his Polish homeland, except in this case the Popemobile was an ancient Ford Granada driven by a fat lad who blew pink gum bubbles all the way. At Gallowgate, Gazza took us to a turnstile in the main stand paddock, had a word with the old chap, shook our hands, and we were in – a good hour before anyone else. Still, we thought, time to soak up the big-match atmosphere…

We lost 3-1. At the end of the season Gazza was sold to Tottenham.

Under that dripping Dunston tree I could have continued with stories about the time I met Gazza shortly afterwards at Waterloo Station – he and Kenny Wharton were waiting for a train to Southampton and eating Mars bars (I kid you not) – or when my son Tom and I met him dressed awkwardly in an ill-fitting suit in the bowels of Selhurst Park and he confided sadly, 'I'm away' – but the sandwiches were eaten, the rain was easing and it was time to be off. I hadn't even started on Harry Clasper. He will have to wait for another time…

We return to the riverside path – and another estate of waterside homes, a rather off-the-peg development of brick boxes. For just about the first time today we meet some walkers coming the other way, an elderly couple from Guisborough. The man stops and in a rather challenging Teesside twang demands: 'What you lot doing?' We tell him; he looks and gives the comic's pre-punch line pause before barking, 'You must be bloody mad,' and walking on.

I stop to get my bearings from a photocopy of a 1912 Tyne map. It's beginning to disintegrate with the rain, but I reckon we're standing on the site of the vast concrete Co-op mills inside which Port of Tyne hydrographer Phil Lynch once smelt the worst smell that ever assaulted his olfactory senses: a floor stacked with long-rotting animal skins. We look across the river at the long, low grey shed in which BAE Systems make what it gnomically calls 'global combat systems'. This was the site once chosen by William George Armstrong for his new works that over 40 years grew and grew until it took up most of the river frontage between the bridges of Scotswood and Redheugh.

Back in the 1850s, this view wouldn't have been possible, for the simple reason that there was once a series of islands in the middle of the stream. The biggest was King's Meadow, nearly a mile long and covering 35 acres. It and its sister, Annie's Island, were officially part of Northumberland, but reading the history, you get a sense they were somewhat outside the law – a bit like Southwark with its theatres and bear pits on the south bank of old

London Bridge in Elizabethan times. King's Meadow had a very lively pub called the Countess of Coventry, which heaved with visitors at weekends and during the regular race meetings held on the meadows. At quieter times the landlady (Annie perhaps) had a more sedate income: she supplied the people of Elswick with milk. However, she and the islands were about to meet their nemesis. Once Armstrong began to build ships at Elswick, the islands became an encumbrance to his business and he prevailed on the Tyne Improvement Commissioners to remove them – and so with little ceremony or fuss, King's Meadow, pub, race track, cows and all, were dredged out of existence and into history.

Fanciful coda: after the closures of Dunston staiths and the two power stations upstream, the colliers and ash-tippers stopped running up and down and traffic above the Newcastle bridges trickled away to virtually nothing. As a result, regular dredging by the Port of Tyne gradually ceased. When I heard this, it occurred to me that the river might silt up again and over time the islands might rise again. When I put this to hydrographer Phil Lynch he gave an indulgent smile and then the measured words of a scientist: 'It's possible – but unlikely.' In other words – dream on, Chaplin…

In short order we're forced away from the river again and back onto Railway Street, via the Colliery Road Garage and into Handy Drive, which leans back towards the Tyne, and the remains of an old quay. Peering over the side, we can make out in the mud the unmistakable shape of a boat keel: for years this was where the two-masted schooner *James Leathard* rested, occupied by a mysterious man about whom I could discover very little apart from the fact that he had a house and a wife elsewhere. I once came here to beard him in his den, ventured up the gang-plank of a vessel that had obviously seen better if less interesting days, called out a greeting, but got no reply. I'm sure he was in residence, but perhaps thought I represented an overdue bill or officialdom. Not long afterwards he passed away, and the boat has gone too. Now under new ownership, we saw it under comprehensive repair at Tyne Dock.

Having touched the river all too briefly, Handy Drive sweeps rather tediously south again and we lose sight of water. However Mandela Way offers liberation from the tyranny of traffic and we head north again, a vast temple of consumerism looming on our left. We leave Costco to its devices and head instead for a little opening in the kind of bland hedge you find on industrial estates. It gives out onto the riverbank – and here we find a man and his dog. The man has some serious binoculars around his neck. Being nosy I go and talk to him.

His name is Stephen Fry. No, not *that* Stephen Fry. This Stephen runs a fish and chip shop in Burnopfield. Indeed his pet, his name and occupation are all referenced in his car's number plate: K9 FRY. It turns out that Stephen visits this slightly unprepossessing spot every single day. The attraction is avian.

'The river's low and I've just been watching some green sandpipers looking for food. It's a great place for seeing waders, the usual suspects like oystercatcher and curlew, but I've seen much rarer birds here too, like ruff, spotted redshank and black-tailed godwit.'

It turns out this little lay-by is also a great spot to watch birds in passage.

'One day I saw these gulls mobbing a large bird and I looked and got very excited – it was an osprey flying north. There've been five little egrets on the Tyne the last few weeks and ringed plovers nest on the gravel at the edge of the BAE car park on the other side of the river.'

Nature being nature, these birds have predators, among them, so it's rumoured, peregrine falcons nesting at St James's Park. (I wonder if Mike Ashley charges them rent?) The delights of the Costco viewpoint include mammals too. Stephen regularly sees seals this far upriver, as well as a dog otter hunting for its family up the River Derwent.

'I live in Winlaton Mill and sometimes I don't bring the car down here, I just walk down the Derwent with the dog and it always amazes me just how much wildlife can be seen in the middle of Tyneside.'

Stephen gets off – it's late afternoon and frying time is looming – and we walk on, passing a white van whose driver is so entranced by the local wildlife he's fast asleep, mouth open and Metro Radio blaring. Mandela Way is again leading us away from the true path of righteousness, but an opening into the site of some former factory appears on our right. Feeling a bit like kids entering forbidden ground, we explore a habitat that seems suspended between industry and nature: the walls have gone but the concrete floor is still in place, but a growing forest of birch and willow is springing up in the cracks. Skirting mounds of dumped spoil, we make for the water. We spot something nestling in the mud: what looks like a bracelet, a dull gold in colour. We all stare at it, intrigued.

'It looks like a Roman torque,' says Charles.

It's rather an unlikely place to find a piece of ancient jewellery, but you never know, so I plodge into the clarts to investigate, making a terrible mess of my boots. The Roman torque turns out to be the remnants of a brown plastic cup. Like a bunch of kids we get the giggles and move on through the undergrowth, slashing through what as kids we used to call 'German rhubarb'. In a glade we find something of greater botanical interest: a small orchard of brambles and wild raspberries, both in fruit.

I start harvesting them, though Charles won't join in; he reckons the ground might be poisoned. I take a chance – the rasps were especially delicious – and I'm still here. Looking across the river at Scotswood, where the steep streets ran down to the river, I suddenly get an inkling of what might once have stood on this side: Dunston Power Station.

A few yards from where I sit writing, a photo hangs on a wall in which the gently smoking towers of Dunston provide the backdrop. In the foreground is one of those sloping streets, and across the street a group of Scotswood children are playing football with a bald man in a suit: my dad. The photo was taken exactly 50 years ago to mark the publication of Sid's novel, *The Watchers and the Watched*, set in the west end of Newcastle. I never pass this photo on the stairs without smiling inside: my dad hated football, and I never once persuaded him to play with me…

Fortified with Tyne fruit, we have the strength for the last leg of today's walk – navigating our route through the Watermark, a business park that stands on ground once occupied by Raine's steel works by the intersection of the Derwent and the Tyne. The tenants with the highest profile are Tyne Tees Television, who moved here from their City Road site in Newcastle, but we've come to see a smaller operation at one of those business park addresses that make me smile – 10 Keel Row. Here Ian Hughes and son Trevor have opened an outlet for Storck, the German manufacturers of electric bikes. I don't know whether they're trying to tempt us into an easier

form of transport for our journey, but Charlie and I both have a test-ride up and down the river path. It's a stylish machine, but when I switch on the assist motor the effect is so spectacular, I can't stop laughing, even though the rain is coming down again. I feel eight years old again. There is such a joy in speed…

Here the day should have ended, but there was a kick in it for Charlie and me. Christy made her way to the station at the Metro Station to catch the train home to Hexham, but my photographer and I were given another ride, this time in a smart Mercedes driven by taxi driver Michael Czuprynski. In strict geographical terms, what happened next should really feature in the next chapter, but given that what Michael told us perfectly fitted the day's theme of play, it's going here.

The adventure came about in a typically serendipitous way. One day I was on my way to a Port of Tyne event in a taxi and I got talking to the driver. When I told him where I was going and why, he said, 'You should put me in your book.' So Michael, here you are.

Michael was brought up in Blaydon, and the river and its shore was a playground for him and his pals. He took us to the spot that was their HQ, where the Blaydon Burn dribbles into the Tyne. We got out to look and as the rain fell, the stories fell too, dating from the early 70s when Michael was between ten and 14, interrupted only by a hurried retreat to the car – my note book was getting pretty damp. In no particular order:

- A little way up the Blaydon Burn there used to be a brick factory. On summer evenings Michael and his mates would wander up there when the workers had gone home and roast potatoes in the cooling ovens.
- Nearby the drivers of Lyons vans used to tip stale cakes into the river. The gang regularly retrieved them and took them home. They tasted fine; Michael's mam was especially delighted with the chocolate Swiss rolls.
- One time the boys dragged some pallets from the brick factory down to the riverbank, lashed them together, filled the gaps with packets of peas they found in a disused food factory and launched the boat on a high tide. They soon discovered, as the boat careered downriver, that they had no means of controlling it and it was only the fortunate arrival of a police launch that saved them from further mishap. Michael's dad was called out – he gave his son a hiding and told him to say nothing to his mam or his younger brother.
- The gang met in a tunnel where they ate crackers and corned beef and wore gas masks they'd found somewhere.

- Using molten lead they poured into moulds, they used to fire homemade catapults at the ash tipper *Bessie Surtees* as it passed Blaydon en route from Stella Power Station to the sea.
- The gang used to jump on coal wagons and cadge lifts to Monkton coke works. These jaunts ended when one boy slipped and lost his legs.
- Once a friend of Michael's discovered a body at the river's edge. The man was wearing a gold watch with Cyrillic letters on the face. The boy took it, but was terrified he would be caught. An inquest was later held; it turned out the man was a Russian sea captain who had got drunk and fallen overboard. The incoming tide had carried him from North Shields to Blaydon.

The tales falter like the tide. Michael sighs, we laugh.

'I shudder to think about all the things we used to do when we were ten or eleven. It's a wonder I'm still here. I guess it was a decaying industrial landscape but to us it was just the most fantastic playground.'

Michael drops Charlie and me off at Harry Ramsden's to wait for our lift home.

After a day weaving along the Gateshead and Dunston shore, of intermittent rain, and diversions both physical and anecdotal, the plate of chips and mug of tea were restorative indeed. Like a childhood pleasure…

⚓ CITY KITTIWAKE

Let's keep you
record breaker
Tyne bridger
edge nobbler
arch lodger
shanty builder
height hugger
wall whitener
dung slabberer
dive bomber
council flouter
face flyer.
Let's keep you
mid-air squabbler
gang rabbler
belly riffler
stunt flinger
spring reviver
self singer
homeward bolter
egg nebber
seawrack weaver
chick bustler.
Let's keep you
Arctic wheeler
heart hauler
eye widener
sky sweller
breeze conductor
lull seeker
memory dweller
eel thinker
light catcher
word maker –

kittiwake

Sweet Thames, run softly, till I end my song, once wrote the poet TS Eliot.

Had the great man chosen instead to refer to the Tyne in perhaps *the* iconic poem of the 20th century, two observations spring to mind: first, he may not of course chosen to call it *The Wasteland*, and second, he certainly would have chosen another adverb – that 'softly' would not have done at all.

For of course the Tyne doesn't meander across several counties' worth of gentle meadow and down. It slaloms downhill at dizzying speed, draining almost 3,000 square kilometers of hill and dale and Pennine fell. And when it rains – and let's face it, this is not an uncommon event in the northern uplands – said drain fills up with impressive speed and force.

Put it another way. If you're standing on the perfect lawns at the front of Bywell Hall, the average flow of the water passing in front of you is 45 cubic metres of water per second (cusecs). But in the flood of January 2005, thought to be the most severe since 1815, a flow of 1,375 cusecs was recorded. Now take your Albert Hall, capacity 90,000 cubic metres: water from a normal domestic tap would take 250 days to fill it. The Tyne at average flow would take just 33 minutes, but that flood – oh, that mighty flood – would have had the hall's cupola overflowing in just 60 seconds.

Don't you just love statistics?

It's in the aftermath of these events that the little *Clearwater* comes into its own. You might have seen it buzzing up and down the river: a Port of Tyne vessel just 15 metres long, painted green, with a tiny wheelhouse at the stern, a flat deck in front, on which sits a crane that offers a clue to the boat's purpose. Its name offers a second. The morning Charles and I went onboard, passers-by stopped and stared. Some took photos, prompting a proud boast from its crew that the *Clearwater* is the most photographed vessel on the Tyne, despite or perhaps because of its unglamorous role as the refuse lorry of the river.

If that's the case, then I suppose skipper Stephen Proud and deckhand David Houshby are the Tyne's bin-men. No disrespect intended: Stephen and Davie are experienced mariners and all-round top blokes, with as it turns out – and here's an apposite phrase – plenty of what you might call *hinterland*. But they have to deal with whatever the Tyne's hinterland coughs up and sends hurrying down to its lower reaches – trees, tyres, the odd dead animal, even the occasional bedstead.

Stephen and Davie pick us up at Fozard's Quay on Newcastle's Quayside on their way up to Newburn to investigate a tree reported by a member of the public beached on a mud bank. If a high tide lifts it off and takes it downstream, it could pose a danger to boats or riverside structures. Hence the *Clearwater*'s crane, cutting equipment and that flat, empty deck. There've been many times when it's been full.

While Davie casts off, Stephen waves to the crew painting a pleasure craft then carefully plots a way round the navigation piles under the Millennium Bridge, now being removed. Stephen has only been on the *Clearwater* for a few weeks after returning to his native Newcastle – he spent 20 years' working on the Clyde with the River Police – and grins when I ask if he's glad to be back. Dumb question. Davie, who's worked on the *Clearwater* for five years, reappears in the wheelhouse. With four of us, it's getting cosy in there, but I see there's room enough for a breakfast bar – tiny kettle and toaster, Weetabix, loaf of bread and fig rolls.

As we move under the bridges, Stephen talks of his growing respect for his ungainly little boat. 'On Saturday we were helping the lads taking out the pilings. The tide was going out with an eight knot current and we had 50mph winds too. The conditions were hellish, but she handled remarkably well.' Despite this, as we pass through the upstream channel of the Swing Bridge, the *Clearwater* suddenly begins to crab sideways, stern swinging to port, and Stephen has to correct it. 'She always does that, she takes a bit of firm handling', he says, of the boat built by Mustang Marine of Pembroke in 2004 as if 'she' actually was a jittery filly.

Reaching Scotswood and Zone 8 of the *Clearwater*'s beat, we slow so that Stephen and Davie can inspect a so-called hotspot where debris gathers, a crumbling jetty on the north shore downstream of Scotswood Bridge. There was a report of a dead sheep here but it's gone, taken away by the tide. That's a relief, especially for today's guests. My job description as writer in residence doesn't include handling dead livestock, but it's a regular occurrence for Stephen and Davie – pigs and horses as well as sheep, and on one occasion a dead porpoise inside North Shields Fish Quay. You might wonder how and why. Natural occurrences perhaps, but there's a lingering suspicion that some corpses at least are the result of the wish of some farmers to avoid more expensive forms of disposal, especially when Davie and Stephen find the late beast's identity tags neatly clipped off.

But the *Clearwater*'s stock in trade is timber. Davie remembers another flood in September 2009 there were bits of trees in Zones 1 through 8. Most spectacularly the boat picked up a tree that was bigger than itself. The same day a car carrier at the Nissan Terminal couldn't leave its berth for the debris around it. At these times the boat's capacity to ride onto a mud bank like an amphibious craft before reversing off comes in handy, though on one occasion the vessel was stranded by a rapidly disappearing tide. Red faces resulted – and a wait of five hours for the next high tide. That month in 2009 a section of quay near the old Spillers mill at Shieldfield began to fill up with the flood's debris; almost 100 tons of wood are there two years later, despite much timber being recycled for compost.

As we approach Newburn Bridge, Davie remembers another weather event: the day last winter when the river froze on the site of an old ford crossing – there was ice all the way across. Here, as the river narrows and shallows, and we approach the river's tidal reach, the water is copper coloured, pure Pennine peat. Finally, on an exposed mud bank, we find the reported tree trunk, but as he suspected David sees that it's one they've tried to remove before, without success. It still has towing wire looped around it.

'That's going nowhere' says Stephen, as Davie turns the boat round. It's at such desolate places that the *Clearwater* sometimes encounters debris of a human kind. Sometimes the outcome is less melancholy; recently the crew helped a disabled woman who went into the river at North Shields and Davie has also received a Police Commendation for helping a woman in her

sixties who for reasons best known for herself climbed over some waterside railings and promptly froze in fear.

Now the tide is coming up strongly and we make slower progress back. Time for the telling of tales.

From South Shields, born and brought up in Laygate Street by the Middle Dock, David followed his father and brother into the Navy, but it was on his own river that he once came under attack.

'We were once passing Bill Point and we got targeted by these lads who were using golf clubs like they were on a driving range. The balls were landing all around, but didn't actually hit us!' Despite this, 'I love working on the Tyne. Me mates say I've got the best job in the world and they're right. I mean, look at it.'

I do. We're approaching the delights of Dunston, but I hear what he's saying.

Stephen's story is of missiles that did hit the target. This Shieldfield lad first went to sea on ships of the Ellerman Line, then as a cook on BP tankers. During the Falklands War, the Government hired his vessel, the *British Wye*, to take 27,000 tons of aviation spirit to the South Atlantic, so that RAF planes could carry on flying. Of course other planes were circling the Falklands too.

'We'd been told that mail would be dropped on board by an RAF Hercules and so one day when we heard an aircraft approaching, we assumed that's what was happening. But it turned out to be a Hercules of the Argentine Air Force. From just 150 feet, the crew dropped eight 500-pound bombs out of the rear doors by hand. Just our luck – one of them hit our foredeck with a huge clang and then bounced into the sea without exploding. A very narrow escape. Three other bombs exploded in the sea but we survived. Not a nice feeling to be bombed when you're sitting on top of a hold full of aviation spirit.'

At this precise moment we're passing under the Tyne Bridge and I look nervously up, but there are no missiles of any description raining down. We cruise past Spillers Wharf to inspect the river's detritus, which rather touchingly includes one small boy's lost football.

Davie laughs, and tells one last story.

'I once found a holdall on a mudbank. It was so full of silver coins I could barely lift it. It was handed over to the police but no one claimed it and after six months it was returned to the Port of Tyne. Not that it did us any good. It was nickel silver and completely worthless.'

Which presumably was why it was flung in the Tyne, most people's natural wonder, but some folks' dump…

DAY FIVE

'One more step along the world I go,
One more step along the world I go,
From the old things to the new,
Keep me travelling along with you...'
Methodist hymn

Our text for today: coal, coal, coal, coal and coke…

For the first four days of our Tyne walk we have often felt the influence of the so-called black gold on the river scene, but today, from Blaydon up to Wylam, it becomes a dominant theme. There's no escaping it: despite its apparent demise, its footprint is everywhere.

On a sunny Tuesday morning, we congregate by a meeting of the waters, where the swift-running Derwent is swallowed by its big sister Tyne. A short diversion seems in order, prompted by an obscure poetic reference and the sight of yet another staith by the waters' meet. Like Dunston's, this has also been blighted by fire-raisers; perhaps the spray-painted names 'Colin' and 'Tommo' nearby are a confession of guilt. A rugby ball floats in the slack water and I wonder where the now-extinct rail line that once ended here began.

And the poetic reference? Once, in a previous life, I went to work for the BBC in Wales. A colleague kindly gave me a welcome gift: a copy of an epic mediaeval poem in the ancient Welsh (Cymraeg) once spoken by the inhabitants of the North East and southern Scotland. The translation of *Y Gododdin* into English was helpful but I wondered about its relevance to me, until my friend told me the poem was an account of a battle in about 600 AD in which the Celtic army was routed by invading Angles at Catterick. One section rhapsodises about the idyllic landscape once hunted by the father of one of the Celtic warriors. It sounds like a veritable or possibly mythic eden.

When your father went to the hills,
He would bring back a roe-buck,
A wild boar, a stag,
A speckled grouse from the hills,
A fish from the waterfalls of the Derwent…

Time then for a little turn off the beaten track. Will we find a surviving waterfall, or even a leaping salmon?

OPPOSITE
Staith at mouth of
River Derwent.

The path up the western bank of the Derwent passes under the Newcastle to Carlisle railway and then a road lined with car showrooms, budget hotels and cholesterol-special fast food joints. A solitary swan leads us towards the growing roar of the A1M. On the other side of the Derwent are two long grey sheds with the name 'Huwoods' in faded lettering. Once upon a time mining machinery was manufactured here, but the site is now operated by Stadium Packing Services. Past the A1, the A694 Consett road on our right, we reach the tidal limit of the Derwent and just beyond, the Derwenthaugh Dam, built in the 18th century so a channel or 'leat' could be run off to the east towards Swalwell to power its brewery, paper-mill and engineering workshops. The bijou dam, once known more prettily as Lady's Steps, was a popular picnic spot in Edwardian times, but its rural ambience was soon to be destroyed. The Consett Iron Company, which began processing iron and steel in 1853, soon acquired or sunk mines by the Derwent to supply its furnaces, and in time realised the fine coal they produced was ideal for turning into coke. In 1928 they established the Derwenthaugh Coke Works just by the dam, connected by rail link to the Consett works and the company's staith on the Tyne a mile or two away. The site was vast, the pollution considerable, as Aidan Pollard, local lad and fishery consultant to the Tyne Rivers Trust, makes clear:

'The works created a lot of pollution, most seriously, for every ton of coke produced, one kilo of cyanide. Most of it went into the river. The lower Derwent was pretty barren as a result. I grew up in High Spen and fished upstream at Lintzford as a boy but even there the most you could hope to catch was common loach and the very occasional trout, but only after heavy rain temporarily improved the water quality.'

Prospects eventually improved for the fish of the Derwent, if not its people. Aidan was one of 3,700 workers who lost their jobs when British Steel closed the Consett works in 1980. Derwenthaugh shut down six years later; the clean-up of the site was a huge operation involving the removal of buildings, plant and thousands of tons of contaminated soil. Standing by the Derwenthaugh Dam now, the river running fresh and clear, mature trees waving in the breeze, red kites wheeling and crying above, it's hard to imagine mineral trains running along both banks, the clang of metal, the roaring of furnaces, the stench of chemicals catching the back of the throat. The site itself is now given over to sport and leisure. Swalwell Cricket Club, Blaydon Tennis Club and Swalwell Juniors FC have made their homes here: a classic post-industrial story.

But it's not quite complete.

Since the 80s, the variety and numbers of fish in the Derwent, including brown trout and grayling, have revived. Salmon have appeared too: Aidan showed me a 15-yard stretch of stones where they spawn, at its centre a two-metre 'redd' in which eggs are laid and fertilised. This is just a few yards below the Lady's Steps, but the fish can go no further upstream because the Derwenthaugh dam is just too forbidding an obstacle.

'Obviously salmon are famous jumpers but this weir-like dam is just too long and high – and you often see them here, waiting in hope of getting over but only very few manage it. That's why the idea for a new fish pass came about,' says Aidan, as we watch the diggers at work on a £350,000 scheme funded by the Environment Agency and Gateshead Council to create two passes at the side of the dam, one for salmon and a smaller one for eels and lampreys. These represent an important step in restoring the ecology of the river to its pre-industrial state.

On the face of it, a plan to increase the Derwent's natural diversity and make it possible to fish for salmon all the way up its waters seems admirable. What's not to like?

Returning to the Tyne, we bump into a friend of mine exercising his dogs. John Adair lives at Rowlands Gill and, it turns out, fishes on the Derwent. He and Aidan have a friendly technical conversation of which I understand very little, and then John goes on his way. Within ten minutes I get a message on my phone from him making it clear that the fish pass scheme is not universally popular among precisely those who on the face of it would seem most likely to benefit – the fishing fraternity of the Derwent. Many who fish the river are concerned that all this talk of salmon will mean they'll be priced out of their patch by moneyed folk who previously would never have given the banks of the unglamorous Derwent a second thought.

All of which goes to prove that you can scratch at almost any issue in England – even fishing, maybe especially fishing – and almost inevitably what seem to be class tensions will rise to the surface, like long-buried industrial pollution.

Back on the Tyne, the walkers amble westwards under a succession of bridges: Scotswood Road Bridge, the old shallow-arched railway bridge and the distinctly unlovely A1M viaduct. Under each is a curious dead zone, land that doesn't seem to belong to anyone, except possibly the spray-painted 'Fatboy' or 'Spike', or used for any particular purpose. The poets Paul Farley and Michael Symmons Roberts have dubbed these places, products of motorways, retail parks and sundry urban blight, 'edgelands', the mysterious, forgotten places that constitute Britain's last real wilderness. Nobody explores them except the occasional naturalist and walker passing through, though a discarded thong (female, I think) suggests nocturnal visitors intent on other forms of exercise. We got to know such places well on our walk, marvelling at the capacity of nature to colonise the bleakest of terrain. Here, for instance, the hardy buddleia is in flower, its brilliant purple flowers the still centres of a minuet danced by a dozen attendant butterflies – a single peacock among the tortoiseshells and red admirals – to the heavy metal music of the traffic overhead.

Finally we crab sideways onto real estate that does have a purpose, or indeed many. The Blaydon Haughs Industrial Estate houses about 50 businesses of varying sizes, many of them involved in the motor or building trades. The biggest enterprise closed just a few months before we came along – the creamery once run by the Co-op and then taken over for a short time by an independent dairy called Medina – to the dismay of its 100 employees and the region's dairy farmers, who now have to send their milk much further afield to be processed. A stack of milk churns, presumably empty, offers a kind of milky monument to what's been lost.

A happier story unfolds when we come across the newest and smallest business on the estate. Housed in a caravan by the side of the road, Lindi Lou's Tasty Bites offers both warm welcome and tempting aroma. As the name implies, this is a mobile eaterie, and Lindi Lou (aka Linda) is frying up some bacon on the hot plate while husband Stan is taking his ease in one of three white plastic chairs on a nearby verge. It's mid-morning and the breakfast rush is done, but a trickle of customers from nearby 'units' are still keeping the couple – on reflection, make that Linda – busy. And the smell of those rashers, even more their symphonic sizzle, makes us pause and stop and chat, and get out the notebooks, cameras, sketchpad – and wallets.

Like many on the estate, Lindi Lou's is yet another SME. The middle-aged couple set it up 19 months earlier, both giving up secure jobs to take the plunge. Linda used to work in catering at Newcastle University, Stan at Nissan, the 6am-2pm daily fore-shift. I ask how it's going, and Linda looks around for some wood to touch.

'Canny. We've got good customers and they seem to like what we serve them,' she says, flipping my bacon over. While Birtley admires the caravan's sign-writing, I try to get my head round the offer of a ten-piece breakfast, the so-called 'Belly Buster'. Linda and Stan arrive early every morning from their Newcastle riverside home and stay long enough to do lunch. The most popular meal is Thursday's mince and dumplings, my boyhood favourite. I make a mental note to return one Thursday – in the interests of research, of course.

In the course of our walk, we encounter many similar caravans on similar industrial estates and business parks, though none with the friendliness and charm of Lindi Lou's. What it indicates of course is the death of the works canteen, a small casualty of the decline of the riverside's big employers. People don't eat together any more in cavernous sheds to the music of the Light Programme's *Workers' Playtime* on the Tannoy. They eat their sandwiches in a grim little room with a kettle and microwave that's stopped working, or they wander off in search of hot grill and banter-filled crack, provided here by Lindi Lou and Stan respectively. It's not hard to see why their SME is flourishing.

'Mind, it's hard work. I've only taken one day off in months and that was April 12th – for the funeral.' Linda steps back from the hot plate, her face clouding. 'I lost my eldest son in March. I don't know what I'd have done without the business. To be honest it's kept me going.'

Suddenly Lindi Lou isn't on Blaydon Haugh Industrial Estate any longer. Linda's in a different place entirely.

We finish our tea and go.

Just down the road, we encounter another singular character, but I never got to find out his name.

He answers to my hollering and appears from inside a big shed at Blaydon Metals, a small scrap-yard that deals exclusively in aluminium. Birtley is much taken with the mounds of silvery metal, surrounded by churned-up mud and puddles almost as deep as the Tyne a few yards beyond. He wants to draw them, so, being well brought-up, I go in search of permission. That's when our friend appears. He has possibly the dirtiest face I've ever encountered, and almost certainly the friendliest. I ask for the gaffer, and he replies.

'You cannot cause he's in Las Vegas. He's always in Las Vegas.'

At least I *think* that's what he said. Our genial host actually has very few teeth, but he instantly agrees to Birtley's request, as if artists come calling here every day. The yard seems quiet, but it turns out that this is because a new gas smelter is being installed. Meanwhile, says our friend, he's 'tidying up' the yard, a task more likely to last a lifetime than a week. While Birtley sketches away, and another scrap-man whizzes around in a fork-lift, shifting massive aluminium ingots from one side of the yard to another, I ask Few Teeth how long he's been in the scrap trade. He grins massively and a tooth stands alone on a gum, like that solitary tower at Dunstanburgh.

'I've only been here five weeks, man! Things'll be better with the new smelter. The power they use here! Costs quarter of a million a year, you know! Most of me life I've worked in construction, but I'm getting too old for that. I was once a coal hewer down Sheffield way but I sharp came back. To be honest, I didn't like the accent down there. Me whole family's from round here. Blaydon, Swalwell. One of me grandfathers worked as a deputy in the Mary and Bessie pits and the other drove shunting engines just along the line here.'

He points at the Newcastle to Carlisle line a few yards away, sighs and lapses into silence, his speech done, having said more interesting things in a minute than some highly-educated men manage in a month. And he's not quite finished, managing a strangely eloquent 'Aye' before he shakes my hand and wanders off.

Blaydon Metals is dwarfed by the much bigger yard of EMR nearby. A couple of dozen of EMR's 3,500 employees at 150 sites around the world are busy weighing, unloading, checking, sorting and cutting up Tyneside's industrial and domestic ferrous scrap. A crane is loading larger items into an awesomely powerful Leimbach shearer where they are cut into pieces no larger than 5 x 2 x 2 feet. Light iron goes into a 'frag-feed', a shredder that reduces the metal to the size of a fist. Cars are stripped of batteries, tyres, electrics, oil and other liquids, and then stacked in dizzying piles. In one corner, there are sections from an oil platform similar to the one we saw at the beginning of our walk, which have come here via the old Swan Hunter's yard; some have been 'half mooned', cut in half lengthways. This isn't the last time we'll see them.

We make our way back to the railway line, and a splendid signal box painted in the original red and cream colours of the North East Railway. Birtley almost purrs as he draws – the emerging image combining twin passions of art and trains – while I work out that the box must have once controlled many more lines than the one that survives. Birtley, who's lived west of here for many years, confirms the suspicion: this was a junction where many mineral lines from local pits used to join the main line.

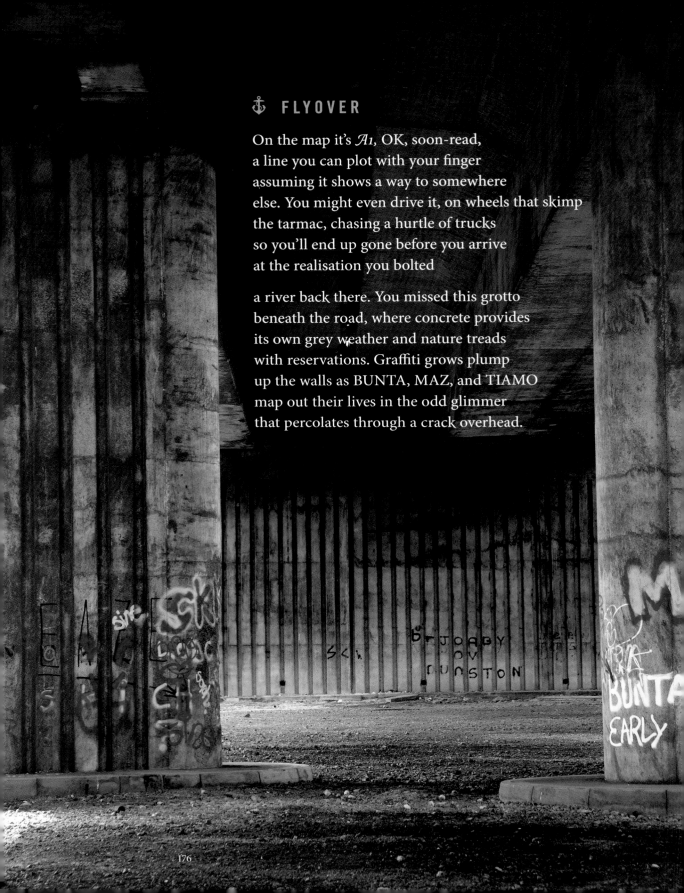

⚓ FLYOVER

On the map it's *A1*, OK, soon-read,
a line you can plot with your finger
assuming it shows a way to somewhere
else. You might even drive it, on wheels that skimp
the tarmac, chasing a hurtle of trucks
so you'll end up gone before you arrive
at the realisation you bolted

a river back there. You missed this grotto
beneath the road, where concrete provides
its own grey weather and nature treads
with reservations. Graffiti grows plump
up the walls as BUNTA, MAZ, and TIAMO
map out their lives in the odd glimmer
that percolates through a crack overhead.

On the other side of the line is a Kingdom Hall of the Jehovah's Witnesses; by the river stand the huge stone blocks of the original Blaydon Quay. A lone curlew pokes about in the mud. As the path rejoins the Tyne, we reach an outfall where the Blaydon Burn drops rather indecorously into the Tyne, above it a stretch of metal railings that invite the passer-by to lean and linger and contemplate. An elderly man called Bill Davison, accompanied by a punkish young woman and a pit bull called Zola, does just that. We start chatting, as men do while so leaning. It turns out Bill hasn't been down this way for ages. The vista of the gently bending river unlocks his memory.

'Once upon a time there was a graphite works over there but that's long since gone. Just upstream here I used keep an old Class One ship's lifeboat. It had sunk somewhere and been salvaged, but I got me hands on it and was doing it up. I used to go out to sea fishing in it, on summer evenings. Smashing, it was.

'Then one time the *Hedwin*, the Port's dredger, went past here far too fast, made a huge wave and smashed my boat up against the jetty wall, damaging the paintwork and all sorts. It always went too fast, that bloody boat.'

I have heard other stories of marine misbehaviour hereabouts: of the ash-tippers serving Stella and Dunston power stations, the *Bobby Shaftoe, Bessie Surtees* and *Hexhamshire Lass,* racing each other downstream and sometimes getting rid of their cargoes long before they reached the open sea. Not true, I'm sure…

We look over the river. The mucky old graphite works has gone, and the box-like offices of the Newburn Business Park have sprung up. Bill doesn't offer the stock response.

'Totally different here now. It's obviously cleaner, and I think it's better. Go and have a look up the burn here, it's lovely up there.'

In fact that's just what we're about to do, in our second detour of the day.

A trim elderly man is waiting for us on the old road bridge over Blaydon Burn. His name is Alan Carr; he lives a few miles away in Crawcrook, where he once worked as a colliery blacksmith. He has an intimate knowledge of the burn: he's regularly walked its length since he was a boy, and like others we've met along the way, he's become an unofficial custodian of its story, which manages to be both remarkable and yet typical of the many little valleys running down to the Tyne.

Alan leads us under the new road bridge and into an open meadow, bounded by the curving burn to the east and a rising bluff to the west, houses climbing its banks. Nowadays this is the home of the rare dingy skipper butterfly, but once it was the site of a works where six million firebricks

were made every year. In the early days – the works was opened in 1838 – the bricks were moulded by hand; a good man could make 2,400 bricks a day. By the bridge are the remains of various kiln backs. It was in these kilns, before the works closed in 1975, that Michael Czuprynski and his pals roasted potatoes on summer evenings. The yard was also the terminus of the Blaydon Burn wagonway, an inclined-plane system that linked all the many and disparate workshops of the upper burn – all relating in one way or another to coal – to the Newcastle to Carlisle rail line by the river. With its mature trees and distant drumming of a woodpecker, it looks and sounds like a perfect rural glade, but not too long ago this was one of the most heavily industrialised parts of the North East. Clues to this hidden past are the hundred or so industrial structures in brick and stone that survive within sight of the next mile of gently rising pathway, connecting what was known as Cowen's Lower Yard and Cowen's Upper Yard, though many are obscured by climbing ivy and shrubs. We start ambling…

As the names imply, all these linked industrial ventures were owned and run in Victorian times by the family of Cowen, a name most associated with a remarkable father and son, both named Joseph, whose business acumen was matched by their passion for radical politics. Both served as Liberal MPs for Newcastle, until Joseph Junior quit Parliament in disgust at the political intrigue he found there, after which he used the family newspaper, the *Newcastle Daily Chronicle*, as the vehicle for his political causes. One of these, which he served with both pen and wallet, was democracy across Europe, especially Italy and Russia. While his father was knighted for services to the Tyne, young Cowen cultivated friendships with revolutionaries from those countries and others, including Mazzini and Garibaldi from the former and Herzen and Bakunin from the latter. It is entirely in keeping with the romantic nature of the younger Cowen, known to enemies and friends alike as 'the Blaydon Brick', that he was in the habit of smuggling secret documents to his dangerous friends abroad in consignments of the family's firebricks. And if you want to see some original Cowen bricks, go and have a squint at the front of the Tyne Theatre in Newcastle's Westgate Road, an enterprise supported by the Cowen family. The white-faced bricks are from Blaydon Burn…

The Cowens lived over the hill in an elegant Elizabethan house called Stella Hall (it was demolished in 1954), from which they kept a close eye on their activities down the Burn. The Joseph Cowens also influenced their business in a rather touching way: they named the pits after the names of their children.

After pointing out the remnants of the many corn mills that preceded industry, Alan stops us in front of a bricked-in entrance to the Edward Pit (with hole to allow the escape of gas), mined from the 1850s to 1896 and

OPPOSITE
Hill of aluminium
scrap, Blaydon.

179

also linked to the much bigger workings at Blaydon Burn Colliery. After the Cowen interests were bought out by another local family-made-good, the Priestmans, they used this as an entrance to the coke and tar works at Ottovale above the valley. Here too was the Newcastle Benzol Works, the first place in the world where petrol was produced from coal. It was known as Blaydon Benzole.

We're walking on a track made of compacted coal waste – periodically, Alan stops to draw maps in it with his walking stick. Here ran the rail line that connected the various enterprises up and down the burn. Every so often, there are little sidings (Alan calls them 'shunts'), long enough to accommodate three wagons on their way down, which would stop here to allow wagons to pass up.

'Each 'train' would have a brakesman riding on one wagon,' says Alan, 'but I also remember kids riding up and down on bogeys with bars you'd move up and down, just like in the silent films.'

As we pass the remains of a tiny reservoir established to quench coke in the works nearby, two lads sitting on its bank and getting stuck into a crate of Foster's jeer out a greeting. Perhaps they're bird-watching: the woodland nearby is a haven for birds like nuthatch and treecreeper. Alan points out steps that lead to the Bessie drift-mine, also linked to the much bigger Blaydon Burn pit. We pass the remains of old hoppers into which the won coal was tipped, and find ourselves at Valley House, the manager's house and pay office but now the home of a nice lady ('a stranger from Morpeth').

Over the lane are the old colliery shops for the Bessie and Mary pits, she tells us, now housing a company making buckets for excavators. Alan laughs and remembers an old pal who worked here, servicing both the Bessie and Mary pits.

'My friend Billy Duddy was the blacksmith at the Bessie Pit.' Beautifully timed comic's pause. 'He could talk to you for 20 minutes and tell you nowt.'

Alan though was destined to work at a pit named after another female Cowen.

'I wanted to be gardener, but my dad said there was no money in that so I came into the pit, the Emma at Crawcrook. It's a rugby field now. My dad got both his legs broken in a roof fall, after that he got light work as a powder-man.'

Alan recalls the delights of the little smithy in which he worked, once recycling hardwood posts from the old Cowen staith on the Tyne for use in the shaft at the Emma, especially eating bacon cooked on a piece of flat plate over the brazier, ideal also for browning rice pudding. He's delighted when I tell him my dad served his time as a colliery blacksmith: how one of *his* favourite memories was the matchless taste of smithy bacon, and the influence of his first craft on the second – the crafting of stories. His eyes light up.

'The characters I knew here, everyone was different, and they all had a story to tell, and they could tell them so well.'

I take him at his word. So what's your story then, Alan?

'After Emma closed in the late 60s I was sent to work at Westoe Colliery in South Shields. It was that much bigger, the shop for fitters and black-smiths was 100 foot long. The first time I went underground we travelled some way and then this lad asked me if I knew where we were. Of course I didn't and he said, why lad, you're under the clock in Whitley Bay!'

Returning to the Tyne, we find we can't keep to it. Repairs are being made to the riverside path and we have to make a detour along the main road from Blaydon to Ryton, which takes us past the aromatic temptations (resisted) of Pumphrey's coffee roasting rooms. Coincidentally, I'd seen the grave of the business's founder, Thomas, Quaker and teetotaler, just the previous weekend in Jesmond Old Cemetery. The road runs alongside what used to be Stella Meadows and the long-demolished house of Summerhill, but history here didn't begin with the Cowens. Oliver Cromwell once stayed in the house after crossing the Tyne by a ford later named after him; Bronze Age bones were dug up here in 1937; and a rise called Image Hill once featured statues of the Greek Asclepius, god of medicine and healing and the god of sun and light, Apollo, who appears to be smiling on us today. The hillside above once featured another statue, of the aforementioned Garibaldi, so-called father of Italian unification, who visited Tyneside in 1854 and addressed open-air meetings attended by thousands of enthusiastic listeners. (Less seriously, it has also been claimed that one day while staying in Tynemouth, he sat on an eccles cake, thereby creating the first Garibaldi biscuit.) His friend and acolyte Joseph Cowen the younger later had a statue erected in his honour at Summerhill. Some time later it was found toppled over in mysterious circumstances. Two explanations for the mishap began to circulate: first, that it had been pushed over by grazing cows; second, that resentful workers of Cowen's had done the deed, not because they disapproved of Garibaldi's politics, but because they'd been obliged by their employer to contribute one penny each to the cost of his monument. (Later on the walk, I heard a third explanation: that Garibaldi's visit to the Pope went down very badly with Protestant elements of his Tyneside support.) The great man now has perhaps a longer lasting memorial: the hill where he walked composing his speeches is now a conservation area, noted for its wild flowers and herbs.

Leaving the main road by a row of aged miners' homes opened by Colonel Sir Frank Simpson in 1934, we turn again towards the Tyne and the site of Stella power station, once the site of those immortal Blaydon Races and now being colonised by a large but tasteful Barratt estate. Turning west by the river we encounter a first for the walk: a field of wheat. To emphasise the rural theme, the path upstream to Newburn Bridge is fringed by poppies and cow parsley. A man is working on power lines 50 feet above us. On the west side of the pleasing blue-metalled bridge, the last on the Tyne on which tolls were levied, we stop by various boat houses, for these are rowing waters, and eat our sandwiches in the sunshine.

Just in front of us people once crossed the river by ford rather than bridge and it was this fact that drew two armies to this spot on 28 August 1640 when a Scottish Covenanter army led by General Alexander Leslie met the English royalist forces commanded by Edward, Lord Conway. Conway, heavily outnumbered, his local militia-men displaying a keen sense of survival, was defeated, and the Scots went on to occupy the town of Newcastle, thereby strangling London's coal supply. Charles I had no choice but to agree a truce, under which the Scottish army would be paid £806 a day, pending a final peace treaty. To raise these funds, Charles had to call the Long Parliament, thus setting in motion a process that would lead to the outbreak of the English Civil War two years later.

On the wooded bank of Newburn Village opposite, the squat tower of St Michael's and All Angels pokes through the trees. This was the formidable vantage-point from which the Scots trained their cannon on the ill-defended

and rather hapless English troops. No wonder they melted away.

A boat appears: the cruiser *Coventina* on its daily trip from Newcastle Quayside with a full boatload listening to stories of Roundheads and Cavaliers, before the low craft turns round, struggling slightly with a strong incoming tide. Time we were on our way too, but not before I point out the spot where a lovely man called Don Graham saw the Tyne frozen over for the first time in a long career spent working by the river for the Port of Tyne. It was a winter's morning in 1982…

We enter low-lying land known locally as 'the scrub', a reference to its bushes and rather struggling willow and silver birch trees, otherwise known as Parsons Haugh and then Ryton Willows. Large blocks of stone are dotted around, remnants of slag dumped here from the site of the Stanner Steelworks in Newburn. Yet the bird life is impressive, and I am soon presented with two firsts for the trip, and personal avian favourites: a gorgeous pink-breasted bullfinch, and an equally rare kingfisher, disturbed from its perch on a branch overhanging the river and darting to the north bank in a blur of orange and iridescent blue.

There's not many other walkers about, but we eventually encounter a dog and then its owner, Elizabeth Tweddle, who stops to reminisce about the Ryton Willows of her childhood, a pleasure ground for locals and trippers from far-off Newcastle and Shields.

'Further along there used to be ponds by the river where people would go curling in winter. We used to sledge down the hill from Ryton village onto the willows and in summer the Hoppings used to come here, the pleasure boats would tie up, and Newcastle folk who'd had a few would fall out and enjoy themselves. Oh, how they enjoyed themselves.'

Among the trippers after the Second World War were two brothers from Byker, who arrived on a flotilla of vessels from the Motor Boat Club on Newcastle's Ouseburn on high days and holidays: Bruce and Freddy Shepherd, who grew up to found and run among other enterprises Shepherd Offshore by the river in Walker. We will meet them later on the walk.

Ryton didn't just have its own pier; it also once had a chain-link ferry, and Elizabeth points to a tiny house on the south side where the ferryman used to live, now under restoration. She points across the river to a place where a wooden jetty stood and we promise to look for surviving timbers when we get there. Elizabeth's dog is pulling impatiently at its lead and she walks downstream while we turn upstream and soon find other decaying timbers: the skeleton of a Tyne wherry, inexorably being received into the gravel and mud of the river-bank. Charlie and I explore its contours, admiring its overlapping clinkered hull and the elegant curve of its wooden rudder. A large metal tub is rusting away in deeper water. Charlie suggests it might be a boiler.

184

Wherries were originally powered by hand with long oars or punting poles, or towed in trains by tugs, but some were later fitted with small boilers and engines. They were used mainly in the Tyne coal trade to bring cargoes from the staiths to sea-going colliers in the estuary. Some 50 feet in length, measuring 35 to 50 tons, they were built to withstand being grounded on falling tides and the occasional collision in the crowded river. Despite their size and weight, their 'Viking' ancestry could easily be spotted in the pointed stems and sterns and the skilful curves of their overlapping planks.

After the war, these workhorses of the Tyne began to fall out of favour. But they weren't sent to the knacker's yard for the obvious reason that there was no scrap value in them, so one by one they were towed to the upper stretches of the tidal river and just abandoned to the elements – the explanation for the various decomposing ribs we'd seen since leaving Dunston. The one Charlie and I explored is thought to have been dumped in 1969. But one Tyne wherry has survived, once used to tow heavy machinery manufactured at Vicker's in Scotswood to ships on the lower river and now beached rather splendidly in the North East Museums' store at Beamish. So if you ever get the chance, go and have a look at the prosaically named but utterly magnificent *Elswick No. 2*, the very last wherry built on the Tyne and launched a few weeks before the outbreak of the Second World War at – where else, given this journey's record in producing the serendipitous – Harrison's yard in Bill Quay.

As Charlie and I climb back onto the riverside path, hemmed in by the Carlisle rail line, we're passed by burly lads in orange jackets carrying wooden posts from a distant van to an unknown destination. This soon becomes clear when we come to a little clearing with a growing pile of said posts and a cheerful gaffer who's content to sit and watch his lads do all the work. Kenny Rutherford's track maintenance crew is draining a man-made pond that has periodically flooded the line, but this essential work has been delayed by a few months. When I ask why, Kenny rolls his eyes.

'It was full of tadpoles, that's why. So we all had to wait till they turned into little froggies and hopped off, didn't we?'

This was said without malice to amphibians, the tone more 'Funny old world.' It soon becomes evident in fact that Kenny is pleased to be doing or even watching this job, since in a long career in rail maintenance from Lockerbie to Dorset, it's one of the few jobs on which he's been able to drive home every night. As we leave, Christy finally recognises him: this cheerful philosopher of manual work – the second of the day substantially missing teeth – has other gifts. It turns out he's a distinguished tar-barrelling guiser in Allendale's famous New Year celebrations, as well as a brass band virtuoso.

Crossing the arid fairways of Ryton Golf Course, we're on the last leg of the day's walk. Then my phone goes. Having tweeted our progress over the last week, I get a message from someone who's been following us. Sarah Raad once worked at Live Theatre and helped promote plays of mine. She suggests our journey cannot be complete without visiting her home village, which is just off our route. So I call her.

'Stay where you are. I'll come and meet you.'

And she does. So begins our introduction to one of the highlights of the trip – and I'm not just referring to the cakes that await us in the miners' cottage where Sarah and her husband Dom live. Within this little settlement there is a whole world to explore: the world of Clara Vale.

Our introduction to it is the short walk off the golf course, over the rail line and up a short hill to a row of neat terraces running north to south. But the moment when the village story really engages, the curiosity beginning to bite, is when, over tea and cakes, Sarah empties a cardboard box onto the table of her stylish kitchen. The sheets of paper are actually paintings of Clara Vale and a series of cartoons featuring two elderly miners commenting on the changes enveloping their home, all the work of a man called Jimmy Curry, the previous occupant of Sarah's house.

Jimmy Curry was a colliery electrician who lived and worked in Clara Vale all his life. After his mother died he lived on his own, having once been disappointed in love. Jimmy was a quiet and fastidious man with a wry sense of humour, a keen gardener who grew beautiful vegetables and keen cyclist who often pedalled to Alston to visit his sister. However his great passion was painting; according to Jean Fox, a neighbour who cared for him as an old man, 'He never had any lessons, he just loved it, he was always at it, sitting at the kitchen table.' After he died in 2009, the house was being cleared, his paintings destined for the tip until his neighbours Karen and Tony rescued them.

Thus we sift through the work of someone who I suppose would now be called a pitman-painter. They might lack the technical expertise of Spennymoor's Norman Cornish or members of the Ashington Group, but Jimmy's work has charm, affection and good humour. I especially like a panorama of the village, with pithead and railway sidings with tank engine in dreamy watercolours, and a cartoon, in which the two old pitmen sit looking down on Clara Vale.

'They reckon there's a different class of folk living in Clara Vale now,' says one.

'Aye, there is that,' his friend says. 'They reckon they get oot the bath if they want a piddle.'

Two pieces of cake later, we go out to look for Clara Vale, old and new.

We are not exactly talking about a settlement that's in the Domesday Book. Clara Vale began life when the Stella Coal Company (head office in Cathedral Buildings, Dean Street, Newcastle) began sinking two shafts down into rich coal seams by the Tyne in 1889. The family who owned the company were the Simpsons, who lived in a fine 18th century house, Bradley Hall, a mile or two to the west (indeed their descendants still do). They operated four other pits in the area, and the story goes that one Christmas, JB Simpson told his wife he had a special gift for her, but it was far too big to wrap up: the pit and village he named after his beloved Clara. Within eight years, the pit was producing 180,000 tons a year and employing almost 1,000 men and boys. The village revolved around it completely.

The first thing we discover about the village is that it's small, almost a hamlet; one road in and one road out. Its streets have differing characters. Edington Gardens, nearest the pit, is what was 'gaffers row', a terrace of pale brick. The house by the entrance to the pit had a window in the side through which wages were paid. The next street along, West View, was originally known as 'sinkers row.' These houses are generously proportioned with yards and front gardens and made of handsome stone. On the other side of the village school, now its community centre, the houses are of a more modest brick, but even so far more handsome than the rather mean pit row in which I began my life 30 miles to the south in Ferryhill. The Simpsons evidently had some sort of social conscience, evident from what they built – the school, for instance – but also from what they didn't; followers of the temperance movement, they wouldn't have a public house. On our ramble we're also tickled to find yet another street named 'Tyne View' and a bench with a plaque announcing, 'The blather seat, in loving memory of Gordon McKenzie'. More sobering, near the substantial Co-op on East View, is the war memorial, 'in proud and grateful memory of the men of this colliery who fell in the Great War': out of less than a thousand pitmen, 56 were killed, including two Burrows, Harry and Joseph, two Johnsons, two Robsons and two Walkers.

In the middle of the village, the community centre is attractively faced with white brick, with red 'string' bands. Posters outside advertise kick boxing classes, Zumba fitness workouts; inside the mother and toddler group is in noisy session as we explore a display in another room of the village's history: a spread in the *Illustrated Chronicle* of 1899 featuring this 'model Tyneside Village'; wonderfully evocative portraits over seven decades of the school's pupils and masters (we note the teacher in 1925, Mark Pinkney, is still there in 1953); black and white photos of a man with pony in ceremonial trimmings, workmates at the pit and a street scene. Then there's the Clara Vale Lodge banner featuring a female figure announcing 'Emancipation of

OPPOSITE
Hall, Clara Vale
Methodist Chapel.

Labour', leading a procession of families, children with hands raised above the final slogan, 'Workers Of All Lands Unite You Have A World to Win'. Finally there are mementoes of the rich social and sporting life of the village: a pennant recording its cricket team as First Division Champions of the Tyne and District Cricket League in 1956; four men in Sunday best including cardies – the NCB Bowls Team 1953; the chapel ladies of 1915; a sewing class outing of 1960; the pit's ambulance team of 1910.

The school closed in 1963, the pit three years later (its flooded workings inundating the Emma pit in nearby Crawcrook, forcing its closure too); the Co-op wasn't long in following. The village might just have quietly died, but it found a new life, with a growing trickle of new residents. One of them was naturalist and museum curator Tony Tynan, who came to Clara Vale in the mid-80s after he met his partner, Karen. He loved it from the start.

'It was a splendid place, very small and friendly, full of ex-colliers and their wives. Over time many of the pitmen sadly passed away, but of course many of their widows lived on to see a different kind of village.'

The physical change began when Gateshead Council demolished the pit buildings. A local man wanted to put a scrapyard on the site, but the village got together and fought the plan, and won. A 'Pit Yard Action Group' suggested that the pit yard should be handed over to nature and the Clara Vale Conservation Group was formed. Gateshead Council approved, fenced off the area and in due course sent a digger to build a pond on the line of a spring fed drain. A long lease on peppercorn rent was granted. Clara Vale Nature Reserve had arrived, the date 1986.

We go and have a look.

The Clara Vale reserve contains habitats – woodland, meadows, marsh and ponds – supporting 100 species of birds, 200 plants and 18 butterflies. Fish weren't introduced but somehow they've got into the ponds, possibly via eggs sticking to the legs of visiting herons and kingfishers. The only remaining traces of the pit are the ambulance house, circular slabs of concrete capping the shafts and the fire-damaged pit baths, operated until lately as a recording studio, enjoying the distinction, or possibly the indignity, of once being used by the band Westlife.

Not far away there's a memorial garden dedicated to the miners who once laboured here, its flower beds and paths tracing the brick foundations of the Church of the Good Shepherd, now demolished, and a community orchard, cleared by half a dozen pigs from Bill Quay community farm (passed on day three) and knocked into shape by villagers as a Millennium project (though Tony Tynan recalls the hardest work was probably filling in the Heritage

Lottery application form). More than 120 apple trees, crab apples and soft fruit now replace a wilderness of scrub.

These green amenities have enhanced the pleasing environment of the old Clara Vale in its setting by the Tyne and made it increasingly attractive to young professional couples, many with children. Among them are Sarah and Dom Raad, who run their thriving marketing and design consultancy Tentspitch from an elegant wooden house in their garden.

'Living in Clara Vale is a bit like stepping back in time. It's a place with genuine community spirit, people socialise with their neighbours, people know your children's names and look out for them, which is the other thing, children play out and do the sort of things we used to do when we were children. It's a bit of a hidden gem really and we feel very lucky to have ended up here.'

The gradual change in the social character of the village over the last 50 years is obvious, but it seems welcome as well as inevitable to this outsider, better in any case than a slow withering, as Tony Tynan, one of the first 'settlers', recognises:

'Of course many of the old timers have passed away, though there are still a few of what you might call the pit widows left. The houses have been done up, and the younger settlers tend to be middle class professionals. You know, we used to take the old Lodge banner to the Durham Big Meeting, where I was one of the 'pole-bearers', with four people hanging onto the ropes. We wrote to the NUM – 'Please can we come etc…' The reply was prompt, and

included a cheque to pay for a coach and the promise of a band to march behind. The community spirit was impressive, and when the Conservation Group celebrated its 25th birthday recently, the spirit was revived, the ladies of the village baked cakes and as one said, 'It's just like the old days.'

Except of course the pit is no more; and maybe less socialism. On our walk around the village, I noticed a sign on a lamp post announcing the last-ever service of Clara Vale's Wesleyan Chapel. Partly out of curiosity, partly respect to my Methodist roots (as a young man my father was a lay preacher), I decided to go.

Some weeks later, on a damp misty evening by the Tyne, I arrived outside the chapel. An owl hooted in the darkness. There was a chill in the air, but inside it was snug and warm. I arrived early, concerned I might not get in, so I have a look around: large organ and pulpit to match, clock in loving memory of Annie Hands 1909-2001, stained glass windows with a touch of the art nouveau, yellow flowers everywhere. An elderly man with white hair and a slight stoop greeted me and asked if I was from Prudhoe. I smiled and shook my head as he turned to a friend who spoke his name: Drag.

The chapel gradually filled – old men in suits slightly too big for them and their exquisitely dressed wives A pianist sat down at the piano and began playing a tune. A murmuring went around the pews and the congregation began singing:

> *Praise Him, Praise Him*
> *Praise Him in the morning*
> *Praise Him in the noontime*
> *Praise Him, Praise Him*
> *Praise Him when the sun goes down*
> *Trust Him, serve Him, praise Him.*

The voice of the old man behind me was reedy but hearty. I looked behind: old Clara Vale was in attendance; new Clara Vale wasn't – possibly watching *Strictly* – though I noticed a small baby being rocked in her mother's arms. There were more women than men. A visiting choir of men in their eighties stood up: the West Ryton Gleemen, which folded in 2010 when their chapel closed down, but reunited for one last gig. They sang 'I hear thy welcome voice'; when they finished, one of them commented slightly too loudly: 'A bit rusty then, lads?' The reading was from St John's Gospel and the minister, Marion Proud, spoke of weddings, baptisms, harvest time, happy times and sad times within those four walls; of the special place the chapel played in the life of the village: 'This is a sad occasion, but also a time to give thanks. In my prayers I have asked what message the Lord would want to pass to the people of Clara Vale. And the answer came – tell them I love them.'

Then while John said prayers of intercession, Drag took around a collection plate that soon filled with notes. The choir finally sang not a hymn, but the old Matt Monro song, *Softly, as I Leave You*. The sound of these old men humming gently was somehow very moving, and soon followed by the last hymn, 'How great Thou art', which I'd last heard at my Auntie Kathy's funeral. I sang along, while an old lady nearby quietly wept.

Afterwards, over home-made sandwiches and cakes in the hall next door, chapel secretary Rosemary Hyman talked of the feeling of bereavement among the dwindling band of regulars: 'It's especially hard for older people as they wanted to have their funerals here. The chapel was built by miners, but there are no miners left. It's closing because the village has changed. It's become a dormitory hamlet, and we only have 14 regular members. We knew this day was going to come.' Two representatives of the new Clara Vale, Gareth and Tamsin Wood, expressed their sadness at the closure, 'But it's inevitable, isn't it?' I wondered aloud what would happen to the organ, the pulpit and pews? It seems likely the chapel itself will become a desirable residence for a family of new 'settlers'.

As I prepared to leave, the elderly man with the curious name called out 'God bless you'. I stopped to have a few words, which led to rather more: the remarkable story of Drag Milton…

It turns out Drag wasn't brought up in the Methodist Church, but in the Greek Orthodox. His original name is Dragisa Milutinovic. Born and brought up in central Serbia, he was a teenager working on a farm when his homeland was torn apart by violence. The Nazis had invaded Yugoslavia, but much of their dirty work was carried out by fascist militia and opposed by Tito's Communist partisans.

'There were lots of killings and everyone was afraid of being caught up in the violence. It was ugly. One day I was taken by the Chetnik militia who collaborated with the Germans. At first they wanted to kill me, but then they gave me a choice. Work with us or we'll kill you. What could I do? I went with them.'

Somehow Drag survived these horrors and three hard years in displacement camps in central Europe before finding a life in the little village by the Tyne.

'About 100 of us volunteered to work in the mines or on farms. I chose the pits, did my training in Scotland and I was then sent to a hostel in Ryton. There were Ukranians, Latvians and Lithuanians there and we all worked in local pits. I was sent to work at Clara Vale and you could say it changed my life around.'

One of the deputies at the pit was 'a very nice chap' called Harry Watson who was also a preacher at the chapel. He invited Drag to attend a Sunday evening service there and then to come home for supper afterwards. It was

there that he met Harry's niece, a young woman called Ellen, and things went on from there. Ellen and Drag have been happily married for 55 years.

'What I want to say is that everyone has been very nice to me. I was very happy to be among these people, I made some good friends and that was how I met my wife, and in all my time here I've never had a wrong word from anyone.'

These words are spoken with deep feeling, but they pale by comparison with the vehemence of what Drag has to say when I ask him about his years working underground at Clara Vale Colliery.

'I worked at the pit for 15 years until it closed, when I became a night-watchman in Newcastle. It was a very bad pit and the conditions were terrible. It was very wet and your boots were always standing in water a few inches deep, sometimes up to your knees. The seam of coal was very thin, only about 12-15 inches thick, and it was really hard work getting it out. This is why I stoop – the pit wrecked my back. It was only after I got out of it that I realised how truly horrible it was.'

I find Drag's words, coming as they do from a man who has known both fear and suffering in a dirty war, deeply sobering.

I suppose there is a temptation among people of my generation, especially those from a mining background, to romanticise the underlying reality of coal culture; to take the kind of strength, solidarity and mutual caring found in pit villages and readily offered to strangers from far away and assume they somehow wiped clean the filth of what awaited pitmen when they went into the cage and dropped into the earth. So let it be said: digging coal was a brutal and demeaning way to earn a living and I for one am glad of two things: that my parents, both clever and resourceful people, somehow ensured I was spared it, and that in Clara Vale in 2012 its residents have found alternative employment, in offices and call centres, or down the garden offering marketing and design expertise to local businesses…

It is a sober but deeply satisfied quartet of walkers that makes the short riverside walk to Wylam Station. We've reached the end of day five and the mid-point of our walk and we celebrate both with a pint of Curlew's Return in the Boathouse. Then we have another pint – and hurry onto opposite platforms for our journeys home.

On our way into Newcastle it takes Charlie and I just seven minutes to travel to the day's start point in Blaydon.

But of course we see only a tiny fraction of what we experienced on Shanks's pony…

OPPOSITE
Wylam signal box at dusk.

Signal box at Wylam
looking east

On The Nent

I once stood on a bank of the Nile.

A substantially bigger river, obviously, than the Tyne, even though it was actually the White Nile, and my vantage point at a place called Murchison Falls in northern Uganda was some 3,000 miles from the point at which the merged Blue and White Nile emerges into the Mediterranean at Alexandria. Even so, this river was w-i-d-e, maybe 200 yards of it, as well as heart-stoppingly beautiful. We took a boat upriver to the falls, past the spot where Ernest Hemingway crashed a plane in 1954, a journey through the most intense verdancy and variety of animal life. Families of elephant were bathing, hippos snorting in the depths, crocodiles glided malevolently alongside the boat, and flocks of kingfishers of many species and the most dazzling colours swooped from nests in a muddy cliff. I thought – this is the closest I'll ever get to a Garden of Eden.

Later on we climbed to the top of the falls and stood on a ledge overlooking the river. At this spot the great river is forced into a narrow fissure in the rock, the resulting torrent spewing into thin air in a blur of violent white motion before falling some 150 feet to resume its meandering journey below. We stood and watched, mesmerised: the young but mighty Nile channeled into a gap that could have been leapt by a long-jumper of average ability. There was no rail separating us from the maelstrom. I felt a visceral sense of fear at the power, and danger, of running water.

Odd, then, to record that the *second* time I sensed this dread, I was perched on the bank of the usually tranquil Nent, only 40 miles from home, albeit in the neighbouring county of Cumbria, on an alleged spring day in 2012. Days of rain had rendered the high Pennines into the fullest of sponges and a goodly portion of its contents had been squeezed into the Nent, bombing past me at a rate my companions estimated at three to four times its usual flow. The primitive feelings inside me, like those I always feel on a cliff-top, alternated strangely between attraction and revulsion: a bit of me wondered what it would be like to surf this foaming peaty torrent; and how long it would take me to reach Spar Hawk, that legendary spot off Tynemouth Pier. For yes, the Nent is a tributary of the Tyne, and the reason why I made this journey on such a day of epic awfulness, meteorologically speaking.

OPPOSITE
Summer by the Nent.

To explain…

You see, if you stand on Wylam Bridge, as we did at the end of day five of our walk, halfway stage and turning point, you can't help but look upstream and ponder with regret all the Tyne places and people we would not encounter on our journey, given that the end result is not designed to run into a multi-volume set. More than that, you reflect on an obvious point: that what's up there affects what's down here, the river being the connecting conduit. This can be, as we heard, travelling timber or the occasional dead animal; it can also be something more insidious, because you can't see it, and potentially a longer lasting problem for the river than a rotting carcass.

So let me speak of the mining of lead.

This interests me for various reasons: I have always loved Allendale, one of the historic centres of the industry in the northern Pennines; I've always been intrigued by the fact that this area and its industrial history so fascinated the poet WH Auden; perhaps most of all because a branch of my family – the Charltons – were Weardale lead-miners who in the late 19th century upped sticks to Shildon, convinced that the digging of coal would be a cakewalk compared to their old calling. And finally I met a man called Malcolm Newson and he told me a beguiling story.

It begins with the Romans: it usually does in my experience. As every schoolchild knows, your ancient Roman was a cut above in the cleanliness department. He or she tended to take a bath more often than your average Goth – and the running water was hot! What made all this possible was the fashioning of pipes from lead. In fact our word for the guy who comes around to your house in an emergency, shakes his head and mutters, 'It'll cost you, mate,' comes from the Latin for lead: plumbum. When the Romans came to the north country 2,000 years ago to build their wall, they found they were in their element: plenty of stone to build, and enough lead nearby, in Allendale, Weardale and Teesdale, for all those bath-houses at Housesteads and Vindolanda, as well as a variety of other objects, including pots and paints, coins and cosmetics. They even added lead to food in the form of lead acetate to sweeten it, which was probably a culinary notion on a par with roast dormouse, but with longer-term ill-effects.

Their preferred method of extracting the metal had its dangers too. In many places in the northern Pennines, veins of lead outcropped at or near the surface, often near streams or becks. The Romans developed a process called 'hushing', a gentle, melodious word for a violent act: the stream would be dammed above such veins, then after a time the dam smashed away so that the resulting torrent would tear away soil and stones below to expose the lead, which could then be worked and washed. The latter phrase rolls easily off the keyboard but was obviously devilish hard in actuality, for many generations of men and boys. In the last few centuries sundry remains of

Roman civilisation have been found in these valley bottoms, among the enormous quantities of debris hushed from the hillsides, in the form of coins, utensils and even stone altars to various gods. One of the latter was discovered in a river-bed at Bollihope in Weardale in the 19th century and found an appropriate home at The Rectory in Stanhope.

As the centuries passed, these surface workings were exhausted and later generations of miners had to start digging down into the hillsides to mine the metal, an even dirtier and more dangerous business. By far the greatest problem was water, by virtue of the area's high rainfall. So in addition to building vertical shafts to gain access to the lead, they also built horizontal 'levels' to drain the water from the workings, which often emerged several miles further down the valley. So Blackett's Level, named after the local landowner and mine-owner, has its entrance in the burn bottom at Allendale Town and meanders for several miles up the East Allen valley towards Allenheads. Even more impressive is the wondrous Nent Force Level, which emerges near Alston's railway station and travels underground for some four and a half miles towards Nentsbury. Often water drained from lead workings in this way would be used to power local industries, but what's remarkable about this underground waterway is that it was built as a kind of canal, nine feet wide and nine feet high (though higher in many places). Miners transporting materials, and sometimes excursion parties of gentlemen and their ladies, carrying lanterns and singing to test the underground acoustics, made their way up it, powering their 30-foot-long boats along with sticks thrust against the roof's supporting timbers. Work on the Level began in 1776 and was only completed 66 years later in 1842, the project having cost its owners, the Commissioners of Greenwich Hospital, the then dazzling sum of £60,000, which gives some idea of the profits to be had from the trade in lead, precious little of which, it's barely necessary to report, trickled down to the people who mined it or the navvies who built this most extraordinary example of Britain's canal age. Its presiding genius was John Smeaton, a man used to engineering challenges: he also built the Eddystone Lighthouse and two bridges I always admire when I cross them, over the Tyne at Hexham and the Tweed at Coldstream.

But – and there is of course always a 'but' – all of this activity had its negative aspects, and not only in the blighted lives of the lead miners and their families, but in an unseen pollutant which affected not only the Nent, but also the Tyne into which it flows. Inevitably, lead itself got into the water system, along with zinc, which was mined separately, and its by-product cadmium, all of which are potentially harmful to humans and animals; actually quite a lot of all three, considering that mining went on for almost two millennia. Over that time, particles of the metals have been swept downriver, much of it buried deep in underwater silts, but at times of flood washed onto its banks. Two examples will indicate the problems this can cause, particularly from zinc. When the Gateshead Garden Festival was held by the Tyne at Dunston in 1990, there was a plan to use Tyne dredgings for flower and vegetable beds until it was discovered they contained potentially harmful levels of the heavy metals. Furthermore, there is rich arable land by the river at Warden and Fourstones producing high-quality cereals that can't be sold for human consumption because of their mineral content.

So now we come back to that sodden walk by the Nent. For a start, Charles can't join us – his footwear isn't up to the terrain – and I nearly lose one welly when a puddle in a field comes to within an inch of the top. But we walk on, we being myself, Malcolm Newson of the environmental charity Tyne Rivers Trust, and Andy Lees, who works for the body governing the North Pennines' Area of Outstanding Natural Beauty. As we make our way upstream from Foreshield Bridge on a tiny path inches from the scary flow, Malcolm explains that while past pollution creates its own problems, the Trust and various other agencies and organisations are working hard to stop or at least slow pollution in the future. While lead mining finished decades ago, its by-products are literally all over the place; liquid pollution gets into the Nent via 'adits' – entrances or drainage tunnels from the workings, while spoil heaps are sources of solid pollution. Further pollution occurs when riverbanks are flooded or crumble into the Nent, so the Trust has commissioned works at these places to control bank erosion using the arcane engineering term 'revetment', coined at a time when fighting natural forces was the engineering ethos – these ones will work with nature. Thus the banks shouldn't be proof against everything. The AONB is trying to encourage the spread of water voles along the Nent and Andy Lees is pointing out evidence of their presence and discussing with Malcolm ways in which the swanky new banks might be vole-friendly.

And then there is the ticklish issue of the Calaminarian Grasslands. Let Malcolm explain.

'In the wonderful way that nature has, there are many species that don't like the presence of these heavy metals and others that positively love them. And what we find on the Nent and on the Tyne are low-level areas that are periodically flooded and on them these rather wonderful plants that absorb the sediments and fix them, at least until the plants die. So they're rather useful to us in the management of this problem, and the other thing is that these colonies are protected – they're rather rare.'

Not so far away the Trust is collaborating with the AONB on another experiment to stop sediments getting further downstream. On a bank of a spoil-heap near Nenthead, they're comparing the results of covering the spoil with different materials (flat stones, coir matting, and a bed of a Calaminarian plant, the spring sandwort) to see which is most effective in slowing the movement of solid pollution into the watercourse. Nearby a team from Newcastle University is trying out the effectiveness of filtering polluted water with, believe it or not, brewery waste.

On the way back to our cars, soaked despite the shelter of my Port of Tyne umbrella, I ask Malcolm how the fish of the tumbling Nent cope with all of these metals in their water.

'Well, being close to the high toxic concentrations, the river is almost fishless, whereas the rest of the Tyne has seen a magnificent resurgence, which shows that the barrier to salmon and sea trout migration lower down was industrial and sewage pollution. Now of course they're thriving as never before.'

Then we come to something quietly amazing. On the bank opposite the Lovelady Shield Hotel, we find a vertical shaft entrance a few yards from the river, now with a protective grille. Peering down into the blackness, I remember something I read about WH Auden, who spent many happy times as boy and adult in these parts; the North Pennines were his 'great, good place'. Once as a young man, he dropped a stone down a similar shaft and waited to hear it strike bottom – in vain. He was forcibly struck by this nothingness; how it seemed to symbolise human mortality, and the short time before we too fall into the dark. He used this image in his verse many times.

So I think of Wystan in that moment, and then of those miners who descended into such depths. I wonder if I might see the lights of those Victorian boat-explorers, or hear the echoes of their distant songs.

But there is only the blackest of black down there and, of course, the sound of dripping water.

HADRIAN'S CYCLEWAY

Ovingham 2
Corbridge 10
Hexham 14

72

HADRIAN'S CYCLEWAY
Newburn 2
Newcastle 10
Tynemouth 20

72

DAY SIX

When I was a boy, I spent my time,
Sitting on the banks of the river Tyne.
Watching all the ships going down the line, they were leaving,
Leaving, leaving, leaving, leaving me.
I've got to leave old Durham town,
I've got to leave old Durham town.

Durham Town, Roger Whittaker

The water dances beneath, skittering madly downstream over a bed of stones towards the distant sea. I have an equally distant memory of standing on this very spot as a boy, feet dangling safely on the road side of the parapet as I alternated between dropping twigs into the river and slow-falling spits…

I am standing on Wylam's elegant little road bridge of 1836. My photographer friend Charles Bell is doing his stuff while we wait for the other walkers to arrive on the train from Hexham. We've arrived by taxi on the north side and as the train arrives on the south, it strikes me that I should go and meet them, otherwise I could be accused of not actually completing the entire walk. So I cross the bridge and walk back with them. We have a guest on today's five-mile amble to Lemington, the filmmaker Charles Bowden, a good friend who grew up near the Tyne at Haltwhistle and spent his professional life reporting the farming scene for *The Journal* before making many immaculate rural and wildlife documentaries for television. With his great knowledge of botany and ornithology, it's good to have him with us: there's also the fact that he's promised to buy the lunchtime beers.

We stop for a moment to mark the fact that we now have the morning sun on our faces: we are heading towards the sea, literally and metaphorically *going with the flow*. Eastward ho! Also, it may be hard to detect – since Wylam Bridge is only 38 feet above sea level – but we're now going downhill…

We make our way past some lovely riverside villas and find a substantial path running east to west – the line of the old railway that ran from Scotswood via Lemington to Wylam and then joined the main line on the other side of the river via a substantial arched bridge upstream of the village. We join the path at the site of the old Wylam North Station. There are walkers about already, including John Short and Christine Curtis from Walker, who are heading west while we strike out for Lemington and, a little way along the old wagonway, a fine stone cottage. An elegant plaque placed on its front wall by the Institute of Mechanical Engineering tackles

OPPOSITE
Old Ryton ferry crossing.

207

the impossible job of summarising the vast achievements of the man born here in 1781. The Institute had an additional reason for conferring this small honour: George Stephenson was their first president. He was also one of the few men in history who can be said to have changed the world. In a regional context, he's perhaps the only native North Easterner to claim membership of that exclusive club. He also happens to be one of my few heroes and one day I hope to write a play about him and his complex relationship with his equally brilliant son, Robert.

So how did Geordie change the world? Put it like this: for centuries mankind moved at the speed of the fastest horse – like the nags that pulled the wagons of Wylam coal to the Lemington staiths – but after the advent of the steam railways, everything about our way of life was altered for good. There were many people involved in this great mechanical, economic and social leap forward, but our George was a key figure – in the development of the steam locomotives that pulled the trains, the tracks they ran on, the bridges they crossed, the tunnels they penetrated, the stations, signalling and all the many other pieces of paraphernalia needed for the railway system. More than anyone else, Stephenson invented the concept of passenger railways and the social mobility that flowed from them. Before him, the poor (and he was one of them) walked everywhere; they could not afford the coach, that preserve of the rich, and incidentally, destroyer of horses – an institutional cruelty that deeply mattered to Stephenson. The man's life was incredibly rich, marked by triumph and tragedy, and a series of battles, most of which he pugnaciously overcame, starting with his boyhood besting of a Wylam bully called Ned Nelson. Despite his success, Geordie never became a tool of the system, turning down the offer of a knighthood and rejecting the opportunity to make a fortune in railway shares. At the end of his life he gave his time once more to gardening – growing grapes in the conservatory of his Derbyshire mansion – and the one mechanical challenge that defeated him: the construction of a perpetual motion machine. It is entirely fitting that the man's motto was 'Persevere'.

Young George lived in the bijou rail-side cottage, now owned by the National Trust and open to the public (the guide tends to wear period dress) because his father, Robert – later blinded by boiling steam in a pit accident – worked at Wylam Colliery, as the fireman tending its pumping engine. The pay was poor and there was no money for schooling – it was his son Robert who later taught George to read and write – so his early education was a practical one. Like Clara Vale on the opposite side of the river, Wylam was a wet pit, and the experience young George gained helping his father ensure the pumps were up to the challenge gave him an early grounding in practical engineering. At 17, Stephenson became engineman at Water Row Pit, before later stints at Black Callerton and Willington Quay completed his preparation for the great developments he initiated first at Killingworth Colliery, then on the Stockton and Darlington, Liverpool to Manchester and countless other jaw-dropping enterprises. Along the way George invented his own miners' safety lamp independently of Davy, while making shoes and mending clocks to supplement his income.

For a little village to have one great railway pioneer to its name is singular enough, but Wylam actually has three, the others being Timothy Hackworth, born here and later contributing much to the building of the Stockton and Darlington, and the pioneering William Hedley, who built two rudimentary locos for local hauling – *Puffing Billy* and *Wylam Dilly* (great names, William!) – before young Stephenson was out of the blocks. Standing on the wagonway all three engineers knew so well, I doff my cap in respect to their collective genius.

Having found one local landmark – it wasn't hard, to be honest – we leave the wagonway to find two more. Both are elusive. I had been told that an outflow from the old colliery workings at Wylam can still be seen gushing into the Tyne, but this morning we can't seem to find it. Following a path through woodland at the river's edge that's alive with bird song, we see the torrent of water we saw tumbling over stones at Wylam bridge has turned to a still and silent flow. The second landmark – the so-called Boundary Stone marking the historic limit of the tidal reach of the Tyne – is equally hard to find. After a bit of fruitless to-ing and fro-ing, we encounter a man of a certain age power-walking towards Wylam. We politely ask him to turn off the juice for a moment and tell us where the elusive stone might be. His directions are confident, but eventually turn out to be – our fault, surely – unhelpful. Meanwhile Charlie Bowden recognises the walker: his name is Alastair Balls, who among other services rendered to Tyneside in his lengthy career in the public service, was regional director of the Departments of Environment and Transport and chief executive of the Tyne and Wear Development Corporation in the 1980s and 90s. The meeting is strangely serendipitious, for I've been looking for people who could guide me through a history of the river and its industries more recent than the age of Stephenson. As for Alastair, he's intrigued by our journey, especially its quest to examine the relationship between the river and the people living along its banks. When this Scot first came to Newcastle in the 1970s, he was immediately struck by the evident strength of this bond.

'I always say that you can get someone in the centre of Newcastle, get them to shut their eyes, spin them round and then when you stop them ask where exactly the river was, their instincts would tell them,' he says.

As we stand in the sunshine exchanging stories, the conversation turns to the clean-up of the river and Alastair recalls a day he considers critical in shaping the political will to start the process.

'When the public enquiry into the plan to build the Kielder Dam was being held in Moot Hall in Newcastle in the 70s, proceedings had to be stopped one day because the smell from the river was so bad. The great and the good were all there and the event got a lot of negative publicity. The later building of the interceptor sewer from Newburn to Howdon flowed, as you might say, from that day.'

Alastair came to Newcastle as a result of meeting a girl on a number 11 bus in London's Strand whose parents were originally from Jarrow. Her Uncle Jim was a Sunday school superintendent who measured insurance claims in the Tyne's industries for a living. Like many shipyard people he wore a bowler hat. When he died of a heart attack, Alastair was invited to the funeral in a Baptist chapel in Jarrow where the men sat on one side and the women on the other. This was his introduction to Tyneside. He took a great shine to the place.

'I was in the Civil Service at the time and in the mid 70s I applied for a big promotion in the North East and was amazed to get it. Then I discovered I'd been the only applicant! It was like being banished to the Roman Wall. No one in London took any notice of what I was doing and so I was left to get on with it. Meanwhile people in the North East had given up on the river and its industries in despair. There were so many lost opportunities, in the offshore oil industry for instance – shipyards in the North East ignored this new market for a generation.'

This chimes with comments I heard before and since, but according to Alastair the lack of foresight wasn't merely confined to industrialists.

'Upstream we saw there could be a need for modern office space so the Newcastle Business Park was established between '86 and '89 and eventually the likes of BA and the AA based themselves there, but the land needed a huge amount of preparation – decontamination of soil, levelling, new roads. The local authorities were rather ineffective at this back then, in fact they didn't seem terribly interested, much more in keeping the bleeding limbs of the old industries going. While I was at the Development Corporation twelve shipyards were closed, all in the face of huge opposition, but my view was that British shipbuilding was gone. The Far East could build ships more cheaply and quickly. British shipbuilders seemed unable to cut costs. The unions had a stranglehold on wage rates that were far higher than the Far East and weak managements seemed to think it was easier to muddle on rather than grasp the nettle and save themselves. When the adminstrators took over Swan's after the building of their last warship, a report to them said that for the shipyard to compete for similar projects in the commercial marketplace it could only afford only one third of its workforce. You could say management and unions were locked in a kind of death embrace.'

Alastair's opinions are both trenchant and contentious (and they'll possibly be countered later on our journey), but they do come from someone who wasn't merely a witness to in the industrial shake-out of the 80s and 90s, but a participant. It should also be said that many of the improvements to what you might call the public amenity of the Tyne that have made our walk so much easier and more pleasant, access to the riverside being just one example, stem from the work of the Development Corporation he headed. A good person therefore to ask about the future of the river and its communities…

'Offshore industry is continuing to grow, and there seems to be a future in sustainable energy, though the Coalition Government suddenly seems rather lukewarm about wind power. In a wider context, if you look at the history of the Tyne it's always been cyclical – good times, bad times. It's been going through the doldrums in the last 30 years but has the capacity to come up again. I think one of the problems is that private industry develops best when working with strong public bodies. Tyne and Wear County Council and the Development Corporation were abolished by various governments and now One North East has gone too. Political intervention on the river is too piecemeal and so I think what's needed is a new body to focus development. Put it like this – it's an idea whose time has not yet come. The era of huge inward investment is probably over and the future is about small businesses starting up in science and technology, just like it was 150 years ago with men like Armstrong and Stephenson.'

LEFT
Alastair Balls (right), talks industrial regeneration and power-walking; guest walker Charles Bowden listens.

Having neatly completed a circular narrative back to the son of Wylam, Alastair switches back on the power and hurries towards the village, leaving us to contemplate his analysis – and find that elusive Boundary Stone.

Easier said than done. A yellowhammer calls out his song – a little bit of bread and no cheese – and a heron lazily rises from the water's edge below us. We come to a high sandy bank with large numbers of sand martins swooping for insects over the water and then returning to their bankside burrows to feed their young. As we stop to watch, Charlie Bowden, keen naturalist that he is, tells a strange tale about the bird. To keep their nests clean, the youngsters defecate directly onto their parents, who then dispose of their noisome cargo outside. This is as strange a definition of parenthood as I've ever heard, but then Charlie spoils it all when he asks himself: 'Or is that the kingfisher?'

But he's on surer ground with his botanical knowledge of the many plants growing by the path: himalayan balsam, angelica, ragwort, vetch, yarrow, fat hen – to me, rather prosaic plants that seem slightly less interesting than their names.

Then I'm able to tell Charlie something, as we come to a patch of woodland with the tell-tale burrows of a substantial rabbit warren. Passing this way a few months earlier, my wife Susan and I came across three young lads, one of their number calling with irritation and then anxiety into the blackness of a hole. It turned out they had lost their ferret. We hung around for a while, but evidently the beast had quite literally gone to ground. The youngest of the boys, he was maybe ten, began to get tearful, his rather touching tough-guy manner falling away. He obviously loved that ferret!

Meanwhile – still no Boundary Stone!

Then we find a tiny path close to the river on a steeply sloping bank. Like a good general I despatch my men to search in both directions while I wait and contemplate the day ahead. I'd been standing there for about five minutes when I realise that in fact I'm staring at the stone just a few feet away, well hidden, tucked in to the bank and partially obscured by shrubs and a hawthorn tree. We go up close and look at its date – 1785 – and the three-castle insignia of the ancient city and county of Newcastle.

The metre-high stone stands beside fast-running shallows called the 'Hedwin streams' and once marked the historic city boundary as well as the river's tidal reach. As a result of dredging between Newburn and Ryton at the turn of the 20th century and the river's increased power moving down its steeper course, the reach has since moved upstream, closer to Wylam, which I guess is one of the reasons why the stone is now so forgotten and neglected. But there's no questioning its symbolic importance, which dates as far back as 1292, when this place was first designated as the western limit of the port of Newcastle, the eastern being a spot off the river's mouth

historically known as 'Sparrowhawk' or 'Sparhawk'. In 1530, the mayor and burgesses of Newcastle were confirmed as conservators of the Tyne by act of Parliament, much to the lasting irritation of the other settlements along the river. It seems possible the resentment survives to this day…

Christy tells a nice story about the matchless artist and engraver Thomas Bewick, who used to walk down the Tyne from his family home at Cherryburn to his workshop in Newcastle in the early 1800s. He became aware that the illiterate stonemason who made and erected the boundary stone had never been paid by the Corporation of Newcastle (why am I not surprised to hear that?) and was living in straitened circumstances. Bewick apparently shamed the 'great men' of the city into coughing up.

At that time, the stone featured in an annual ritual mounted by the corporation: the 'surveying' of the city's bounds from Tynemouth to Hedwin Streams every Ascension Day. The worthies would make their way upriver in the corporation barge and alight by the stone, where the Mayor would kiss whoever he judged to be the prettiest of the Heddon girls assembled before him, presenting her with a golden sovereign. For this reason, the marker became known as the 'kissing stone', and for the avoidance of doubt it should be made clear that over time the point of the ritual segued from the ceremonial to the social: basically, it became the most tremendous piss-up. The last annual survey was held in 1851; afterwards it was held every five and then seven years, before being abandoned some decades later by the more upright worthies of the Tyne Improvement Commission, possibly because proceedings got rather out of hand, as this tasty account of the Ascension Day ceremony of May 1818 suggests:

'On arrival, the river jury took formal possession of their boundary stone as the mark of their utmost jurisdiction westward. Mr Ostle, the harbour master, an individual of considerable proportions, with the help of the largemen, placed himself at the top of the stone with a glass of wine in his hand and said: In the name of the King and the Corporation of Newcastle upon Tyne, I take formal possession of this stone: it has been theirs from time immemorial and will be theirs for all time to come; and I therefore propose the health of the King and the conservators of the River Tyne, at the high water mark.

'This address was warmly cheered, while the pit lads began to fire off some cannon, the band to play, and bottles of wine to empty of their exhilarating contents; dancing parties of men and women also began to form as if by instinct.'

(Yes, the party's shaping up nicely, but wait…)

'A cottage a little distance from the boundary stone, named the Cat House…'

(Honestly, I'm not making this up…)

'... was inhabited by a gentlewoman whose face bore evident marks of acquaintance with the middle of the last century; on this occasion she appeared at the door to greet the party, in a silk frock and a diminutive lace cap. Every gentleman uncovered in her presence...

(I think the writer means they took their hats off...)

'... a token of respect she acknowledged with a very low courtesy (sic). She was plentifully regaled with wine...

(I bet...)

'... for which she returned a flood of compliments, and then modestly intimated to the bottle holder that it was customary for the bottle to be left at her house and she thought it a pity to let old customs go down.'

It seems to me that a strong case could be made for the revival of this ancient ritual. If so, I'd like a ticket please. I'd certainly enjoy the spectacle of the current Harbour Master standing on top of the stone with a bottle in his hand and a loyal toast on his bibulous lips...

More seriously, the assembled walkers agree it's a shame this ancient monument of the river is so hidden from view.

A little further downstream we see a tern dropping into the river and find remnants of the Ryton Ferry, further on the handsome cottages of Blayney Row, and remnants of another pit that commemorated a coal owner's female relative, the Isabella. It was at the nearby and aptly named Water Row that the young George Stephenson tended Robert Hawthorn's pumping engine, but as we cross the little New Burn, it's a surviving pumping station, now The Keelman pub and Big Lamp micro-brewery, that provides the next landmark. Built in 1854, it provided the citizens of Newcastle with water of a rather salty and gamey flavour. The products of its successor on the site bear no such health risks, but we decide to take our lunchtime pint by the water's edge, at the Boathouse. The sun is high, the temperature rising, the river surface a shifting mosaic of golden ripples. A chap on his second pint could easily nod off but for the surfeit of nearby visual stimuli that trigger conversation – and wonder: especially, on the pub's front wall, the impossibly high flood markers of days of less benign weather, from 1832, 1851, 1858 and the daddy of them all, 1771, which stands about nine feet high. There's also, on the exterior of the Tyne Rowing Club, the familiar and yet mysterious image of the River God Tyne that also appears on Newcastle's Civic Centre and on one of nine arches symbolising Britain's mightiest rivers at Somerset House by the Thames (that piddling puddle). This splendidly mad image from 1786 features a god whose voluminous beard suggests the uniting of the South and North Tyne, who bears flaming coals on his head and is surrounded by further symbols of the river's industries, including pick and shovel and fishes and nets. Taking all of this in, you can't help wondering of the sculptor – what exactly was he on?

Eventually the glasses are empty and time to move, Charlie Bowden leaving with the excuse of a lunch date, the rest of us muttering that it's all right for some. But onwards! We decide on a short diversion, to walk up the bank into Newburn village to have a snoop around, especially at the church tower from which Scots artillery-men lobbed hot iron at nervous Newcastle militia men on the south side of the river, until such time as the latter made their excuses and quietly left.

But first we come across a row of fine almshouses built in 1870 by Hugh Taylor of Earsdon, a bailiff for the Duke of Northumberland. A man approaches, jingling keys for one of the houses. I ask him about Hugh Taylor. He laughs.

'Oh, I think he built these to buy his way into heaven, don't you?'

Of course he wasn't alone. The spire of the church near my boyhood home, Holy Trinity in Jesmond – my sister was married there, the obsequies for my father spoken there – is topped by a boat, symbol of the trade, and possibly guilt, of the man who paid for it, a ship-owner who had lost more than one shoddily maintained vessel with considerable loss of life. At least that's what my dad said, but then he also claimed the vertiginous boat was big enough to hold three boys, which is plainly bunk. He was a man who just couldn't resist gilding a story…

The scheme established by Hugh Taylor in Newburn is still in place, administered by eight trustees who sift applications on the basis of the founder's original conditions: residents have to be born in the parish, and must come from that section of society beloved of eminent Victorians, the 'deserving poor'. I wonder how the trustees define that nowadays.

The first thing to say about St Michael's and All Angels, Newburn, is that it has a lych gate with welcoming inscription ('Come unto me, ye that labour') to match the beauty of its name. Recently restored after a calamitous fire, it's associated with the Spencers who ran Lemington's great iron works in the 19th century (of whom more anon) and two of Wylam's railway pioneers. A fine window was dedicated by William Hedley by whose 'inventive genius the locomotive engine was brought into operation'; and George Stephenson was married here not once, but twice, the string quartet that decorated the second ceremony symbolising Geordie's rise through the ranks of Georgian England. The afternoon sun casts multi-coloured shadows on the stone of the cool interior and I almost fancy I can hear the scraping of ill-tuned violins, but then the church clock chimes three, the quiet nave echoing with its slow sonority and I think not of weddings, but funerals – and the solid names of Newburn's 165 dead of the First World War, as recorded on their memorial nearby, a painfully high toll for such a small parish. However, the most sobering aspect of our visit is another inscription, on an ancient gravestone, one of many marked with Masonic symbols, in the quiet yard: 'Remember man, as thou pass by, so art thou so once was I, so art I so must thou be, prepared for God and follow me'. It stops me in my tracks; and I do remember.

Down the hill and back to the line of the Wylam wagonway, we encounter that ubiquitous feature of contemporary Tyneside, the industrial estate. As usual I note down its tenants: steel stockholding warehouse, aluminium depot, 'out of town party warehouse', café named 'Snax Factor' (for such enterprises punning titles seem de rigeur), offering all day curry and chips; and Warburton's depot with three grain silos and hovering miasma of pungent yeast. Driven slightly mad by the smell, we sit on a grass verge and demolish yet more sandwiches, before returning to the wagonway, and one of the discoveries of the day. In fact this apparently endless wooden shed with its fading rust red paint, missing timbers and badly-holed roof is one of the most extraordinary structures of the entire journey. Eventually we find the entrance – and current use: 'H Pringle, the largest indoor auto dismantlers in the North East'. With a friendly nod from the gadgy, we have a look around the interior: car wrecks as far as the eye can see, stacked in crazy piles. A stream of men wander around, looking for second-hand clutches, exhausts, windows. I ask the man what this extraordinary building used to be. The answer is obvious, once you've heard it and consider the shed's great length: it was a rope works.

Just up the hill is the site of the Tyne Ironworks, once the biggest in the world, originally established in 1797 'for the cast iron extracting by the action of fire in large furnaces from ironstone… to produce everything from an anchor to a needle', then taken over by a typical Victorian industrialist called John Spencer and reopened in 1871 as the Tyne Haematite Iron Company, using Spanish ore. Not content with re-titling his works, Yorkshireman Spencer also wanted to give a new name to the locality: New Sheffield. He did not get his way – his employees were rather attached to the ancient names of the surrounding settlements and it's not hard to see why. The name of the old parish of 'Sugley', for instance, may sound rather industrial, but in Old English it actually means 'where the sparrows are'. (Remembering how my Northumbrian grandfather always called these little birds 'spuggies', perhaps the place was originally 'Spuggley'?)

However, Spencer managed to be more persuasive in a matter of lasting significance: he leant on the Tyne Improvement Commissioners to fulfill their responsibilities at this end of the river, and in the 1880s, Dutch engineers led a scheme to alter and widen the course of the river at Lemington and Blaydon Haughs; another of the lost Tyne islands, Dent's Meadows, was removed at the same time and the entrance to Lemington Loop was cut off and subsequently silted up. This area is now called 'the Gut'. This huge project made it easier to get the products of Spencer's works to market, including sections of the *Mauretania* taken down the Tyne to be assembled with the rest of the ship. There were other industries that benefited, among them Lemington glassworks, founded in the late 18th century and taken over in late Victorian times by the Gateshead glassmaking family of Sowerby. This company is long since gone, but survives in an unusual form: one of the great plays of Edwardian England, *Rutherford and Son*, written by Githa Sowerby, daughter of the man who drove the company to success. Forgotten for decades, it's recently been revived by Northern Stage and put in its proper local context, which is more than can be said of a previous revival at the National Theatre in 1994, when it was claimed that the play was set in North Yorkshire. What I loved about the play when I saw it was the insight it gave into the family lives of the great Victorian industrialists of the North East, and the human cost of their ambition and work ethic, which often wasn't limited to their workers but also affected their wives, sons and daughters.

Of course the ironworks, glassworks and the other industries of Lemington benefited hugely from the plenitude of cheap coal nearby. The settlement's staiths were the termination of many coal wagonways, including the Wylam and the Walbottle. When a proper rail line from Scotswood to Wylam was laid in 1876, a new Lemington developed 'up the bank', north of the railway line – and it's this platoon of Victorian terraces marching up the hill towards

the line of the Roman Wall that we're heading for this afternoon.

The old wagonway path is busy, with a party of schoolchildren on mountain bikes, scowling lads a-lurking and smiling, fresh-faced girls of a similar age bouncing along with bairns in pushchairs. Above us is the site of the old Percy pit, below a posse of stabled ponies like the ones we admired so much at Bill Quay. The entrance to Lemington is quite literally fruity: the trees and bushes by the track include apple, cherry, plum and blackberry. I fill my cap with their bounty, but once again can't tempt Charlie Bell. The track climbs to the site of Lemington's long-gone station, an ideal spot for the partaking of view. We admire the long curve of the Tyne as it bulges towards Blaydon. Below us at Lemington Point, there was once another island, known during the First World War as 'Canary Island' after its munition works and the yellowing effect the explosive lyddite had on the skins of its unfortunate female workers. The land was reclaimed after the Second World War and in 1958 the Anglo Great Lakes Corporation built a plant for the conversion of carbon into graphite for use in the nuclear industry. This area has been redeveloped again in the last decade as Newburn Riverside – our starting point for day seven of the walk. For today, we're mesmerised by the elegant shape – and 1.75 million bricks – of Lemington's last surviving glass cone, now beautifully restored and housing a showroom for stoves and cookers.

We're about to hear a story about this structure and I might as well tell it here: once upon a time a highly agile cat was chased up the cone by a dog, reaching its overhanging rim more than a hundred feet above Lemington, where of course it promptly got stuck, and loudly miaowed its misery. The story has a happy ending: an elderly lady living nearby took pity on the cat and paid for a steeplejack to rescue it…

We leave the wagonway by a tattoo parlour and the finest *Tyne View* sign we've yet encountered, heading for an audience with a man who has chronicled this little place in paint for the last 50 years. His name is John Peace and I've known him all my life.

John gives us his characteristic welcome and we make our way to the kitchen where he puts the kettle on for the tea while we admire the pictures and objects, including a booler, the so-called 'ring of burnished steel' that children rolled along cobbled streets in the early 20th century. One such played a key role in my mother's young life, the day in fact she took her 11-plus exam at her primary school in Ferryhill 25 miles south of the Tyne. Hurrying to school with her parents' injunction to do her best ringing in her ears, she didn't notice someone's booler lying in the gutter and so tripped over it, injuring her arm and knocking out her front tooth.

Her mouth pouring with blood, she was taken to a dentist to have it seen to; as a consequence she missed the exam and there was no opportunity to take it another day. She was therefore denied the high school place her intelligence and wit merited – and all because of a booler. Despite this, as she wrote years later, 'I've had so much good luck throughout my long life, I can hardly grieve over that one piece of bad…'

Pouring the tea, John tells my friends that he has spent his entire life, apart from a period at art school, in Lemington. As I've indicated, there were once many industries nearby, a railway a few yards away and inclined-plane lines uphill to the Percy and Blucher pits, but very little remains of them all now.

'I feel really sorry that there's no evidence they ever existed,' he says. 'The pit heaps have gone, all the buildings have gone. Why remove everything? Why pretend they never existed? I don't understand this at all.'

Perhaps by way of compensation, John has recorded many images of the culture in which he grew up. On my walls are two prints of local scenes that I adore: *The Bridge Over the Incline*, showing a crumbling wooden foot-bridge over the Blucher line, and *Eric's Café*, the last surviving building on a site of cleared Victorian cottages in Blaydon, a rather forlorn fish and chip shop. There are no figures in these landscapes – perhaps the reason I find them so haunting.

But behind the images are stories, and John has many, and so we listen.

'I remember when I was a boy, coming home from school one day I saw some women waiting for their men to come home from the pit. A man appeared, exchanged words with one of the women, and she threw her pinny over her head and the other women followed suit. I've never forgotten that gesture – and the terrible keening sound that followed. A man had been killed in the pit.'

Nearby was a street of houses called Bells Close that backed onto a stream that ran down to the Tyne. 'They had no back windows because the pollution was so terrible. This was ironic given that once there had been salmon netting stations on the river at Lemington.

'I was told by an old man that many of the streets of Victorian Lemington have a connection to the Percy family, the Dukes who owned the land in these parts – Algernon Street, Percy Street, Hugh Street and so on. I grew up in Loraine Terrace.

'One of my earliest memories is visiting Blaydon when I was three or four, on a ferry, actually a rowing boat oared by an old man, and using a spoon to dip in the water which my father took off me. We visited my dad's aged aunt – she seemed so very old to me – and I was given a piece of cake. I found a tooth embedded in it. On Sunday mornings I used to go to Marchetti's ice cream parlour in Newburn, which had knickerbocker glories and marble tables. Mr Marchetti made the ice cream on the premises. I went to school with his son Dino, who later on ran another family business, the billiard hall nearby.'

The Peace family had an enterprise of their own – a general store that served the working-class community 'up the bank', started by John's grandfather, who died before he was born. John laughs as he recalls the stories about him. He was evidently quite a character.

'A woman once stopped him in the street and asked him how many children he had. Seven, he said. Oh, said the woman, I thought you had more than that. Oh well, he replied, if you're counting girls, I've got twelve.'

John grew up above the shop and used to love to come to the bottom of the stairs to a spot where he couldn't be seen by anyone – the chocolate counter hid him from view.

'I used to sit on a step and listen to the conversation between the people who came into the shop and members of my family. It was interesting what they said. Warm and comforting too.'

Then came a day when it was anything but.

'I was there one day, it was the spring of 1940. I suppose I was about six. My Uncle Pat was holding up a newspaper with the banner headline 'France Falls'. Here we go again, he said. One woman in the shop said there were stories of German atrocities, tales of how their soldiers were using babies as footballs and so on. Then I heard my mam speak up. She said, they'll never get my bairns. How come, asked the woman. I can hear me mam's quiet voice now. I've got a little bottle, she said, I'll sprinkle it on their pillows and they will die gently in their sleep. They won't suffer. The words sank in slowly. I was absolutely terrified. For nights I lay in bed fully dressed, one foot on the floor, window open. I had a plan – if I heard her coming, I'd slip out of bed, open the window, slide down the canopy above the shop and jump to the ground and run away.'

John laughs.

'Funny, the things you remember,' he murmurs.

Of course Mrs Peace never came in the night, John didn't have to slide down the canopy of the family shop or run away. In fact he and his wife Rosemary – in the adjoining room recovering from an operation – made their home in Lemington, brought up their children there and remain still, John continuing to draw his considerable inspiration from its landscape.

But in a way he did escape. The combination of his own talents and the financial security of the corner shop provided the footing for an education at grammar and then art school that ensured that John has led a very different kind of life and made a very different kind of living from what was once the norm hereabouts. Thus John was, like me, part of the social revolution that accompanied the economic changes running up and down the river since 1945.

As we're leaving for home, I ask John where the folk of Lemington work nowadays?

'Good question. I honestly don't know.'

I suspect many drive along the Scotswood Road into Newcastle, others making their way into Newburn Riverside Business Park, where we will start day seven the following morning, when after a couple of days out in the country, we will again be walking an urban river.

But whatever else the people of Lemington do for a living, there are no longer any women who wait anxiously on steep streets for their men to come home, who throw pinnies over their heads when they hear the news they've dreaded, and weep bitter tears.

⚓ TIDE STONE

I've been admired by artists, remember,
And quite right too. I'm the standard bearer
For those who prefer their sense of boundaries
Set in stone. It's true, I love the Tyne dearly
But let's be honest, she's quite unstable
And spends too much of her time round people.
Give her an inch, she'll flounce up to Wylam,
Griping on about how I confine her,
But she'll be back. She always sees reason
In my adherence to rules and custom.
Without me, she'd have no sense of structure
To regulate her murky adventures,
So rather than judge me as out of date
Consider me whimsy's counterweight.

A Grand Day Out

The Ascension Day survey of the boundaries of the River Tyne by the Mayor and Burgesses of Newcastle, May 1818:

'I rose early this morning, having resolved upon accompanying the barges as they are popularly termed. The morning dawned beautifully giving promise of fine weather for the festive occasion. I sauntered down to the Quayside, where great numbers of persons were engaged in decorating the various boats which were intended to take part in the procession. As I did not possess a boat, I took a seat in one of the wherries, which from being vessels of great size could accommodate a great number of persons. At 5 o'clock the boats began to arrive from various parts of the river and to throng about the front of the Mansion House where the embarkation was to take place. There were observable at the oars of the various boats a host of fine athletic fellows in clean white shirts and trousers, dashing their slim vessels over the smooth surface of the stream with admirable ease and dexterity. Almost every boat had secured some itinerant musician, no matter of what talent, and at intervals the dissonance of their music would be hushed for the purpose of listening to the wild but melodious strains of Jack, the Howden Pans fifer, whose notes sounded sweetly along the surface of the swelling river. At a little before 6 o'clock the guns of the old fortress above sent forth their thunder, the bells of St Nicholas rang their merry peals, and the shipping hoisted their flags: every boats oar fell from its perpendicular into the water, as the procession began to move eastward to the harmony of a party of musicians on board the Mayor's barge.

'On reaching the bridge the music struck up *Rule Britannia*, gladdening the hearts of the spectators who even at so early an hour lined the edge of the Quay to the amount of some hundreds. As the barges with a numerous retinue of smaller craft sailed down the river, the men were repeatedly saluted with shouts of gratulation and the report of cannon from the numerous founderies and other manufactories which constitute one of the chief features of the banks of the Tyne. While passing 'bonny Sandgate', the band played '*Weel May the Keel Row*', which elicited much cheering, together with a due share of squalling approbation from a numerous concourse of 'keel deeters', 'kelp carriers' and 'market lasses'. The Royal Standard floated majestically from the summit from Hawks's iron works and their artillery

DAY SEVEN

Quayside Walkway

Newcastle Arena
International Centre for Life
Central Station
see locations listed below
see locations listed below

Guildhall
Trinity Maritime Centre
St Nicholas' Cathedral
Bessie Surtees House
Tyne Bridge & Views
High Level Bridge & Views
Tyne Ferries

'It's just a rumour that was spread around town
Somebody said that someone got filled in
For saying that people get killed in
The result of this shipbuilding
With all the will in the world
Diving for dear life
When we could be diving for pearls...'

Shipbuilding, Elvis Costello

I spot a patch of colour near the riverside path.

Thinking it's a flower, I go to investigate and find three colours and three materials: the pink of a burst balloon, the white of a silky ribbon and the sky blue of a label. On the latter is a message from the person who let go of the balloon; his name is Ryan Chandler. The message begins with the printed words, 'When I leave Malins, I hope that…' to which Ryan has added in his neat, painstaking script, 'I can be a professional footballer in London.'

It takes me a while, and a bit of computer time, to work it out. Malins Close is a primary school in Blyth; the school term ended a couple of weeks ago and I guess there might have been a passing-out ceremony for those about to go to the big school. Hence the coloured balloons – imagine them all taking off from the school playground, cheered by lots of reedy voices; except Ryan's pink number didn't fly with the prevailing wind out across the sea in the direction of Norway, but dribbled rather anti-climactically back to Newburn. But I suspect there are worse places for a downed balloon with a message to end up than on the bank of the Tyne. And if you're out there, Ryan, I hope you get your wish one Saturday afternoon one of these days…

All of which makes me ponder, on yet another sunny morning, on childhood dreams. Speaking for myself, the footballer thing also applied, on the playing fields of Newcastle rather than London, but this ambition came a distant second behind becoming a driver of steam locomotives like the ones I saw a few yards from my grandparents' house in Ferryhill. British Railways' abandonment of steam within a few years meant I had to search for a new goal, and in my mid-teens I found one: to become an actor. Thankfully for audiences everywhere, this ambition was never realised and I stumbled almost by accident into the trade of journalist and writer. As for my fellow walkers, the young Christy Ducker wanted simultaneously to be a

PREVIOUS PAGES
Dunston Rocket (deceased)
and distant Angel.

palm reader and forensic scientist (which seems to confirm what a curious soul she is, in every sense); writing was also in her thoughts but she didn't think it constituted a proper job. Birtley had no childhood ambitions, while Charles simply can't remember – it was after all quite a long time ago. How odd then that during the course of this seventh day of our Tyne peregrination, we will encounter in one way or another characters who did realise their dreams…

We begin the day by going backwards, not as we have so often in time, but in direction. The previous afternoon's diversion from the riverside path to visit Lemington means that we start two miles west on Newburn's industrial estate. The previous day we were temporarily intoxicated here by the yeasty aroma of Warburton's bakery; this morning we resist the smell of frying bacon at the latest in a series of walk-side cafés with imaginative names, Breakfast at Tiffany's. Skirting a puddle the size of a small lake, we reach the river and contemplate its progress around the big bend of Newburn Haugh. There are no people about, but masses of birds: the cries of curlew and oystercatcher on the wing, a lone cormorant sitting on a rotting post, and most spectacularly, about 40 lapwings directly overhead, plunging dramatically like synchronised swimmers, their hypnotic flight accompanied by strange fluting noises that explain the much older name used the length of England's east coast: peewit. We once visited friends in Copenhagen and spotting a carved wooden lapwing, I asked our host for its name in Danish. I was delighted by his reply: our Viking relatives call this sociable bird the vibe, pronounced 'veebit'.

The tide is out and the water low, the reason for all those wading birds. An oystercatcher picks its way carefully around a marooned lifebelt from the Swing Bridge. At Lemington Gut, a squadron of about 30 mallard ducks are feeding on the mud. Nearby a skeleton of the boat *Brekaer* is subsiding into the bank, its faded blue hull a counterpoint to a cloudless sky. On the swanky new Riverside Business Park a flag flutters, though not at half-mast, over the headquarters of One North East, the regional development agency that will soon go out of business. Outside the regional headquarters of the North East Ambulance Service, a group of women stand together, gossiping and smoking furiously. We pass the Tyne Cruising Club and move towards the various Scotswood bridges and a procession of household superstores.

Here, once upon a time, straddling the old railway bridge on the Newcastle side was the works of the famed sanitary ware manufacturer Adamsez of Scotswood. It's possible that men of a certain age will be more familiar with the name than women, as most of us cumulatively spent many hours staring

at it, emblazoned as it was on the urinals of our youth. This was certainly the case with me: that funny name was the one comforting aspect of the outside netties at Sandyford Junior School. It turns out the name was simply a phonetic representation of 'Adams's', the family that started the business at Scotswood in 1880 and oversaw its growth over the next century to a bathroom brand leader. Exploiting clay deposits and the tiny Scotswood drift mine nearby, with the river and a rail line literally on their front and back doorstep, the Adams twins found Scotswood a perfect place to do business. In 1904 Moses J Adams began the manufacture of 'Adamesk' art pottery (everything from fern pots to bird baths to baptismal fonts), but it was under the leadership of the splendidly named Adam H Adams that the company found its heyday before and after the Second World War, when their wares, heavily influenced by art deco design, managed to capture both the mass and luxury markets in sanitary ware. A catalogue from 1937 marked by the three-castles crest of the city shows an aerial view of the works and head office ('Telegrams – Sanifera, Scotswood; Telephone – Lemington 85 and 86'). They cover extensive river frontage – various Tyne wherries are tied up – extending towards Lemington and then north to the drift mine entrance cut into the steep hillside. The goods on offer include 'the Alps urinal with armour-plate glass anti-splash plates, as seen in a Scarborough convenience' and the circular 'Radio urinal, as seen at Southend on Sea'. The catalogue also features a charming lino-cut vignette of the company's base, with the old Scotswood suspension bridge wreathed in mist in the background, and the inky swirling Tyne below.

I suspect you're beginning to fear the worst. What happened to Adamsez? Well, the truth is that this family firm did indeed go bust, in 1977, and then west, after the Adamsez name was acquired by a company based in Dundonald in Northern Ireland, where it appears to flourish. Thus the last link between Scotswood and the bathroom business is now a tile warehouse...

Negotiating some decidedly manky walkways under the roundabout at the northern end of the more utilitarian successor to the suspension bridge, we explore the desolate dead zone by the river. A beached coconut – perhaps a discarded memento of the recent Hoppings on the Town Moor – adds a touch of the exotic to the plastic-strewn water line, but out on the water, the fish, in the shape of two sinuous salmon, are jumping. All that muscle-bound energy provides a useful example: we start striding up the Scotswood Road. It's late morning now, and the last few days of semi-rural walking and the availability of riverside pubs has given us a taste for a lunchtime pint. You'd think we'd be OK on this mythic highway for pub-crawlers of the past, but not any more. Fifty years ago, when my father published his coming-of-age novel *The Watchers and The Watched* about a young welder from Scotswood called Tiger Mason, many of its best scenes took place in pubs. In the summer of 2011, we actually didn't encounter any (other than as mirages in the heat), these temples of the communal now being heavily out-numbered by showrooms for upmarket cars, symbol of the individual. So we had to make do instead with a *conversation* about Scotswood's pubs, which was interesting but hardly nourishing, and as it turned out, not terribly comprehensive. We couldn't remember many of their names, so here – to be intoned like a beery poem – are the public houses of the Scotswood Road, all 50 of them, with street numbers attached:

- 2 King's Head
- 32 Rokeby
- 42 Golden Eagle
- 46 Graham's Arms
- 48 Durham Ox
- 52 Golden Fleece
- 76 Somerset
- 78 Marlborough
- 96 Blenheim Hotel
- 98 Farmers' Inn
- 110 Elswick House
- 126 The Fountain
- 146 Lord Wharncliffe
- 157 Duke of Cumberland
- 174 Maid of Derwent
- 203 New Burnt House/ Shipwrights' Arms
- 222 Royal Oak
- 266 Green Tree
- 305 Bath
- 336 Falcon
- 403 British Lion
- 404 Park Road/Clasper Arms
- 420 Freemasons' Arms
- 427 Caledonia/Flax Mill
- 450 Grapes
- 467 Ordnance
- 505 Whitworth
- 523 Atlas
- 528 Lincoln
- 531 Shell
- 534 Gladstone
- 534 Plimsoll
- 543 Rifle
- 630 Dene
- 640 Vulcan
- 662 Blast Furnace
- 676 Bridge End
- 688 Foresters' Arms
- 692 Mechanics
- 734 Crooked Billet
- 746 Miners' Arms
- 766 Forge Hammer
- 802 Moulders
- 818 Gun
- 876 Elswick Hotel
- 903 Hydraulic Crane

And on the un-numbered section west of 'Paradise' (of which more later):

- Boat House Inn
- Delaval Arms
- Robin Adair (19th century)
- Ord Arms (rebuilt as the 'new' Robin Adair)

That morning in the taxi on our way to Newburn, there'd been another conversation about these establishments. Like all taxi drivers, our Brian has both a pessimistic take on human frailty and a disdain for easy sentiment. His response to our bout of reminiscence was to recount how towards the end of the old Scotswood in the 1970s he would drive strippers from one engagement to another in one dreary, near empty but certainly dying pub after another. Their time had come. We got the message, Bri.

But the names continue to fascinate. Of course many of them – the Rifle, the Ordnance, the Vulcan, the Forge Hammer, the Gun, the Hydraulic Crane – were given in tribute to the vast works where many of the drinkers laboured, what they did there and the man who dreamt it all up, the afore-mentioned William George Armstrong. His fledgling business first came to a five-acre riverside site at Elswick in 1847 to develop Armstrong's hydraulic crane, but as it diversified with staggering success into guns, ordnance and ships, it grew and grew over the next 60 years until it consumed almost two miles of river frontage. A key element in that growth was a partner-ship between Armstrong and Charles Mitchell, who like Andrew Leslie, his fellow Aberdonian immigrant to Tyneside, established a shipbuilding business on the Tyne, in his case at Low Walker. Under this agreement the joint enterprise would launch a major push into the building of warships at precisely the time when there was a surge in demand for them around the world. Between 1885 and 1918, the Elswick yard built 90 warships, along with pioneering submarines and oddities like a royal yacht for the Sultan of Turkey. The building of the Swing Bridge and the dredging away of King's Meadow – the island in the stream – made this activity possible. The first vessel launched from the Elswick Yard on 13 June 1885 was *Panther*, a torpedo cruiser for the Austro-Hungarian Navy, followed in 1887 by the Royal Navy battleship *Reknown,* later renamed *Victoria* in honour of the Queen's Golden Jubilee. Sadly she didn't rule the waves for long. During training manoeuvres off Lebanon in 1893, a bungled order by Sir George Tryon, Vice-Admiral of the Navy's Mediterranean Fleet, led to a collision with the battleship *Camperdown*, which caused *Victoria* to capsize and sink within ten minutes, taking with it 358 men, including the unfortunate Admiral Tryon, some of whom died an appalling death in the 'scalding milk' of the water thrown out by exploding Armstrong boilers. (By the way, Tryon's blunder has a curious filmic echo in the Ealing comedy *Kind Hearts and Coronets*, in which one of Dennis Price's rivals for aristocratic succession, an incompetent admiral, triggers just such a collision.)

In the three decades leading up to the outbreak of the First World War, Armstrong's expansion went into overdrive as the world's great and emerging powers re-armed themselves. By 1886 the Elswick Works was employing 12,000 people, but that doubled within 20 years, as the company – as the result of another merger now named Armstrong Whitworth – opened another factory at Scotswood to produce shot, shells and fuses, and another to build motor cars. During this period, Armstrong personally nurtured growing relationships with the navies of foreign powers, including Portugal, Norway, the United States, Chile and China (there are headstones to various Chinese sailors in Elswick Cemetery), frequently entertaining admirals and ministers at his Cragside retreat. Perhaps the most enduring was with the Imperial Japanese Navy, for whom Armstrong's built a series of warships in the 1890s and 1900s, usually launched with the ceremonial release of flocks of pigeons from baskets on the ship's bow. There are some beautiful relics of this relationship in Newcastle's Central Library. The yard produced 'launch cards', given to visiting dignitaries to mark the big day when ships went down the slipway, with a painting of the ship on one side and helpful information on the other. Sometimes they listed the pre-launch entertainments laid on by the ships' crews, including dance, drama and music. The cards for the launches of Japanese ships like the *Tokiwa* and *Asama* were obviously influenced by the art nouveau and oriental design movements; they are quite exquisite. The eventual fates of the ships and their crews were rather less so: no less than three ships built at Elswick were sunk on the same day in the first few months of the Russo-Japanese War in 1904-05: the cruiser *Yoshino* and the battleships *Yashima* and *Hatsuse*, with the loss of almost a thousand men. However, the following year, the fleet largely built on the Tyne and commanded by Admiral Togo, once entertained at Jesmond Dene House, destroyed the Russian Imperial Navy at the Battle of Tsushima and the war was effectively won. Some of the heroes of this climactic battle returned to Tyneside the following year to man the last Japanese warship to be built at Elswick, the battleship *Kashima*. They were treated like royalty. A hundred men were invited to St James's Park where they took tea with the club directors and were cheered by the crowd as they took their places in the main stand. A photograph evocatively records the moment. The team did their bit too – they beat Stoke 5-0.

Of course that war far away was only an overture for the epic tragedy to come. Again Elswick, and the company's new Walker Naval Yard, did their bit, producing killing machines in vast numbers. During the First World War, 78,000 people worked at Elswick, 21,000 of them women, making 13,000 guns, including a 12-inch howitzer mounted on its own rail bogie, 12,000 gun carriages, 18 million ammunition rounds, 109 warships, 230 armed merchant ships, 102 tanks, two train ferries and a floating crane.

By then William Armstrong was dead: he passed away in 1900, as a less innocent century began and, with it, a new era of industrialised warfare. What he made of that, and the role played in it by his amazingly successful enterprise and his own engineering and organisational genius, we don't of course know, though I've often mused that there's a play in it. But I do know that although only a few miles from the paradise of the Pandon Dene where the young William first contemplated the power of water, his vast Elswick Works of 1918 inhabited a very different moral and spiritual universe. Was this the kind of future he dreamt of as a young man?

Perhaps I am being overly harsh: Armstrong benefited from but did not create the unstable world order that eventually exploded in 1914, but in so doing he provided employment for thousands of his fellow Tynesiders and conferred generous gifts on the city he loved, from which I and thousands of others still benefit. As I've said before, make up your own minds…

⚓

All of which reflections provide a useful diversion from a growing thirst as we slog up the Scotswood Road. On our right is the long, apparently endless, grey shed of BAE Systems' Armstrong Works, reputedly the longest industrial building in the country, but also possibly the most featureless. This is the last surviving remnant of Armstrong's Tyneside empire. In 1918, as warships became bigger and bigger but the gap left by an open Swing Bridge didn't, the last to be built at Elswick, the aircraft carrier, *HMS Eagle*, was launched, and nine years later Armstrong Whitworth merged its most important activities with Vickers of Barrow in Furness to create Vickers-Armstrongs. Local control of the business thus began to slip away and over the years this process accelerated and the company concentrated its Scotswood activities more and more on the production of guns, tanks and armoured vehicles. It made a major contribution to the war effort during the Second World War; 17,000 people were employed at that time but in peacetime that figure soon fell to 11,000.

One of the latter was a young apprentice called Alan Reece, who first arrived on Tyneside in 1944 to study engineering at what was then King's College. 'It was the only place in Britain where you could study engineering without having learnt Latin. How crazy was that? I was a Londoner but as I walked out of the Central Station the first thing I saw on the front of a bus was the destination Scrogg Road. I knew then I'd come to a place with character.'

Back then, Professor Reece, a man who later invented and built a range of specialist vehicles and created two of the most successful companies of modern Tyneside, was an active and proselytising Communist. Yet this didn't blind him to the realities of life at Vickers in Scotswood.

'By far the cleverest people were on the shop floor. Management didn't really run the place – they were a shambles – so it was the workers who kept the place going. There were some slackers, but in my experience the natural inclination of people is to work hard and at Vickers it was no different. Despite this, it seemed to me the management held the workforce in contempt. They really hated them. A typical example is that the factory shut on the dot of 5.15 and thousands of people streamed out onto the Scotswood Road to try to catch one of the many trams lined up on both sides. I thought then, why don't they stagger the finish time? It would make life so much easier. But it never occurred to the management, or if it did, they didn't care. As a young man, this confirmed my gut feeling that the world was very badly organised, especially perhaps in industry.'

After the war, Vickers went into decline and by 1980 the Scotswood site had gradually shrunk towards the Scotswood Bridge end (where locomotives had once been made) and the workforce had fallen to 3,500. The surviving rump is now owned by BAE Systems, the British-based defence, security and aerospace multi-national, which acquired Vickers in 1995. In 2010 the Government awarded a £500 million contract to a rival firm, General Dynamics UK in Wales, for the manufacture of new armoured Scout vehicles and training equipment. BAE had warned the Government that more than a third of the workforce at its Scotswood Road site would be at risk if it did not get the contract, and the following year the company cut 100 jobs from its workforce. Work here on the manufacture of the Terrier armoured vehicle runs out in 2014.

We approached BAE Systems to ask if we could look around this historic site, but were turned down for the first and only time on our walk, perhaps for reasons of security and confidentiality. One last observation: if you visit the company's extensive website and type the words 'Scotswood', 'Armstrong Works' or 'Newcastle upon Tyne' into its search engine, no results appear.

Today at least the works' car-park is full and I stop to see if there are any nesting plovers to be seen between the Micras and Corollas. Not a sign – perhaps the fledglings have flown the scraped nests in the pebbles.

Other local residents have disappeared too: the community that grew up to service Armstrong's works is much smaller, and the people who lived in those steep terraces running off the Scotswood Road and drank in its pubs have moved away, many to live in T Dan Smith's infamous 'vertical villages'. Yet that old Scotswood still survives, in the wonderful work of a man called Jimmy Forsyth.

Jimmy was a Welshman who came to Newcastle to work as a fitter during the Second World War; a few years later a sliver of a chisel he was working with flew off and penetrated one eye, rendering him unfit to work. A single man who lived on his own, his all-consuming passion became photography: more specifically, recording the lives of the people among whom he lived for most of his life. He lived on National Assistance and therefore the edge of poverty: his first camera was ancient, acquired second-hand. He developed his prints at Boots, finding the wherewithal for new work by selling prints of his old to people who didn't possess cameras of their own. To begin with, he recorded events – fires, the aftermath of car accidents, a road race to celebrate the 100th anniversary of the Blaydon Races. He also chronicled the demolition of the streets around him and their replacement by tower blocks; one sequence shows the unveiling of a modernist sculpture ('The Monstrosity', as he called it, later sold for scrap) at the opening of the Willow Flats by Labour leader Hugh Gaitskell and Dan Smith, then-leader of Newcastle City Council in June 1962. He loved the Tyne, and caught the river in its many moods: ships being launched, Stella ash tippers hurrying towards the sea; the Swing Bridge etched in snow on a winter's day; the demolition of the old Scotswood Suspension Bridge (he climbed to the top to capture it). Not having a job – at least not one for which he was paid – he wandered the streets and was often in the right place at the right time, when, for example, a Vickers Armstrong tank was caught on a road test by the Gloucester Arms one day in 1957.

However, for me, Jimmy's greatest achievement is a portfolio of portraits, mostly taken on his wanderings in the open air: a demolition gang leaning on the bonnet of their truck, feet resting on shovels; two teddy boys, who turn out to have been rent collectors; a pair of old boys off to the pub. Then there are the children: two swaggering lads on the cusp of manhood; two beautiful sisters in party dresses standing in a tiny front garden, a pigeon caught in flight above them; a little girl in a coat slightly too big for her, standing in bright sunlight against a brick wall. At the bottom of the photograph there's a shadow I found hard to make out until I realised it was the photographer, his old camera at one good eye. The image is typical in a very particular sense: the obvious trust and affection between the man with the camera and his subjects. You sense they were prepared to give themselves and their lives to a man who was one of them, not an outsider. He was just 'Jimmy'. As a result his photographs are powerful and touching, an insight into the souls of people whose way of life was gradually being taken away from them.

I treasure the three Forsyth prints that march up the staircase of our house, and the two books signed by Jimmy in his shaky handwriting. Whenever I go to the Discovery Museum, I stop by the monitor that shows a loop of the short but epic journey in the mid 1990s of Parsons' *Turbinia* from the Museum of Science and Engineering to its present home. One shot shows a little old man running ahead of the huge truck, camera in hand: Jimmy, then in his eighties, desperate to catch the defining shot. I finally met him not long before he died, at his last exhibition, held in the retirement home where he spent his last years; he'd just woken up, was almost blind and pretty deaf, but received our compliments with the lightest of handshakes, and the sweet smile of someone who knows he has fulfilled himself.

Jimmy's photographs played on a slide show inside my head as we pass the visual emptiness of the BAE works and its neighbours. But something interesting is about to happen: further up the Scotswood Road, we are about to enter Paradise…

Here works a man whose enterprise has hugged the riverbank for a century or more and remained steadfastly in the hands of the family that started it. What's more, Tim Jobling-Purser isn't merely content to be interviewed, but positively enthusiastic. It turns out he's an enthusiast about many things, but with a nice line in ironic humour. The tale he tells is fascinating.

Jobling Purser's Paradise Works – the name derives either from the bucolic beauty of this part of Elswick in pre-industrial times or the comment of a local vicar who once caught fat salmon on the site – sits in the middle of what was once the vast Armstrong works. The company first came here in 1917 from a site by the Walker Naval Yard; they effectively did a swap with Armstrong Whitworth. There's evidence of earlier industrial activity along the quarter of a mile of river frontage in the form of three old mine shafts and the decaying remains of an abandoned wharf. By the time it arrived here, the business, then known as the Tyne Oil and Grease Works, had been going for some 70 years, set up by a savvy lawyer and entrepreneur called Mark Lambert Jobling. He was well connected, a Sheriff of Newcastle, and a leading figure in the city's Masonic lodges; he used his contacts well.

He was one of the investors behind the sinking of the infamous New Hartley pit, in which 220 lives were lost after an explosion in 1862 broke the beam of the colliery's only shaft. At that time, before roller bearings were invented, the wheels of industry were greased by, well, grease, originally from animal fats. In the 1860s the Grease Works passed to Jobling's son, James Augustus, a man described by our host as 'a philanderer who never married'. He smartly developed another business, based on the unwanted contents of the river's ballast hills. At that time, as we've heard, Tyne colliers took cargoes around the world: one of their longest journeys was to Royal Navy coaling stations in the South Atlantic, including the Falklands. One collier returned with a load of Chilean guano, which James Augustus promptly snapped up and then sold to local farmers as fertiliser. Tyne keels and wherries also delivered cargoes of phosphates in the form of fossilized guano from North Africa to the Paradise Yard. Another smart cookie then, but the best was yet to come.

James Augustus' sister married a Dublin lawyer with whom she had six children before she was widowed. In the fullness of time, one of her sons came to Newcastle to work, firstly for another Irishman, Charles Parsons, who pioneered the use of steam turbines in ships and power stations before diversifying into optical equipment. The young man was Ernest Purser, and he arrived at just the right time. A rush of technological developments meant that Tyneside in the 1890s was like the Klondyke, a kind of Silicon Valley with dirt. The Tyne was awash with money, and young Ernest wanted his boat to come in too. And indeed it did, after he went to work for his uncle.

Another of James Augustus' ballast cargoes was manganese, which he sold to Greener's of Sunderland for colouring glass. When Greener's went bust in 1886, it was acquired by its principal creditor, but James Augustus did little with it until 1902, when he gave it to 'the boy' to run. Ernest then transformed the company with two big ideas.

First, he was fascinated by the burgeoning oil business. The navies of the world, those good customers of Armstrong's, were very interested in this new fuel because it produced less smoke than coal and so ships were less visible on the horizon, as well as easier to handle, not requiring the immense labour of stokers. Ernest forged contacts with a young company called Shell and did an advantageous deal with them. From then on, the glass business – soon renamed Joblings – ran its ovens on oil. Ernest further revitalised the company with an investment programme using new American and German technology. In 1921 he acquired a licence from the Corning Glass Company in the States to manufacture and market Pyrex heat-resistant glassware in Great Britain and the Empire. This enabled Joblings not merely to survive the depression years, but to flourish with a range of decorative 'art glass' using mechanised presses.

Not surprisingly, Ernest didn't have time to marry, especially after he'd packed off James Augustus to retirement on the family estate in Argyllshire (won by Mark Lambert in a game of poker), in return for which he agreed to call himself Ernest Jobling-Purser. Eventually though, he met and married a much younger woman in 1937, and their son was born four years later. One of Tim's earliest memories is opening food parcels from friends in the USA: the Houghtons, the family who founded and ran Corning Glass, and to whom Ernest finally sold his Sunderland factory after the war for, says his son Tim, 'a packet'.

And now we're returning at last to the Paradise Works and the last of Ernest's big ideas.

Through his contacts with Shell he acquired a licence to emulsify bitumen with water, to make road surfaces, a huge new market in the making. Ninety years later his son is still in that same business in Scotswood.

It wasn't exactly meant to be that way.

'In 1948 my dad took his family back to Ireland to live but I came back here to school where I decided I wanted to be in trade. After university I became a chartered accountant in Dublin, and started a business importing BMW cars. Jobling Purser was still owned by the family and in the early 70s I came over to appoint an MD, but ended up becoming MD myself. I've been here ever since.'

As it turns out, this is not strictly accurate. The long relationship with Shell continued until the late 80s when Tim finally succumbed to a handsome offer and Jobling Purser ceased to be a family firm and became a tiny part of a huge multinational.

'We used to distribute Shell bitumen which came here from Ellesmere Port by rail. We finally sold the business to them in 1987 – they'd wanted us for a long time – but under a clause in the original contract I bought it back in 1992.'

I ask why.

'I was bored,' says Tim with a laugh, as he shows us around the site, and his current pride and joy, a new £4 million stone-coating plant (the stone comes from Northumberland quarries). Not many companies are investing in a recession, but here's one. Tim's optimism is the result of a familiar theme in this family saga – technological innovation. Each carbon zinc battery, for instance, needs a drop of bitumen to make it work.

With 36 employees and a turnover of £11 million, Jobling Purser may not be the biggest enterprise on the Tyne, but I find its story heartening as well as fascinating. There's something striking about the way the company has reinvented itself time and again in its 150-year history, embracing and nurturing technological change. I also love its denouement, that precedent-breaking buy-back from Shell. If only the many Tyneside industrial concerns that have gone to the wall in the last 50 years, most of them vastly bigger than Jobling Purser, had been as smart. When I mention this to Tim, he grows thoughtful, then trenchant:

'If you're not in control of the equity of the company, control goes south to people who know nothing about the business and care less. This helps to explain the pattern of underinvestment in industry in the North East. So the spiral of decline begins. This tends not to happen in companies that remain under family control. Just look at our old business in Sunderland. The Pyrex factory was eventually bought by a French company specifically to close it down and eliminate competition, it being more expensive to make French workers redundant than Mackems.'

'Sometimes of course, family businesses fail too. There are usually three stages: 1. The pioneer starts the business. 2. The next generation expands it. 3. The third generation isn't interested and manage to screw it all up.'

So how have Jobling Purser managed to avoid this fate?

'What can I say? Luck! Brilliance! No, I suppose with this business each generation has come to it late, almost by accident. That was certainly the case with Ernest and then with me. It's the same with my two sons, Evan and David, who went off to do other things in the timber industry and oil-rig design and have come to us and brought something fresh.'

Tim laughs again, we shake hands and leave the Paradise Yard.

Walking back to the Scotswood Road, passing a refuse treatment centre and a plant where car doors are pressed, we encounter a remnant of the Victorian industrial scene. On the north side of the road, some blokes in high visibility jackets are standing around a hole in the hillside. A metal grille guards a brick wall, through which clear water trickles out. This is the entrance to the old Delaval drift mine, one of many workings into the coal-rich banks of Scotswood and Elswick to be exploited by riverside industries over the past 500 years. These City Council engineers are satisfied; today's flow from the flooded workings is an improvement on the torrent emerging earlier in the week.

A further example of the power of nature, in this case political, lies further east along the south side of the road. A corner of the Paradise Works has been designated a Site of National Conservation Importance, the ballast on the old railway line making an ideal home to four of the five colonies of dingy skipper butterflies in Newcastle. Tim Jobling-Purser had not been impressed: 'I mean, come on. Have you seen a dingy skipper? Why do you think it's called dingy?' We stand by the fence for five minutes in the hope of spotting one, but the only evidence of wildlife are the

JOBLING

PURSER

LTD

twitterings of goldfinch. I try to remember the collective noun for this brightly-coloured little bird – one of my favourites – but can't. I look it up when I get home and discover there are actually four such nouns: the entirely appropriate *charm* or *chirm*, the slightly less *drum*, and the rather mysterious *troubling*. Aren't collective nouns brilliant?

There's more wildlife-spotting to come as we walk back down to the Newcastle Business Park on the riverside. There's a fine view to the south, the Angel of the North peeping out from behind the Dunston Rocket. It's appropriate that the Royal Society for the Protection of Birds has its regional office here: the Tyne is a flyway for wading birds heading west towards the vast feeding grounds of the Solway Firth. The squadron of lapwings we saw this morning at Newburn was small beer: a concentration 25 times that number was seen here a few months ago, and on one spectacular occasion a greater concentration of golden plovers. There are shelducks in the water below – a creche of chicks with one supervising adult. One of the thousand or so kittiwakes nesting on the Tyne flies past, and a pair of common terns, perhaps from the colony at Blaydon Ponds. So we sit and eat our sandwiches and watch avian TV for a while. Then I remember another lunch, on the shore opposite, and the story of the Dunston lad that got postponed by heavy rain.

Harry Clasper was a Tyneside sporting hero of the Victorian age, whose arena wasn't a muddy field, but the water in front of us: he was a professional rower and boat builder at a time when the sport was hugely popular and big crowds lined the Tyne's banks to watch races with big prizes. After working at Jarrow Pit he became apprenticed as a ship's carpenter in Brown's Boatyard. Later he piloted a wherry for the Garesfield Coke Company at Derwenthaugh before forming a racing crew with his brother William using a boat named the *Swalwell*. They began to win races and then Clasper took over the tenancy of the Skiff Inn, where he began to design and build boats himself. In his skiff *Young Hawk*, he won the Durham Regatta Single Sculls in 1842, while his foursome team began to dominate the Tyne rowing scene. The same year he challenged a crew from the Thames; the race was held on the Tyne later in 1842 over a five-mile course from the Tyne Bridge to Lemington for a stake of £150 a side. Clasper's team lost heavily and he realised that he needed to design and build a much lighter boat for future races. His new boat, *The Five Brothers*, complete with outriggers, made an appearance at the Thames Regatta in 1844 when the Derwenthaugh crew won a prize of £50 and narrowly missed winning the £100 top prize, the Champion Fours. The following year Clasper took another boat, the *Lord Ravensworth*, to the Thames Regatta, this time entirely crewed by the four Claspers and won the title of World Champions. On returning to Newcastle the team was given a royal welcome and the canny Clasper sold the winning boat for £80.

251

In the next 15 years, Clasper won the Champion Fours at the Thames Regatta six further times, his last victory in 1859, when he was 47 years old. As a successful coach, he recommended rest, light and regular meals, walking and running, as well as two sessions on the water each day. As an innovative designer, he pioneered the development of the racing shell and is said to have invented spoon-shaped oars. After his death in 1870, the coffin was transported by paddle tug from one of the many pubs he ran, the Tunnel Inn, by Newcastle's Ouseburn (he also owned the Clasper Hotel on the Scotswood Road) to Whickham on the river that had seen so many of his triumphs, watched by thousands of Tynesiders.

Clasper is barely remembered now, but many writers have been drawn to his story; in the last 25 years I must have read three or four film scripts for Clasper biopics that haven't been made, possibly because it seems hard to make rowing races visually exciting, the reason I suppose why the university boat race generally ceases to be interesting after the first bend. Maybe one day someone will crack it.

Lunch over, we wander further along the Elswick shore to a waterside office block, the regional base of the Environment Agency, which works to protect and enhance the quality of our rivers. Here Anne Lewis, regional freshwater conservation officer, gives us a quick tour of an environment that has changed so radically since she first saw it, beyond the wildest dreams of those who worked on the river in its (literal) dark days. In the early 1980s Anne worked for Northumbrian Water and used to trawl for marine samples from a survey vessel on the Tyne.

'Back then we'd only catch fish in the lower river. The Victorian system was a muddle of sewers and private drains that by the mid 1960s was discharging 700 gallons of sewage per second into the Tyne. Because of the complex flow pattern of the river it took up to ten days for this pollution to reach the sea. All this changed very quickly once the interceptor sewer was built. It might have cost £150 million and taken 20 years to build, but with it in place, by the late 1980s we started catching fish all the way up the river.'

Anne points out other recent changes. Since dredging above the bridges ceased 15 years ago, the mudflats at low tide have got bigger and bigger, especially here at Elswick – a haven for wading birds like the curlew, not usually known as an urban dweller. Anne is also delighted that the concrete banks below us are being colonised by salt marsh plants like the edible sea aster (if anyone's interested in a bit of foraging), as well as teasels, buckthorn, gorse, alder and ornamental escapees from the business park. From her office window, Anne regularly sees otters, but despite the glut of

...with great and buried industrial ...the Tyne

...of 1993 the scheme, as e... ...Northumbrian Water has ...much of it from ...the North East, in ...rtant project. It ...fe to the water ...vironment of ...d helped ...regens...

No... sche... huge ... of the riv... at the coas... outfalls and ...treatment w... Wallsend.

good news, there is one significant environmental danger facing the river: when a combination of high tides, low pressure and rain in the Pennines could make a perfect storm to threaten riverside communities with a catastrophic flood.

Not, however, today. As we walk the last mile to the Quayside, it's balmy, mild, a cloudless sky framing the bridges ahead. On our left on the northern bank once stood the familiar landmark of the shot tower of the Elswick Lead Works. A man I met not so long ago told me the tower featured galleries at two or three levels of its elevation which were used by spectators during the great Harry Clasper rowing races of the 1840s and 1850s, but later by the workers at bait-time: the view was outstanding. Alan Edgar, who worked as a chemist at the works after the Second World War, was one of them. His reminiscences are both fascinating and touching:

'When I started, the works was very busy. The inputs were lead ores mainly from Allendale, Weardale (the best ore) and Teesdale, and secondaries – drosses from manufacturing processes, old batteries, and scrap lead. These were smelted in furnaces, then treated in the refinery, where copper, tin, antimony and silver were removed from the lead, which was then cast into one hundredweight pigs. Much of this was taken by barge to the Hayhole works at Howdon, where red lead litharge and white lead (much of which went for paint-making on the river) was made. The slag from the blast furnace was recycled to reinforce the riverbank on the north side between Newburn and the Hedwin streams.

'Lead shot was made from an alloy of lead, antimony and arsenic, the concentration of which was critical for the formation of spherical shot. This was determined by a method that seemed to be black magic! The metal was hoisted to the top of the tower and melted in a small pot, then poured into a steel bowl pierced with holes of the desired shot size. The lead drops fell 180 feet into a very large barrel of water where it set. The shot was transferred to the sorter, which consisted of a series of inclined planes made of polished mahogany where any non-spherical shot was removed, later recycled. The perfect shot was sorted for size, then packed into bags by one of the women, Mary Ellen was her name. They had to carry 12-stone bars of lead on their heads up ladders! The chap who poured the shot was called Sammy Hawkins, and he claimed he had the highest job on Tyneside.

'In my early days at the works I noticed how clever many of the older men were. No doubt they had to leave school at the earliest possible time and start work to bring some money into the house. Who knows what they could have gone on to do if they'd had a chance?

'The Elswick Lead Works was a magnet for characters. Some truly wonderful chaps worked there. Their wit, antics and tales of what they'd done caused much laughter. As a sort of memorial to them, some of their names were: Bill Landless, Big John MacLain, a Polish chap called Jonny Zelcs, Sam Sterry, and a comic genius called Bob Griffiths, who was kept on long after his supposed retirement, I think because he made people laugh so much. What a man, they don't make them like that any more! To me, there's a certain sadness that the place is no more. It was a Newcastle institution in its heyday, and a great many very fine people worked there.'

The works was one of a number of companies along the river processing lead, including Cookson's of Wallsend and Blackett's of Hebburn, which amalgamated before becoming a subsidiary of the metal multi-national Rio Tinto. Elswick Lead Works closed in 2002.

As we walk under the Tyne bridges to the Quayside, two things happen at once: inside the old fish market, a drummer who's obviously listened to Ginger Baker starts practising solos for that night's gig; and up on the High Level, a woman waves down at me. I don't wave back – play it cool, I think – then my mobile trills. The mysterious come-hither female turns out to be my wife, come to take us for tea. I really must get some new glasses.

It's an early finish – mid-afternoon – and the combination of a cursed Protestant work ethic and the fact that it's Friday (which has since time immemorial been my going-to-the-pictures day) gives me an idea. After the tea and cakes are done, I walk past Bessie Surtees House (and the site of the elopement of a couple who acted on their emotions and were richly rewarded) and up an alley and a flight of stairs to a dream palace of another kind: the home of Amber Films.

The Tyne hasn't featured in many films, but often when it has, it has been to significant effect. Mike Figgis's *Stormy Monday* made much of the Quayside, albeit rather oddly dressed to make it look like a waterfront on the Lower East Side; Mike Hodges' *Get Carter* featured among other memorable sequences that epic shoot-out on the mid-Tyne ferry; and then a mostly forgotten but rather good British thriller from 1950, *The Clouded Yellow,* features some superb sequences of the riverside, including the arrival of Trevor Howard and a young Jean Simmons at the Tyne Tees Wharf by boat from London, a journey I'd love to have made. (The film also features a delicious moment in which the pair get on a yellow bus by the Town Moor, and Howard's clipped

RP English delivers the immortal line: 'Two for Jesmond, please.') Television drama has often featured the river, mostly to rather disappointing effect. Unquestionably, to me, the finest representation of our river culture hasn't come in a single film, but in a remarkable body of work executed by the group of people who've clattered up and down those worn steps a few yards from the Tyne over 40 years, and worked to a governing ethic.

To explain…

Once upon a time there was a man called Murray Martin. Together with a group of other film students at London's Regent Street Polytechnic, he came to Newcastle in the late 1960s to make a film. (He'd previously studied fine art at Newcastle University under Richard Hamilton and Victor Pasmore.) The Amber group never quite left, and settled in the city and went to work, forging a distinctive philosophy: to work in film and photography as a collective, sharing both the vision and the craft in an egalitarian way; committed to long-term relationships with working class and marginalised communities in the North East; the end product characterised by what might be called social realism.

Their very first film, made as students in 1969, set the tone: *Maybe* is a ten-minute hymn to the transience of life, set on the ferry *Tynemouth*. Shot in black and white, and bookended with Louis Killen singing that haunting Northumbrian folk song *Sair Fyeld Hinny* on the soundtrack, the film features the reflections of the boat's engineer as he sits at his controls. Two important elements of the Amber style are already present: there's no commentary to interpret or distort what we see and hear – the old man is allowed to speak for himself; and the lyrical fascination with industrial processes – the ferry gliding across the silvery surface of the Tyne, the almost balletic movement of its engine's rods and pistons.

In my viewing session I'm intrigued to see, or see again, later films in a similar vein, especially those that touched places on our walk: *Last Shift*, for instance, made in collaboration with the industrial archaeologist Stafford Linsley (see his magnificent photographic archive via Newcastle University's website), recorded the end of a tiny Swalwell brickworks making fire-bricks for Adamsez of Scotswood, which was itself about to close. (The brickworks drew its water supply from the Derwenthaugh Dam referred to in chapter four.) *Glassworks* from 1977 is a quietly staggering film about the pride of Lemington, in which an apparently mundane industrial process is rendered as a thing of beauty and grace. By this time, Amber had developed its photographic work – Sirkka-Liisa Konttinen's matchless *Byker* project spawned exhibitions, books and films – and its social campaigning. Based on the Quayside, Amber successfully fought Newcastle City Council's planned redevelopment of the neglected quarter that subsequently became the city's chief heritage asset. One of the weapons in this campaign was 1979's *Quayside*,

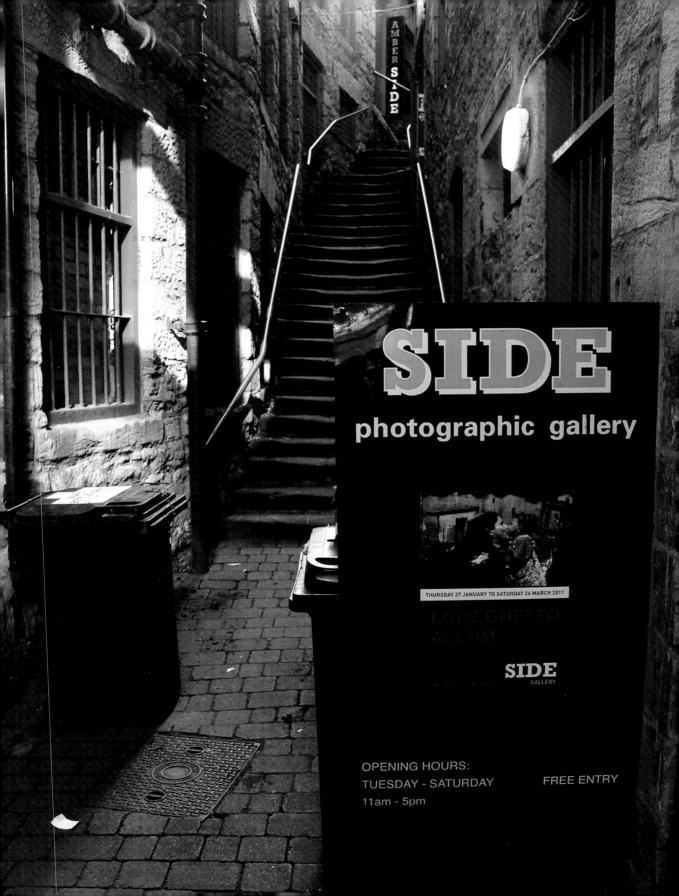

a 17-minute film that managed to celebrate as well as lament. The following year the group made the rather longer *Tyne Lives*, an impressionistic journey accompanying the ash-tipper *Bessie Surtees* from Blaydon to the sea, featuring pub drinkers singing, tap-dancing girls, reminiscing butchers and some semi-fictional scenes featuring the North Shields playwright and fish merchant Tom Hadaway. Just as pertinent to this walk, Phillip Trevelyan's *Ship Hotel Tyne Main* lyrically recreates the atmosphere of a riverside pub (in Gateshead, now renamed the Schooner) and features the Newcastle poet Tom Pickard and his wife Connie. (It also gave me an idea for a drama, very definitely another story…)

But of all the Amber films that feature the river, my personal favourite is *Launch* (of the super-tanker *World Unicorn* at Swan Hunter's Wallsend yard in 1973). It's only ten minutes long but is more eloquent than films ten times its length. The usual Amber trademarks are evident: lyrical and lingering black and white photography; a highly evocative soundtrack without commentary; the faces of the workers and their families, people leading dignified and honourable lives. Two other things struck me: just how antiquated, and sometimes downright dangerous was much of the equipment they were using; and the fact that the local community wasn't allowed anywhere near the launch, like Princess Anne and the local great and good, but forced to peer over the yard's walls. One such spot, at the end of a street of terraced houses over which the great ship hangs like a colossus, provides *the* shot of what is for me, *the* film about the river.

After the champagne has crashed against the hull, the film cuts to a long shot from the other end of this street. The great ship begins slowly, imperceptibly, to move, then picks up speed, and appears to wipe the frame, watched by the crowd, a man arrives on a motor bike, followed by a dog. It looks like a piece of cinematic trickery, but it isn't. It happened.

Never mind films about the Tyne, this is one of the most amazing shots I've seen in *any* film. The kind of image film-makers might capture once in a lifetime. The kind of image viewers usually see only in their dreams…

FROM THE ABOVE WINDOW
ON NOV 18ᵀᴴ 1772
BESSY SURTEES DESCENDED AND ELOPED WITH
JOHN SCOTT LATER CREATED 1ˢᵀ EARL OF ELDON
AND LORD CHANCELLOR OF ENGLAND

⚓ LEAP

Sandhill, 1772

Then all at once, the walls went up,
flirting was shut down, talk turned
to heirs and his Grace fat Henry.
Duke of the West, he'd come to snoop
round Bessie's home and pull rank
on the men downstairs who shadowboxed
about her future. He tainted rooms
with a black pomander stink

till she *had no choice but to leave,*
to press through the window then bloom
out among the weathervanes
before ske-laddering down to love,
to John and a journey through night
over the border from wrong to right

Countless times during the ten days of the Tyne Walk we mused on the waters of Tyne. This after all was the point of the exercise.

But more than once we mused on the Waters of Tyne (note those caps), that traditional song on traditional themes: the woman separated from her true love, her beseeching of the boatman to speed her to him and a sadness, surging like an incoming tide, swollen by a plaintive tune, that the doubtless-cheating beggar had in fact gone for good.

This set in motion a riverside conversation about other songs of the Tyne, ancient and modern, and so I began to keep a list of our Water Music, which I'm sure is by no means comprehensive, but even so surprisingly lengthy as well as eclectic. Still, I never thought I'd actually find an excuse to write about these songs, until a small and rather strange boat sailed up the Tyne and docked by the Millennium Bridge, with music rather than cargo in its manifest. This was ~*Flow*.

As vessels go, it's not the most elegant, but is certainly intriguing, with a passing resemblance to an idealised image of Noah's Ark, without the animals: a side-on wooden house perched on a metal pontoon, with tidal water-mill providing the power. Inside the house are instruments you've never seen or heard before, though no musicians play them. Not wholly true: the river plays the melodies, an ambient sequence of ghostly clicks, sighs, beeps, bubbles, hisses, creaks and groans. Who says the devil has all the best tunes?

To explain…

Funded by Arts Council England at a cost of £500,000 as one of 12 public art commissions to mark the 2012 Olympics and Paralympics, ~*Flow* was built to house specially designed electro-acoustic musical machines that respond to the constantly changing environment of the river to produce, if you like, the sound of the Tyne.

It's the brainchild of Gateshead-based art and music producer Ed Carter, who collaborated with Nick Spurr's Amble Boat Company (Tyne-trained, he built the vessel), David Willcox (he designed and built the waterwheel that powers the equipment) and the Owl Project (the Manchester collective of musicians and engineers who designed and made the instruments). The salinity sampler sequencer, with its wooden conveyor belt and electronic sensors, makes a tune from the tide by 'playing' hourly water samples, with salt levels controlling the instrument's pitch. The bubble synth and giant bellows create sounds from resonating bubbles, controlled by the chemical composition of the river. A turbidatron generates sounds according to the muddiness of the water, with gears and cranks driving a laser beam of light through water.

The whole is a delightful combination of low- and hi-tech: Wallace and Gromit meets The Chemical Brothers. As for the music, it won't set the foot tapping or bring a tear to a sentimental eye, and it wouldn't be one of my Desert Island Discs, but it's got something quietly haunting that I couldn't quite put my finger on – until I imagined myself squatting on the muddy bed of the Tyne under the Swing Bridge, the peaty Pennine flow pouring over my head. This is the kind of aural universe I might inhabit…

I was there one sunny Sunday when ~Flow was opened to the public. More than a thousand people turned up and though there were some puzzled looks, most people, especially the children, entered into the spirit of the thing, twiddling knobs and pulling levers to manipulate the sounds. After a while, I leaned on a railing, looked at the sun on the water and contemplated the Tyne's considerable musical inheritance.

When I was a boy my dad sometimes took the family record player from its usual place in my bedroom and had his own spin session. While I played Cream and Canned Heat, he loved the jazz rhythms of Duke Ellington and Jack Teagarden and the more traditional songs of the High Level Ranters and his pal Alex Glasgow, perhaps most famous for his recording of the traditional song *Dance Ti Thi Daddy*, which became the theme for the hit TV show to which they both contributed scripts, *When the Boat Comes In*. The two of them also collaborated with Alan Plater on that epic musical history of the Durham miners, *Close the Coalhouse Door*; the almost unbearable poignancy of its theme song never fails to raise the hairs on the back of my neck, especially when sung by actor Joe Caffrey, as it was during Alan's funeral. Alex also wrote a brilliant polemical song about unemployment called *Hands*, but was equally keen to re-work the songs of Tyneside songsmiths of earlier times, including pitman Tommy Armstrong (*Wor Nanny's A Maizor* and *Durham Gaol*) and Joe Wilson, a printer-turned-publican, who, like a contemporary popsmith, turned out many anthems of Tyneside life, some jaunty, some definitely not, including *Geordie Haud the Bairn* and *Keep Your Feet Still, Geordie Hinny*. Indeed Alex wrote a terrific one-man play about this beguiling and slightly tragic man (he died of TB at 33) called *Joe Lives*; well worth a revival. But for me the masterpiece of the Glasgow canon also has the best title: *The Tyne Slides By*, a sweet and evocative song-cycle – and indeed life-cycle – contrasting the fortunes of two Tyneside boys who are dealt very different hands through the random accident of where they're born. The political edge of the piece is typical of its writer, a committed International Socialist who once stopped speaking to my dad for a whole year for the crime of accepting an OBE from the Establishment; I think words like 'lackey' or 'lickspittle' might have been used. But as always the quality of the man's writing stops the songs from becoming overly preachy and didactic. One of the songs is *Saturday Afternoon*, an affectionate hymn to communal prayer in Bobby Robson's 'cathedral on the hill' at St James's Park. Notice how that sentence doesn't quite have the same quality when punctuated with 'Sports Direct Arena'…

Meanwhile the High Level Ranters tended to focus more on work songs, many of which focused on or at least mentioned the Tyne: *Doon the Waggonway* for instance ('There's nivor a lad like my lad drives te the staiths on Tyne…'), and a personal favourite, *Byker Hill* ('… and Walker Shore, collier lads for ever more…') which I used to love singing for the simple reason that it's designed to be belted out and can't be ruined by an indifferent voice.

I'm fond too of songs about local characters. At Sandyford Road Junior School we used to sing *Adam Buckham*, a song about a famous Newcastle busybody who lived in one of the chares of Newcastle's Quayside, and the street hawker's song, *Buy Brown Buzzems*. Way back, this was performed by a blind fiddler known to all on Tyneside as Blind Willie, who for a small consideration would add extra verses as plugs for local tradesmen. I also loved, and amazingly still remember the lyrics to, the compellingly catchy *Billy Boy* ('Where have you been all the day, Billy Boy, Billy Boy?') This traditional song has travelled the world: the composer Ralph Vaughan Williams heard it on his travels in England in 1912 and transcribed it; a version of the song was later 'collected' by the American musicologist Alan Lomax in the Deep South in the 1930s.

There's a rich canon of songs specifically about Tyne keelmen, the men who ferried coals from upriver staiths to colliers near the mouth: the jaunty *The Keel Row* of course; the rather more anxious *My Bonny Lad* ('Have you seen owt o' my bonny lad, An are ye sure he's weel, O?'); and the lament of a lovesick keelman, *Cushy Butterfield* ('She's a big lass an' a bonny lass an she likes hor beer…')

My mother once gave me a treasured gift, the lovely *Beuk of Newcassel Sangs* collected by the Newcastle rope manufacturer and artist Joseph Crawhall in the second half of the 19th century, and illustrated with his own striking woodcuts. What's striking about the songs is how many of them are unknown to me. After the familiar *Bobby Shaftoe*, and *The Bonny Pit Laddie*, there are many strangers: *Cappy's The Dog,* for instance, the pungent *Newcastle Beer* and the splendid *Hydrophobie*. I hope one day to hear them sung…

There are equal riches, and oddities, closer to our own time, though perhaps the range of songs has narrowed somewhat. There are fewer work songs, fewer character songs, but many, many more focusing on that time-less experience of countless Tynesiders – leaving the Tyne, and finally returning. Naturally many of these songs have been written by people who've had precisely that experience.

Mark Knopfler has been especially prolific in this sub-sub-genre. His *Fare Thee Well, Northumberland* sets the tone ('Come drive me down to the Central Station, I hate to leave my River Tyne, For some damn town that's God-forsaken, Fare thee well, Northumberland… Roll on, Geordie boy, roll on, Roll on, Geordie boy, roll on…'). I like his narrative history *Sailing to Philadelphia* and *5.15am*, his take on the gangland murder of Angus Sibbett that also inspired CP Taylor's play *Bandits* and Mike Hodges' classic film noir on the Tyne, *Get Carter*. Not content with all that, Knopfler also produced other Tyne anthems like *Why Aye Man, Down to the Waterline* (which refers to the Dog Leap Stairs) and returning to that ubiquitous theme, *Southbound Again*. Going further back, The Animals reworked *The Waters of Tyne* for their song *The Immigrant Lad* (as has Kate Rusby for her haunting *Bring Me a Boat)*, but perhaps suggested a less sentimental attitude towards their home town in the classic *We Gotta Get Out of This Place*, which to be pedantically correct was originally written by Brill Building luminaries Barry Mann and Cynthia Weil for the Righteous Brothers. Alan Price wrote the more specific *Jarrow Song* about the town's Crusade of the 1930s while his ex-colleague Hilton Valentine touched a more familiar theme in *River Tyne*. The song *Back Home Once Again* by a band called Renaissance was chosen as the theme tune for the 1970s ITV children's drama set on Tyneside, *The Paper Lads* (my old man wrote episodes for that too) and I vividly remember *The Five Bridges Suite*, commissioned by the Newcastle Festival and written and performed brilliantly by Keith Emerson, the rest of The Nice and orchestra at the City Hall on 10 October 1969: I was there! In later decades I saw Lindisfarne at the same venue at one of their legendary Christmas concerts; that evening finished with – what else? – *Fog on the Tyne*, when the roof lifted, though I have a possibly ironic regard for Gazza's version. Talking of football (and I do, often), matches at St James's Park are usually bookended by Knopfler's wonderful theme for the film *Local Hero* and the nauseatingly sentimental and irritatingly catchy *Home Newcastle* (another of those songs) by Busker. This song has celebrated, and sometimes mocked, countless Newcastle performances, good and bad, in my presence. I prefer to remember the great, the latest being *that* recovery from being 0-4 down against Arsenal to drawing 4-4 in season 2010-11. Even I was humming the wretched song that afternoon. By the way, is it the cynic in me that makes me wonder why the slushiest of the songs about returning to the Tyne are written by folk who no longer live anywhere near it and indeed have no intention of doing so?

Songs featuring the Tyne aren't merely the preserve of locals. The car in that great song *Driving in My Car* by Madness (don't you love Madness?) '*was made in 59 in a factory by the Tyne*'. Two equally brilliant songs by Elvis Costello – *Oliver's Army* and *Shipbuilding* – reference the river, while Blur's *This is a Low* mentions its section of the shipping forecast. The country singer Gretchen Peters does a kind of lament-for-home-in-reverse in *England Blues*, pining for Tennessee 'holed up in a hotel room on the River Tyne'. The middle European band Asonance wrote an elegy for the landscape at the Tyne's source in *Kopce U Promenu Reky Tyne*. I would tell you how the song develops, but sadly my Czech is a little rusty…

Then there is the river as torch song. Jimmy Nail's *Big River* is a lament for the death of the river's heavy industries wrapped up in a slightly misty-eyed optimism that 'This is a big, big river, And in my heart I know, It will rise again, This river will rise again.' It's rich stuff, but for my taste rather overdone; when you get to the end it feels like you've eaten far too much chocolate. Rather more to my taste is *Great Northern River*, written by Graeme Miles, which I first heard sung wondrously by the Unthanks in 2011 at the *Songs From the Shipyards* event at the Tyneside Cinema, sponsored by the Port of Tyne, a collaboration between the cinema, the band and the film-maker Richard Fenwick, who crafted archive film about the industry to the accompaniment of some brilliant songs. I hope the Unthanks record the song; their evocation of a lost culture is both beautiful and profoundly moving.

Finally, there is Wallsend's Sting, who has written many great songs touching on the river and its people. What I like about them, apart from their superb musicianship, is a spare elegance and subtlety. Sometimes they appear to be about something else. On first listening *I Was Brought to My Senses* appears to be a straightforward love song, but the clues are there for the cognoscenti: a reference to 'where the river meets the sea' and a plaintive folky fiddle. Sometimes the clue is more obvious: Kathryn Tickell's Northumbrian pipes, for instance. Many of Sting's love songs of another kind – to the river of his youth and imagination – feature on the superb album *Soul Cages*, none finer than *All This Time*, an elegy for his late father Ernest, a milkman who always wished he'd become a sailor. It begins atmospherically, and builds movingly to the final, most tender service a son could perform for a father, in this case only fulfilled in song:

I looked out across
The river today
I saw a city in the fog and an old church tower
Where the seagulls play
I saw the sad shire horses walking home
In the sodium light
I saw two priests on the ferry
October geese on a cold winter's night

And all this time, the river flowed
Endlessly to the sea…
If I had my way I'd take a boat from the river
And I'd bury the old man
I'd bury him at sea

So there we are: if push comes to shove, and *The Tyne Slides By* runs it very close, this is my favourite song of my favourite songs about the Tyne. But I accept you probably won't agree with any of it.

So make your own list.

DAY EIGHT

TYNE-TEES
STEAM SHIPPING
COMPANY LIMITED
REGULAR
LINER SERVICES
BETWEEN
NEWCASTLE SUNDERLAND
AND
LONDON
ANTWERP
ROTTERDAM
AMSTERDAM
DORDRECHT
HAMBURG
BREMEN
GHENT
AND
NORTHERN FRENCH PORTS.

ALSO
MIDDLESBROUGH
AND

'And all this time, the river flowed
Endlessly to the sea...'
All This Time, Sting

I don't suppose there could be a more fitting place to start a day's walk along our river than underneath the Tyne Bridge – or indeed, on this fine Monday morning, a smellier place, given the proximity of the kittiwake nests in the superstructure above our heads and the ammoniacal stench drifting down from them. Of course the smell isn't the only hazard of standing here.

So having registered a symbolic point, as we wait for our fellow walkers, Charles and I move to the corner opposite, under the famous sign of the Tyne Tees Steam Shipping Company, with its list of exotic destinations including Bremen, Dordrecht and Middlesbrough. Once we're all together we get the show on the road and move along the Quayside. It's a Monday morning and the riverside is busy, especially by the Crown Court, where two TV crews are setting up: there must be a tasty case on today. The coffee shop on the corner of Broad Chare is packed with defending barristers and their clients and wives. It's easy to tell them apart, but I'm not talking wigs: the latter have deep tans and plenty of bangle. We won't get served here inside half an hour, so we cross the road and head downstream.

Broad Chare is worth exploring. It's home to the astonishing Trinity House, headquarters of the guild established in the 16th century to regulate shipping on the river and a hidden treasure of the Tyne, and next door a building that has played a significant role in my creative life since I first got involved with the company in the mid-1980s: Live Theatre. Ten years earlier the fledgling theatre had bought for a song a crumbling medieval warehouse that had latterly seen service as a marine supplies store and which has since undergone a series of sensitive redevelopments. Meanwhile the theatre has built an unparalleled reputation for creating plays reflecting, exploring and celebrating the culture and people of the North East. I've had countless great nights out in this warm and intimate space, some of them watching my own work being rendered impeccably by wonderful actors and Live's gifted and equally self-effacing artistic director Max Roberts, but mostly watching in admiration the plays of other writers, including Tom Hadaway, CP Taylor, Lee Hall and Alan Plater. Inevitably some of this work has featured the waterway lapping at the quay a hundred yards away.

The most memorable was also the shortest: a masterly adaptation of a short story of my father's by Alan for a show called *In Blackberry Time* that we worked on together exactly 25 years ago. *Where Is My Old Friend Bing Crosby Tonight?* describes a chance encounter by a deserted river late at night between a troubled young man and a washed-up singer visiting Tyneside for a gig. As a novice at the writing game, I thought this atmospheric but sketchy piece of prose un-adaptable, but the master was equal to the challenge, producing something that said more about human frailty and loss in ten minutes than the vast majority of plays manage in a hundred and fifty. It was an object lesson in the great truth that 'less is more' – and I have never forgotten it. So thank you for that, Alan – and for many other things…

One of the reasons why that story resonated so much was that by the 1960s its haunting sense of mortality applied to the setting as well as the inner lives of the two characters. Over the next 20 years the smell of death settled like a sea fret over the whole of the Quayside. But as we've heard, community action helped to lift the gloom, and the river frontage on both banks of central Gateshead and Newcastle has been transformed in the last 30 years. As it turns out, it's not the only place on today's walk: on this first day of a new week, this sense of rebirth will strengthen and grow to become the dominant and entirely encouraging theme of today's walk.

As if to nail the thesis, the first thing we encounter on the Quayside proper could barely have been imagined a few years ago. OK, the beach arranged rather incongruously around John Wesley's centenary memorial of 1891 may be composed of imported sand, but this summer initiative of the city's promotional agency NE1 is easy on the eye. We eschew the buckets and spades but enjoy a game of volleyball with soft balls (the proper ones have inevitably all gone into the water), and then sit on deckchairs for a natter with the man in charge. It turns out Gary was born in Walker but after his family emigrated, grew up in Adelaide. When he came home on a trip, he met a girl – as inevitably you do – and after he went home to Australia decided he couldn't live without her. 'I guess this is my home now', he said, gesturing to the Quayside's answer to Bondi. At the mention of home, we all turn to look at the river: the tide is coming in, almost imperceptibly.

We finally get our morning teas and coffees from the back of one of those nifty little beverage vans. Nearby are the Pitcher and Piano (where I celebrated my 50th before we boated down to the piers), the Malmaison hotel and a cluster of upmarket offices belonging to law firms. They all provide a good trade for the mobile barista, who started his business four years ago after many years' catering for another sense: he used to work for Bang and Olufsen. Opening a book, he shows us a photo of the precise area where we're now standing, once known intriguingly as the Swirle and commemorated in the name of the modern pavilion nearby. At the heart of it

was a pub called the Half Moon and a grocery to service the ships tied up nearby. The sailors have nearly all gone, replaced by people who sit behind desks. Despite the fact that they provide his business, our friend thinks this is a shame – the Quayside has lost some of its character, he says. Then again, black and white photos always lend a patina of down-at-heel glamour to places in which none of us would actually wish to live or work, bearing in mind that before Alastair Balls and the Tyne and Wear Development Corporation got to work here, the riverside warehouses were derelict and stacked only with carcinogenic debris. Also, looking back upstream at that matchless view, it strikes me that the contemporary Quayside isn't exactly short of that elusive 'character' either. To top it all, some real actual sailors turn up. It might be a yacht tying up, rather than a butter boat from Esbjerg, but I scurry over nevertheless to see from which exotic port the crew of the *Honour Bound* has arrived. It turns out they've just popped down the coast from Blyth.

Paper cups in hand, we stroll down to the point where the Ouseburn ends the 14-mile ramble from its source near Callerton. Once Tyne wherries used to moor here, but today there's a cluster of small boats, old fishing cobles among them. As always I inspect their names, for the simple reason that I enjoy musing on the stories that might lurk behind them. So I wonder about the girl who might have inspired the *Molly* and the relationship behind the *True Friendship*. I'm standing on the spot where as a boy in short trousers, I first had a proper look at the murky Tyne of the late 1950s. Something made me shiver that day, but I didn't know then what I know now: on the ground beneath my feet once stood the little building where bodies found in the Tyne were laid out for identification. And here's another evocative name, this time grim rather than uplifting. The Victorians didn't go in for euphemisms. It was called the Dead House.

Behind us, up the Ouseburn, a new building is going up, or rather a restoration of an old one – the Toffee Factory, the home of Maynard's best from 1906 until the 1970s. Along with a new barrage regulating the flow of the Ouseburn, this is a sign of the quietly astonishing regeneration of this small quarter of the East End between the outflow of the stream from a hillside under Byker Bridge and its disappearance into the Tyne. It's quite a story. Back to those short trousers…

On Sunday mornings our house was a place of sensory torture: the tantalising smell of roasting beef and saccharine sounds of late 50s 'pop' on *Two-Way Family Favourites* often drove me out, not to play with my pals (forbidden on a Sunday) but to go for a walk with my dad (permitted because

of its improving nature). These walks often went towards the Tyne, via Sandyford and Shieldfield. Once there was a detour through Jesmond Old Cemetery where Dad showed me the headstones of eminent Victorians who built lasting Newcastle brands, among them Christopher Maling, Thomas Pumphrey and Emerson Muschamp Bainbridge. I was more interested in the grave of a man eminent in another way, William Campbell, at 53 stones once Britain's heaviest man. At various points, Sid got out his notebook and scribbled something down. This wasn't an unusual event – he always carried a thick notebook, ruining many jackets in the process – but it was years later before I discovered exactly what he wrote down in this place: names for the characters in his novels. Then we walked on, passing down Goldspink Lane, crossing Warwick Street, skirting the running track and under the railway bridge to descend to the bottom of the Ouseburn valley, an unlikely destination given that it was rapidly becoming a sink-hole of abandoned mills, tumbledown cottages and fractured hopes. Not a place to linger – the Ouseburn was rather smelly and had a vague air of menace – but my dad had a gleam in his eye. He loved this place, for professional rather than aesthetic reasons: he was writing a novel about it.

Having arrived in Newcastle in 1957, Sid had developed a vision to write a different kind of novel, a genre he called 'social thrillers', to be set in his new home. He wanted to examine how the old working class values that had shaped him would survive in a new world of tower blocks and consumer culture. In *The Day of the Sardine*, this tension is focused around one Arthur Haggerston, fatherless child and secondary mod no-hoper, who makes the same journey as we had down into that valley, a crucible in which his mettle will be tested, a place of temptation, sin and unlikely redemption, where Arthur might find his own moral compass and become a man:

To get there it's a mile across the wreck of an ancient village. Every so often bulldozers come and have slum clearance fun. Result: open spaces ideal for dumping old beds, decrepit settees, ancient prams, sometimes the odd body. You can walk across the scrap without putting your foot on the ground. Skid down a wilderness under the railway viaduct and slopes pockmarked with old clay workings, you find a filthy burn and No Man's Land – a few houses occupied by scrap-men, hawkers and drabs, with gas lamps outside, which don't lighten the dark. Further down the burn's tidal. Sailing ships once came up here, but the quays are idle now. For some reason they call it Venice Steps…

Well, actually they don't, in fact they never did: my father's little joke. But the rest is spot on. The Ouseburn – once a hotbed of industry – was dying, its death throes drawn out over five decades, but the lower Ouseburn still had its own Motor Boat Club, a motley fleet of small vessels, usually decommissioned lifeboats from cargo ships snapped up by working men for as little as £10, which organised sea fishing trips and armadas upstream to the Hoppings on Ryton Willows. Among the passengers, incidentally, were two Byker lads called Bruce and Freddy Shepherd, of whom more anon…

In the summer of 2011, at more or less the same time as the Tyne Walk, I returned to the lower Ouseburn in preparation for adapting *The Day of the Sardine* for BBC Radio 4's *A Book at Bedtime*. And lo, as the man said, what a transformation was there!

Mike Mould can be said to have started it. In 1970 Mike came to Newcastle to work as an actor at the University Theatre. He found digs in Byker and made a habit of walking to work every day via the Ouseburn. A few years later he set up the theatre company Bruvvers and began looking for a place to rehearse. To begin with, the company used the old Imperial Cinema in Byker, but then Mike got his eye on the old Ouseburn mill designed by John Dobson and after a protracted wrangle with the car auction company that owned it finally bought it for £30,000, with the help of a loan from his actor brother Roy Marsden and the sale of a house in Walker which Mike had first squatted and then acquired. In 1982 Mike and his family moved to the Ouseburn Valley.

'The whole area was pretty derelict. Few people actually lived there. The Ship pub under the bridge was kept going by the few locals and a group of social workers who'd adopted it. The houses next door had been demolished after sustained vandalism – tearaways used to lob bricks off Byker Bridge

'The transformation has been amazing but it's happened everywhere – Soho, New York, so why not east Newcastle? Developers look for a profit wherever they can find it – first it was going to be social housing, then upmarket flats and when they couldn't sell those they went for studios. As for us, we just wanted a cheap place to work and when it came to letting the rest of the building, being socialists, we didn't want to screw people and we still don't.

'Actually what strikes me most now are the trees down here. When we first came there weren't any, now there's loads, and 50 feet high too.'

And that's not all. I tell Mike the lower valley now has its own pair of nesting sparrowhawks, often seen swooping through the arches of John Green's railway bridge and Ove Arup's equally elegant Metro bridge to take out the Ouseburn's hapless pigeons.

I suppose like Mike I too have a sentimental attachment to the old Ouseburn, grim as it was, largely because it inspired one of my father's finest novels, but there is life there now, and the sound once more of children's voices and children's laughter, inspired by lots of other books. Sid wouldn't quibble with that, and neither do I.

One of the 16 potteries in and around the Ouseburn was a great Newcastle name: Maling. In fact the name is actually French, the Malings being originally Huguenot refugees who came to Newcastle after the Napoleonic Wars via the slightly circuitous route of Scarborough and Sunderland. The business prospered tremendously in the 19th century, largely from the manufacture of marmalade and jam pots for Keiller's of Dundee and Cooper's of Oxford: nearly 750,000 items were made every month. Much of the profit was invested in a vast 14-acre site in Walker half a mile away, serviced by its own rail siding. In the early 20th century, the workforce, again mainly female, was making everything from bedpans and urinals to beautifully designed home ware, culminating between the wars with a fabulous art deco range. Their designer was another Frenchman, Lucien Boullemier, a talented chap who, when he worked in the Potteries, had a second job on Saturday afternoons: he turned out for Port Vale. In the 1930s Maling's also benefited from a partnership with Rington's Tea and I suspect there are many local households, like ours, that contain richly decorated tea caddies marked with the names of both of these iconic Tyneside brands. Sadly the famous pottery was not to last: increasing competition from abroad and, I suspect, a wavering commitment to the business from the Maling family meant that after the Second World War, it was sold to the local removals firm Hoult's before it briefly flickered back into life and then finally closed in 1963. However, the great Maling buildings are still there, now marketed under the name Hoults Yard, converted in the last ten years into office and workshop space for dozens of small enterprises specialising in media, PR, marketing and design, sometimes known by the modish acronym 'KIB' (knowledge-intensive businesses). The pottery that once prided itself on the largest concentration of furnaces and kilns under one roof has found another temperature. This so-called 'creative village' is now officially cool.

Back on the Tyne two hundred yards away, there's another piece of regeneration going on: the old Spiller's flour mill is being demolished, bit by painstaking bit. The crew from Scarborough reckons the vast bomb-proof mill is one of the toughest jobs they've ever had: 'We're ten weeks in, six months to go. It's a bugger to pull down.' Not that much pulling is going on this morning: the crane hydraulics have gone and the lads are waiting for new parts to arrive. In the meantime, three of them are fishing. When I wish them luck one calls out, 'We've only had one flattie, so we won't be putting on the chip-pan just yet.'

We hurry on: we have an invitation for tea up the hill from two other working men at Auto Diesel, a workshop repairing starter motors, fuel pumps and batteries. As it turns out, we barely have time to sip from our giant mugs for laughing.

Products of the small parish of St Lawrence, Joe and Dennis have worked together for many years. When they talk, the sentences overlap, each man eager to reach the punchline first. This is a double act in more ways than one. My ancient shorthand just about recorded everything that was said, but not always who said what.

'We used to play on what we called Byker Sands when we were lads, swinging on capstan ropes over the water. By, it was hacky back then.'

'We served our time at British Engines down there and our foreman there, Gordon Johnson, once went into the river to rescue someone and knackered his kidneys.'

'Once I saw a car go into the river, so I tipped off Tyne Tees Television and got a £3 reward, which was nice but a bit disappointing. It would have been five quid if someone had been in it.'

'I started as an apprentice electrician in 1960. I was at work for a week and then I was on strike for two! My dad was the best welder on the Tyne, or so me mother used to say,' says Joe. Dennis takes over.

'Our old boss at British Engines started Auto Diesel and wanted us to take it over. So we took the plunge in 1988. I'm more the salesman. In the old days I'd drive round NCB opencast sites drumming up business, Joe was

back here. He has everything in his head, he doesn't need diagrams or owt like that.'

There's a short pause in the patter and I take the chance to look around. The first thing I see is assorted cheesecake on the walls: I didn't think they made calendars like that anymore. The rest of the workshop is a glorious jumble of oily parts, but I notice something else hanging on the wall: a rather battered bugle.

'Oh aye, we got that off a rag and bone man once.'

'We often blow it when it's dinnertime, like.'

I have no idea whether this is true or not.

The bugle isn't alone: the workshop's collection of instruments also includes two mouth organs, an accordion, a guitar and a violin.

'We once did a job for a lad who did house clearances and we didn't charge him anything. He said if we fancied anything, he'd get it, and something made me say if you come across a fiddle, we'll have that. And he did, and we got it.'

As far as I can make out, no one actually plays any of the workshop's instruments, apart from a mysterious man called Davie, who used to be a busker and sometimes plays solo jam sessions in the workshop.

'I suppose we're just hoarders,' says Dennis, unnecessarily.

There's a third member of the Auto Diesel team who's off today. The men keep referring to 'the young un'. It turns out that Stephen came for a three-month trial when he was 18 and ('the best thing we've ever done') has been here ever since. The 'young un' is actually now 37.

Tea drunk, we have a look around. Joe shows us two Volvo pumps sent for repair by a dockyard in Gibraltar. 'To tell the truth, it's a dying trade,' he says, pointing at a fuel injection engine. 'There's 300 parts in that and how they all fit together isn't easy to learn for an old chap like me. But it's been a good living and a good laugh, always a pleasure to come to work. Good business too – it would be a shame if it all went when we retired.'

So I ask the awkward question about what will happen and get a slightly awkward reply.

'Well, we want to do something for the young un, but it's not easy.'

We return to safer ground – the telling of tales, in particular about a 'real hard lad' from the old days at British Engines called Slash Macleod. Listening with a smile on my face, I remember all the older men we've met on the walk whose eyes grew misty when they described the laughter and camaraderie of the yards and workshops of their younger lives. Practical jokes often featured. Joe and Dennis do not disappoint.

'Once upon a time, Joe found a little bonsai tree. It was dead basically, but he swore he'd revive it.'

'I brought it into the workshop and every day I carefully watered and tended it. Then I came in one day and it was like magic! It had come back to life!'

'What he didn't know was that me and the young un had got hold of these little leaves from a hedge and stuck them on with superglue.'

'I was overjoyed!'

'We could have left it there, but we couldn't resist it. One night after Joe had gone home, we cut all the little leaves off.'

'I came the next morning and I was dismayed. Oh Dennis, I cried, it's gone and died!'

'And I said, "You soft bugger, it never was alive!"'

We reluctantly leave the pranksters of Auto Diesel and walk down the hill to the river, passing the base of the Royal Marines Reserve Tyne and a rare spot where cars have direct access to the water, aka 'Joy Riders' Quay'. Beyond is St Peter's Basin, one of the first regeneration schemes on the Tyne of recent times and our chosen lunch spot. On a bench by the water, we munch our sandwiches but for once don't look at the water, but a 'kit' of racing pigeons circling overhead before heading back to their crees high on the bank of the Newcastle shore behind us. They're not the only active avians around: I can hear goldfinches and magpies chuntering in the shrubbery nearby and as my watch nudges 2pm, a rather confused cock crowing from the direction of Bill Quay community farm. Nearby a buddleia bush is in impressively purple bloom, but Charlie wrinkles his nose. He tells us he has never been able to stand its smell. Funny the things you learn on a walk.

Heading on downstream, we encounter traces of the river's poisonous past: beyond St Peter's once stood the Locke, Blackett lead works and then the St Anthony's tar works. A 'Keep Out' sign warns us to stay away from the shore, still contaminated by the latter. The following day, as if the deadly buddleia wasn't enough, Charlie develops a mysterious rash on his shins.

And so we come to the big bend of Walker, the western limit of what was once the Walker Naval Yard, to meet two men of similar age from the same part of Newcastle, whose lives have been shaped in one way or another by this stretch of river. One of them is a man called Bruce Shepherd, who with his brother Freddy operates a substantial and successful business along the next mile or so of river bank, and the other is my older brother, Chris, who once worked here. There's another riverine connection: like me, Chris once lived near the Ouseburn in Jesmond Vale, while Bruce was brought up lower down the stream on Byker Bank, going to school in that wacky building with a pagoda roof mentioned by Mike Mould. Later he worked in London for a fruit importer in Floral Hall at Covent Garden market ('We were serenaded

every day by the opera singers rehearsing'), while brother Freddy went to sea on a BP tanker at the same time as Chris joined Ellerman Lines as the lowest form of life in the engine room. But first came an apprenticeship in the yard that was once the eastern outpost of Armstrong's mighty empire but by 1959 owned by Vickers Armstrong. And here he is, returning to the site for the first time in many years, and despite the fact that the Naval Yard is now the Offshore Technology Park and it all looks very different, Chris soon gets his bearings. We stop by some new houses on Malaya Drive, the site of the yard's main gates, and he smiles at the memories drifting into his mind after 53 years:

'I used to come on my bike – there were thousands of bikes, very few cars, kept in sheds down there, none of them locked – for a 7.30 start. You were allowed to be late once a month. If you were late a second time you were sent home and docked half a day's wages. At 15 I got 26 shillings a week; at 16, £2; at 18, £3, 10 shillings. There was always overtime.

'I remember a couple of things about going-home time. Of course the gates were shut, but a crowd of men would gather behind them a few minutes before the hooter went. On odd occasions we'd be searched by the gatemen. The word soon spread through the queue and then all you could hear would be bits of metal hitting the ground. Men used to take orders for little things they'd make in the workshops. I remember making pokers. It was a kind of perk of the job, but a sacking offence if you were caught. People used to take home firewood too. Mind you, I heard the gatemen often tipped the wink about an upcoming inspection and everyone knew it was going to happen.

'After the gates opened, we'd all run up the hill to get away. When I started, I noticed these children standing to one side, begging for food. When I told Mam she made extra sandwiches I gave out at the end of every day. Strange that, isn't it? Like it was the Great Depression, but it was 1959.'

And the year of Conservative Prime Minister Harold Macmillan's great General Election boast: 'You've never had it so good.'

'First I went to apprentice school for four weeks, then I trained on the job for the next four years. I was put with a different journeyman every day, different men for different tasks, for instance a man who taught me about capstans and windlasses, a man for steering gear and so on. I must have worked with six or eight of them, and most had followed the same route as me, starting onshore and then going to sea where you really learned your trade. There was one journeyman I worked with, he was called the sketcher, and he'd make intricate drawings of nuts and bolts and other metal pieces which would be made up in one of the shops. He also drove the yard's launch, showing visitors around the Tyne.'

At the bottom of Malaya Drive, Chris points out where the joiner's shop, fitting shop, electricians' shop and general store once stood. As we clatter down metal steps towards the riverside, he points out the site of the tanks where steel was cleaned by pickling in acid, a place of terrible memory.

'A lad once fell into the pickling tank. His own father saw it happen and actually pushed him under with a pole. An act of mercy, I suppose.'

We pause for a moment in silence and move on, towards the great yellow 'hammerhead' crane that stills patrols the riverside. Christy needs a loo – often a problem on this walk – and goes to ask at the nearest security gate, but is denied, the gadgy telling her she'd have to go on an induction course first. Meanwhile the rest of us press our noses though a fence, looking at landmarks that are no longer actually there.

'The yard's slipways were to the east end of the yard, facing upstream and getting bigger as they went west, from small naval vessels to cargo ships and liners. When a ship was launched, the drag chains would be pulled with the ship and make this amazing noise and you'd see rats running for their lives. After the ship had gone into the water the wash would come surging up the slipway. One launch I do remember was a beautiful liner called the *Princess of Canada*. I got a ticket for my mother. I later sailed on the *City of Port Elizabeth* that had been built at this yard.'

We walk on. Chris laughs again. We've reached the site of the old black-smiths' shop, just by the test shop for ropes and shackles.

'I was once summoned by the foreman in there because I was going out with his niece and he wasn't very happy. I got a warning about my behaviour.'

He explains that each of these shops was a little empire with its own emperor – the head foreman. They usually had offices in the crane gantries running above the workshop where they could keep an eye on the workforce.

'If an apprentice got stroppy for some reason, the older men would have ways of dealing with it. I remember apprentices having their overall arms fixed into two vices and being left there as a punishment.'

'You tended to work on one ship at a time, so there was strong team-work and a good atmosphere – lots of practical jokes and laughs every day. But when you needed help you got it. I remember just here a man fell from scaffolding on to a steel post. The first aiders went to help, the post was cut and the lad went to hospital with it still in him, but he survived. I was amazed and was inspired to train as a first aider myself.'

We walk back towards Chris's car, where the yard office once stood ('Working men were never allowed in there!'), the pattern shop where wooden representations of ships were meticulously laid out to scale and the plate shop to which new steel was brought from Consett by train. The biggest ship built here in Chris's time was a 65,000-ton tanker, but he once enjoyed leaving the Tyne on another tanker for its sea trials off the Northumberland coast, where it ran a measured mile off Newbiggin while performing to spec. Shortly afterwards Chris left the Naval Yard and went to sea.

By his car, a kestrel hovers overhead and Chris reflects on what the Yard meant to him and his life: 'I loved working here – it gave me so many skills and good experiences.'

It's easy to see why. The technical training he received was obviously of a very high order, but that wasn't all. The apprenticeship system delivered lessons in life as well as engineering and the experience of working so closely in teams, in good times and bad, gave young men a solid, structured framework in which both to learn skills and to grow up. Looking at the young men of Walker today, one wonders what has taken its place. As it was, Chris was part of the last generation to benefit from it.

'The yard was always incredibly busy. I had absolutely no idea that it would all fold as quickly as it did. It happened so quickly.'

We look back at the kestrel and Chris drives away.

In a smart boardroom by the Tyne a hundred yards away, propped up on a model of riverside holdings at Walker stretching for two kilometres, there's an aerial photo of the Naval Yard taken in the late 1970s, not long before it closed for good. The slipways are empty, the site empty and desolate, but somewhere amid the ruins is the Portakabin where Freddy and Bruce Shepherd once had a rather less salubrious office. This was the beginning of the quiet Tyneside phenomenon that is Shepherd Offshore, to which my brother paid a characteristically quiet tribute as he left.

'But I must say it's nice to come back and see the old yard so busy in a different way.'

The Shepherd piece of Tyneside essentially consists of what were once two shipyards – the Naval Yard and the Neptune Yard, acquired in 1986 and 2008 respectively, with sundry pieces of real estate near and far. As we saw, there's very little remaining of the Naval Yard's former use, which has been gradually cleared and prepared for new enterprises, mostly in the offshore industry. Shepherd Offshore hugs a thin slice of the bank, to which around 250 vessels come every year to load equipment and supplies for rigs and facilities in the North Sea. The brothers started with just 15 employees, but now never employ fewer than 200; more to the point, the tenants of the site, including other offshore companies such as Wellstream, employ more than 2,000. Their neighbour, Duco, which every year makes 300 kilometres of steel, electrical and thermoplastic 'umbilicals' (tubing and hosing, basically), coiled around vast 350-ton reels, is about to embark on a £30 million expansion. The Neptune site is also undergoing major redevelopment, in the expectation that 2,000 people will soon work there too. In total, Shepherd Offshore and the other companies on the two sites are currently investing,

with help from the Government's Regional Growth Fund, £120 million in new infrastructure and manufacturing capacity. Unquestionably then, this stretch of the Tyne is, along with Nissan, an investment hotspot of north east England.

Clearly, the brothers have quite a story, but have rarely told it. Despite, or perhaps because of, their lengthy and sometimes controversial involvement in Newcastle United FC (for the best part of two decades they owned a significant chunk if it, while Freddy was chairman for some years, before the current owner, Mike Ashley, bought them out), they have maintained a low profile as far as their family business is concerned. Yet when I buttonhole him at the launch of the new Port of Tyne dredger *Sir Bobby Robson* and tell him about this book, Bruce instantly agrees to be interviewed. Entering his company boardroom without jacket, he offers a firm handshake and invites me to fire away.

I start with the family: I usually do. It turns out that Bruce's great-grandfather was a shipbreaker on the Ouseburn, but 'mind you, the ships can't have been very big then'. Freddy and Bruce were brought up in Wilkinson's Court on Byker Bank, the last working farm in the East End, where their father's haulage business was based. Their uncles ran the famous Tyneside scrap business nearby. After the post-war Labour government nationalised the haulage industry, the family moved to a Sydney suburb.

I ask when they came home. Bruce smiles.

'When the Tories de-nationalised it. My dad bought the business back.'

Just think – if the Conservatives hadn't won the 1951 General Election, the Shepherds would have grown up with an Oz accent and might have taken over a prominent Aussie Rules club.

'My brother went to Raby Street School – he was head boy – and I went to Ouseburn School. Our entire childhood was shaped by that little area. East Newcastle was very important to us – it still is.'

After leaving school, Bruce went to work for those fruit importers in Covent Garden ('7A Floral Hall!'); his customers included firms in Newcastle's Green Market. When I mention I once had a summer job there, he asks who I worked for. When I say I can't remember, he reels off a dozen names or more, only one of which I can remember: Dady's. Maybe I worked for them. But I'm impressed by my host's feat of memory: a man who doesn't miss much.

Spinning forward into the 1970s, Newcastle City Council compulsorily purchased the haulage yard of CH Shepherd and Son at 72 Byker Bank to make way for the Byker Wall – the family could maybe be forgiven for thinking the Labour Party had something against them – and the two brothers bought an old Whitbread brewery by the river at Walker and began working with oil companies starting to exploit the energy fields in the North

Sea, handling materials onshore and offshore. This remains the core of their business 40 years later.

'We didn't just work in the North Sea, we worked in the Middle East, we worked in Kazakhstan with British Gas. We worked with Americans, Dutch, Germans, Indians and Chinese, forging relationships, buying companies and then selling them, and over that time the Tyne has gone from shipbuilding to oil fabrication to subsea work. And we've been part of that.'

This may seem like an obvious business strategy, but oh, for the wisdom of hindsight! Even in the 1970s, there were many who questioned it, as Bruce remembers all too clearly.

'Years ago I went to the Port of Tyne's head office near the Central Station – it was there because all the top men lived in nice houses in the Tyne Valley – and the topmost man, a very nice chap, gave me coffee and a chocolate biscuit and asked me why on earth we were bothering with this offshore work? It would never amount to much, he said. In the nicest possible way, he kind of patted me on the head. Well, look where we are now! If only all those shipbuilders had got into offshore work rather than trying to compete with Koreans and Scandinavians in building ships, the Tyne might have had an easier time of it.'

Bruce Shepherd speaks crisply, without pauses. From time to time, he asks me questions: 'What do you think?' comes more than once. At first the tone seems challenging, aggressive even, then I realise, a) he seems genuinely curious to hear my opinion, and b) the apparent gruffness is a bit of a front. There's humour behind it, as well as strong feelings. At times, in our two hours together, he positively *twinkles*.

I digress…

As shipbuilding and other heavy industries declined, the Shepherds snapped up land, especially on the river itself. They bought the Wallsend shipway and the old Mercantile Dock at Jarrow; this is now leased as an aggregate depot. That wasn't all.

Propped up against a wall in the boardroom are two paintings of a building I recognise: the old La Sagesse school in Jesmond that the brothers bought a few years ago and plan to redevelop. They've already done that with the old garage on Osborne Road that's recently become a Waitrose store: I use it myself when I can get past the posh students at the champagne counter. Then there's the 5,000-acre Mitford estate on the River Wansbeck in Northumberland, with its centerpiece of the magnificent late Georgian hall designed by John Dobson in his pomp.

But let's go back to La Sagesse. Its development potential wasn't the only reason the Shepherd brothers became interested in it. This was also where Charles Mitchell, the man who founded the Naval Yard in 1852, chose to live. Evidently the man on the other side of the table has a keen sense of history

– and he acknowledges the fact with a smile.

'It's funny. Life's a circle, isn't it? The Mitchell connection is intriguing, but in the end we want that development and others to fund investment down here on the river. We've poured millions and millions into these two sites and that's going to continue, especially on the Neptune yard.

'Continuity. It's been going on for almost for 40 years now but we've stayed the same, especially in one way. This is a family business: we've turned down many, many offers to sell out. The reason we've done so is that we like what we do and also we want to serve the East End of Newcastle, which is where we come from. We want to employ people from round here – they're hardworking and good at what they do. People talk about the so-called loss of skills, but if you go to places like Aberdeen and Falmouth they're full of engineers and technicians from Tyneside. They'd love to be back here, they should be back here. Some companies might employ people from abroad but maybe that's because they're cheaper, not because they're better.'

Outside the late afternoon sun is shining. Bruce asks if I'd like to have a run around the Shepherd empire. We set off in a company Landrover and he shows off his pride and joy: the bigger of the two old Naval Yard cranes, 89 years old but recently upgraded to lift up to 300 tons – reels of umbilicals used offshore are getting bigger and bigger. On the quay are the *Fugro Saltire* and the *Seven Navica Subsea 7*, offshore supply vessels, the latter just leaving.

Then Bruce drives to the Wellstream car park, where he invites me to guess at its apparently hidden significance.

'It's full?' I suggest.

'Not just that. What else?'

'Erm…'

He grins.

'Nice cars. New cars. People here don't get paid Mickey Mouse money.'

Nearby are bases for a cluster of smaller businesses associated with off-shore – New Arc Equipment, Bewick Engineering – and one or two that aren't, including the Dodgy Clutch theatre company and Mullen's Bakery. We move east, off the Naval Yard site and onto the Neptune Energy Park. Here the Shepherds are preparing the ground for the expected growth of the renewables sector.

'Neither Labour nor the Coalition has really grasped the opportunities but there has to be a huge development in sustainable energy. Wind, wave, all these things will come and we'll be ready for them. I'm a great believer in UK plc, especially this bit of the UK.'

On the site where the Walker boneyard used to stink out the East End of the city, there are some remarkable and little known stories. A new plant is being built for Bridon Ropes, which has operated the ropeworks at Willington Quay (formerly the legendary Haggie's) for many years, but is now investing in a new plant making steel and wire ropes for use in the world's most challenging environments. Yet another new plant is being completed nearby, originally earmarked for use by Clipper Windpower, the Houston-based wind turbine manufacturer that put its Tyneside plans on hold in 2011, but now occupied by a company with much closer links to the Tyne. Soil Machine Dynamics has grown into the world's primary designer and manufacturer of remotely operated subsea vehicles and recently won two consecutive Queen's Awards for Innovation. Two hundred yards upstream is Pearson Engineering, an equally successful company that's become a world leader in de-mining equipment, winning contracts from the British Army and the US Marine Corps, doubling its turnover in the last financial year to £116 million, with profits of £31 million. Beyond their proximity and the fact that they're both specialist engineering companies, there are two other aspects of SMD and Pearson that tie them together: their products are essentially refinements of one of mankind's oldest and most humble of inventions – the plough; and they both owe a great deal to the ingenuity and flair of a man called Alan Reece.

Once upon a time, Dr Reece was an apprentice at Vickers-Armstrong's in Scotswood and then what used to be called a boffin, working at Newcastle University for 27 years in the Department of Agricultural Engineering as an innovative researcher and passionate teacher. His big idea lay in pioneering the application of soil mechanics principles to the design of earthmoving equipment. In the 1970s, the foundations for the global economy and information age were being laid, quite literally, in the form of undersea pipelines and telecoms cables. But as fast as they could be laid on the seabed they were damaged by trawler drag-nets. Extrapolating from his agricultural experience, Alan Reece designed a highly efficient undersea plough, slashing the cost of installing cables and pipelines safely below the seabed. Soil Machine Dynamics began life as a three-person operation, camping out in the front room of his house. In year one, turnover reached £100,000. In year two, it was £1.5 million. By then employing eight graduates from Newcastle University, the company went on to sustain an annual growth rate of 20 per cent, achieving an annual turnover of £60 million by the turn of the new millennium. Along the way, Dr Reece also took over and established Pearson Engineering as global leaders in the safe removal of land mines, most recently in Afghanistan, a destination for 2,000 anti-mine 'roller' vehicles manufactured by the Tyne and bought by the US Department of Defense. Though SMD is no longer under family control, it remains on Tyneside and retains its original ethos, and between them the two companies have a combined turnover of £250 million a year, employing 700 highly qualified staff. To date, more than £400 million worth of business has been brought

to Tyneside by Alan Reece's companies, demonstrating the following: how huge an asset our universities can be to the region, Tyneside can still cut it in the business of cutting-edge engineering, and finally, that immense benefits can flow from managing people fairly and in a collaborative spirit.

'I've always had confidence in our engineering, but I also wanted to get away from the poisonous 'Them and Us' ethos that I experienced at Vickers-Armstrong's as a very young man and which has done such damage to this country's industry. I'm semi-retired now, but I when I arrived at work in my modest Saab the first thing I did was change into my work clothes and get down on the floor. That's how it should be, but in my experience the managing directors of many companies are just never seen by their employees. We have always been literally hands-on.'

And here's another harmonious note.

My wife Susan is in a choir. During a break one evening, she learnt that a fellow singer worked at an engineering company that provided its staff with free breakfast and lunch, encouraging them to use the time and space to get to know each better, and address work issues in an informal and collective way. The company was SMD – and how different is their ethos to the rigid class structures of the old industrial titans, where the gaffers wore bowler hats and ate in the management canteen and the workers wore caps and ate their bait on the job. A quiet cheer then to Alan Reece, mountain-biker, alpinist and skier as well as engineer…

While we drive across the bustling site, Bruce Shepherd makes the point that before any of these exciting new ventures could begin, the groundwork had literally to be laid. Three of the Neptune yard's dry docks have been filled in with cleaned and graded soil, while the biggest, 200 metres long, has been refurbished as a facility for testing subsea equipment underwater. There's a helipad. The quays have been reinforced to become 'load-out pads' to take bigger and bigger pieces of kit. A new rail line is being built to move materials around the site.

We stop at the far end of the site, where a tunnel and rail line used to connect the Neptune Yard with Swan Hunter's next door: the perfect spot to draw a telling comparison between the developments upstream and the un-cleared site downstream.

'Now do you see? We've done it here, but it's hardly been started there. It's a huge job of work and costs a fortune, but it has to be done. We're funding the vast majority of the work, but nobody knows about it, or gives us much credit for it. Now why do you think that is?'

I suggest it's maybe because Shepherd Offshore is a private company, with

OPPOSITE
Regeneration at work: Neptune Yard being prepared for new industries.

no apparent need to promote itself. Bruce nods. I suspect the bad publicity surrounding the Shepherds' long association with Newcastle United may also have encouraged a bit of a siege mentality. The company will soon have to face the issue of dynastic succession that in the past sometimes made or sometimes broke many famous Tyneside companies. The brothers are nearing the end of their careers; some of their children are now working in the business. I hope it's a smooth transition. The East End of Newcastle needs Shepherd Offshore, and what they've brought to Walker.

Looking back upriver, another question occurs: what would the dismissive doubters of the 1970s have made of the importance of offshore energy to the river 40 years later? When I mention this, Bruce laughs and tells me that when the Port moved from their old offices in Bewick Street to Tyne Dock, the furniture and fittings were auctioned off. Freddy bought much of the specially made furniture while Bruce bought portraits of the whiskered Victorian commissioners that used to hang in the boardroom. They now decorate the dining room at Mitford Hall.

Suddenly my driver asks: 'Are you bored yet?'

I tell him I have a high boredom threshold and he pretends to be offended, before driving to a warehouse a mile away and handing me over to its guardian with the instruction to show me 'the corner'.

Tucked away behind materials bound for offshore is a rather wonderful collection of vehicles, both motor and horse-drawn: among many, a huge farm cart, Wells Fargo stagecoach, beautiful 1954 Bentley and a rare Ferrari (of which only eight were built). However what strikes – and touches – me most are a Mercedes 230CE Coupe driven in the 1980s by the brothers' mother Margaret and two Foden lorries, restored and repainted in the original livery, that once belonged to their father's haulage company, CH Shepherd, 72 Byker Bank, Newcastle.

Family and history are big words in Shepherd language, and Bruce touches on the latter to give me a chapter-closing quote.

'I love the history of the Tyne. I love the stories of the old merchant venturers, who used to trade right across Europe, and the Victorian giants who made their own world. The thing about history, if you understand where you've been it might be easier to work out where you're going and how to make things anew.'

I can't disagree. The words encapsulate one of the main impulses of this book.

⚓ AUTO DIESEL JOE AND THE TREE

No-one stared, some even believed,
when Joe brought the tree in
turned up the heating and breathed
on its little black bones,
hoping for buds in St Lawrence
by spring. He sang it songs,
warming its roots with milky tea
to see it through the frosts,
and when new shoots began to sprout
he missed the joke at first,
that all the buds had been stuck on
by workmates keen to soften
a tree as bald as the question:
when Joe retires, who'll take over?

Peter Hope grew up in Heaton in Newcastle. In the mid-60s
he and his father Harold sometimes went fishing with family
friends Trevor and Wendy Welch. He recalls their adventures.

I remember the early start and then the very long haul from the Ouseburn where the boat was kept out to fish off Tynemouth. Trevor Welch said he knew a good fishing area with a depression in the sea-bed where the fish congregated and which he could find by transit points on the shore. It seemed to work and we caught heaps of fish. I once won a fishing competition, although some of the others on the boat may have contributed to my catch. I won a multiplier fishing reel that I kept and used many times until I took it to the Med one year and left it on a Sunsail yacht. (I rang the skipper in Greece but he never sent it back). I thought it was a pity we caught so much since a lot of the beautiful cod and pollack went off because we couldn't eat it quickly enough or freeze it.

There could be quite a swell and I was sometimes seasick and would go and sleep in the boat cabin. Once I came on deck and we were motoring alongside a huge oil tanker anchored off Tynemouth. It was quite frightening being about 20 feet from such a huge cliff of brown steel, and past the enormous propeller, thankfully stationary.

The long trip back up the Tyne was tedious and cold and I would usually sleep again in the noisy, warm cabin that stank of diesel. The river itself was particularly foul with turds and condoms floating merrily down out to sea. We would eat our tea on plates that Trevor would then wash in the Tyne water. It doesn't bear thinking about, but I was so hungry after a day's fishing I just didn't. I don't remember any safety equipment either and the boat was rudimentary. It was a converted ship's lifeboat, apparently. The hull was made of aluminium and quite sturdy, but it was the only part of the boat that was.

On occasions Dad and I fished off the North Shields fish quay. All we caught were the most disgusting-looking small green fish (I don't think they were graced with a name) which always swallowed the hook completely and had to be cut up (still alive, of course – they were impossible to kill) to retrieve it, risking injury from its vicious spines or the hook itself. I remember my utter shame when Dad bought an expensive paternoster fishing trace (at that fabulous fishing shop in the Haymarket with a vast array of fishing rods and the sweetish smell of decomposing worms). I was so excited to start fishing that I attached the connector wrongly to the line (I can remember to this day the mistake I made) and when we cast it into the water the trace detached itself and sank into the Tyne. Our fishing trip lasted a grand total of two minutes. Neither Dad nor I needed to say anything to each other.

What was spectacular was going to the fish auction on the fish quay. The fish were huge and many were unrecognisably exotic. You would never have thought the North Sea could produce such fabulous fish. It was incongruous that such catches came from boats that were tiny, rusty heaps. One fishing boat had such a primitive single cylinder engine that you could hear it fire about once a second at tick-over – positively Victorian engineering.

I used to practice casting at Ravenswood school field but never managed to reach that magical 100 yards. I made my own weights by pouring molten lead (heated on the Calor Gas) into a spoon mould, with a loop of wire. They worked well and I managed to avoid disfiguring burns. Dad (no surprise) made a fine fishing reel from brown Formica but the bearings weren't quite good enough to cast sufficient distance. Dave Storey and I had had great fun casting though, fending off jibes about how we'd never catch anything on the school field.

The only time Dad and I went fishing off the rocks was with the Whitley Bay Fishing Club, and we felt rather inadequate when we saw the fantastic gear the other fisherman had. Our line got snarled upon the rocks and I dashed forward to retrieve it before being rugby tackled back to safety as an enormous wave nearly swept me to oblivion.

We never went again.

Peter Hope became an orthopaedic surgeon and now lives in Hitchin. He has fished in various parts of the world but hasn't yet experienced the renaissance of fishing in the Tyne.

DAY NINE

And the Tyne slides by
And the seagulls cry,
And the ships lie safe and silent
By the riverside...

The Tyne Slides By, Alex Glasgow

Day nine of our Tyne Walk is a slightly maddening and schizophrenic day: maddening, because the concentration of enterprises hugging the river bank makes it all but impossible to stroll by the water itself; schizophrenic, because it consists of two modes of transport – our own two feet and a motor car. The latter isn't a cheat, but an opportunity to acquire some tasty stories – tales of the riverbank, you might say, but not the kind featuring Toad, Rat and Moley.

To explain...

Every morning and evening of the walk, my three companions and I have been picked up and deposited elsewhere, courtesy of East Coast Taxis, by the estimable Brian, who has also kept us entertained with his own brand of storytelling. Everywhere we've been, Brian has chipped in with tales culled from a lifetime spent by the Tyne and 32 years of driving cabs along, under and over it. Tersely sardonic, bleakly humorous, Brian has often topped our own tales, and undercut any tendency towards sentimentality about the river and its people. I suppose most taxi drivers are realists, sometimes seeing mankind at its worst, but beyond Brian's 1,000-yard stare is a man with an obliging and helpful nature, married for 33 years to the same girl, an animal lover with the memory of an elephant...

So when we were on the Quayside, he added a tellingly rich detail to our memories of its Sunday morning market: an escapologist who used to tie himself in chains and then jump in the river, safely emerging a few tense minutes later to empty a hat full of coppers. On the now-empty and land-scaped Pottery Bank in Walker ('once the roughest street on Tyneside') he told us about its two lost pubs – the Raglan and the Ellison. When he first went into the former in the 1970s, 'There was an old woman with one tooth propping up the bar and a kid braying another with a snooker ball inside a sock. People were hard. More people were stabbed in in the Winc (the Wincomblee pub nearby) than anywhere else in Newcastle.'

But today, Brian comes into his own: we are entering his patch – Wallsend

PREVIOUS PAGES
Messing about on boats at Willington Gut marina.

OPPOSITE
Derelict Russian ice-breaker *Paadeberg* about to meet its maker – the scrap man.

303

and environs. So the observations from our ramble will be accompanied by his special brand of memories and reflections, many touching on the river and its communities, though he was actually born and brought up further north, in the then leafy lanes of Battle Hill.

'When I first knew it, Battle Hill was all farmland – it's full of houses now – and the Rising Sun pit was still working nearby. We lived on the other side of the Coast Road, which they were building then, six miles of road at £1 million a mile – I remember people saying it was the most expensive road in Britain. Our home was in Rose Hill, but it's called Howdon now.'

He takes us there. Newton Avenue is a little cul-de-sac of post-war council houses. A solitary mature tree is set in a broad pavement, but once there were seven, in a row.

'I once climbed one of them. I was holding a rope and a lad on the ground pulled it and I fell and fractured my skull. I was in hospital for a month.

'There was only one car in the street, it belonged to a school teacher. No one had phones, there was a callbox round the corner. As for us, it was tin bath, coal fires, the lot. Mam was bringing up five boys and two girls on her own so there wasn't much cash. Every so often she'd say, Brian, we need some coal and me and one of me brothers would push a pram to a rail siding near Rising Sun Pit where coal wagons would be lined up. We'd climb under a wagon, pull a lever and tons of coal would fall out, and we'd fill our pram high and push it home.'

This wasn't the only unofficial source of fuel: the man in the corner house at Newton Avenue was a pitman at Rising Sun who used to sell coal from his allowance for sixpence a bucket; a pramful could also be had from the gadgy at Howdon coke depot for a few shillings. The land was bountiful too.

'On Sunday mornings we'd take our dogs – we always had lurchers or whippets – up Battle Hill and catch rabbits or hares for our Sunday dinners, and dig up turnips or carrots from the fields to go with them.'

Brian carries on driving and we come to a place – the course of a stream, where a tip used to be. He and his mates would catch newts and frogs and pour tinfuls of water into holes in the tip. Rats would appear, thinking they were being flooded out, and the dogs would chase and kill them.

Brian entered the world of work early, for obvious reasons: working a milk round in his teens from 4.30 every morning until he went to school. By now Brian and his mates had discovered the rich playground that was the Tyne.

'We used to go to this scummy little beach on the river we called the Alamo. I'm not sure why, except that was the first film I ever saw. When I was 15 I took it into my head to swim across the Tyne – I suppose I just fancied it, I was a good swimmer – and I made it but hadn't reckoned on the current. It carried me two miles downstream and I had to walk back through the pedestrian tunnel in my shorts and bare feet. I got some looks but it was OK. We used to love riding our bikes dead fast through the tunnel.'

But we're getting ahead of ourselves, geographically. Brian will return…

Day nine begins where day eight ended, at a little lane between the Neptune Energy Park and the remains of Swan Hunter's shipyard. In the warm sunshine we make our way down to the spot where the mid-Tyne ferry used to dock at the Wallsend landing and Michael Caine once did his stuff with a shooter in *Get Carter*. Today the scene is more peaceful: cabbage whites fluttering near a stand of buddleia, sunlight dancing on the still water, blue skies counterpointed by the fading colour of the derelict Russian ice-breaker upstream. We linger for a few moments, then reluctantly leave the Tyne. At the top of the lane we stop by the boarded-up wreck of a pub inevitably called the Ship, its gardens returning to nature, colonised equally inevitably by ubiquitous buddleia. Brian later confirms that the pub had been closed two years earlier – hardly surprising, given that it's hard to imagine a place with less passing trade – though he adds a delightful story of when it catered for the workers of two flourishing yards, sometimes in surprising ways.

'There was a high fence between the pub and Swan's, but back in the day one of the yard's cranes often lifted about six blokes in a round bucket over it so they could have a few drinks before being lifted back. The gaffers turned a blind eye to it.'

BELOW
Roman wall, Wallsend.

We skirt around the Swan Hunter site, walking along the old riverside rail line, passing what's now the excavated Roman fort of Segedunum and its museum. The reconstructed white painted bathhouse seems rather surreal in this scene of post-industrial Tyneside, but once another Wallsend institution stood on this site. Simpson's Hotel had nothing to do with its swanky namesake in the Strand, but it did run to 300 rooms, catering mainly for sailors and other transient workers, testimony to the flourishing marine trade of the Tyne during most of the 20th century. By the 1970s Simpson's was catering for a different clientele. In 1981, not long before it closed for good, homeless men could secure bed and breakfast here for as little as £2.90 and a week's full board for the curiously exact sum of £22.96. (There was another Simpson's in Hebburn, known locally as 'the

house of broken hearts': the young Tom Kelly wondered about this name until he went inside one day and found it full of 'sad men sat alone'.) Legend has it that when Simpson's was finally demolished in the 1980s, stones from the Roman Wall were found among its foundations. We stop for a cup of tea in Segedunum's Chariot Café, once Swan's canteen, and I wonder what became of the men who once ate pies and peas here and the lonely men who lodged nearby. The fine house next door used to be the yard's drawing office, but today it's visiting schoolchildren, one sticking out his tongue, who are using pencils and rulers on big bits of paper. Making our way back to old rail line, we cross the bridge over the road running down to Swan's main gate, and stop to look; rather curiously, a young woman is pushing a rack of clothes towards the 60s building that once housed the yard's management. What can this mean?

A few weeks later I find out.

One of the very first things we observed on our Tyne Walk, as we waited to get the show on the road at the tip of South Shields pier, was a curious structure moving slowly toward us from the south west. Later in the day, as we passed the Customs House, it moved slowly upstream: a 50-metre super-structure welded onto a barge and pulled by a tug, one of eight 'topsides' and eight 'jackets' weighing 1,000 tons and more which saw long service in the Indefatigable oil-field in the southern North Sea and ended their lives on the Tyne. Over several months they were cut up and processed by 70 workers employed by the environmental services company Veolia, most of the disassembled metal being then taken to EMR's yard at Blaydon industrial estate – another spot on our journey – where 98 per cent of it was recycled.

Before the job is completed, Veolia hold an open day at the old Swan's yard. Two of the structures are still standing, one inscribed 'Shell/Esso 49/24-L'. About 30 people turn up to hear this worthwhile story, but it soon becomes clear that most, men of a certain age, have to come to take a look at their old workplace, not gaze at disused oil rigs. A few drift away to look through a fence at the last remaining slipway. I walk over to join them and hear their reflections. David Brown from Wallsend, now 77, served his time in the Merchant Navy and then worked at Swan's as a marine fitter. Indeed he worked on some of the last ships built here, including *HMS Northumberland,* and *RFA Fort George,* which, ironically, was broken up in 2011. David's mood is rather melancholic.

'I can't believe how empty it is. I've lots of relatives who worked here as well and I'm kind of upset thinking about how wonderful the ships were that we built here, the best in the world, and how it all came to an end.'

His words are heard by the other ex-Swan's men and a lively discussion begins among the workers about what was to blame for the demise of the yard and many like it. One man had no doubts: 'The workmanship was

OPPOSITE
Dead pub, Wallsend, where once customers arrived by crane.

tremendous but the management were hopeless. They didn't know what day of the week it was. Lions led by donkeys!' One of his ex-colleagues wasn't so sure: 'The unions were to blame too – all the stupid demarcation rules and negative attitudes to new methods. Maybe management and unions deserved each other.'

Curiously, Brian added his own insights into this issue, delivered with characteristic pungency, on his tour-de-force tour of Wallsend. After he went wandering around England, labouring on a farm, working on the line at the Vauxhall plant in Luton, where he lodged with a bagpipe champion ('We got free drinks everywhere we went, but I got sick of the noise'), he returned to Newcastle to work on the bins: 'The best job I ever had – every day you'd make enough from scrap and rags to go on the drink.' Then his wife's father got him a job at a marine engineering company where he was a gaffer. Brian worked in the foundry. Or maybe that should be 'worked'.

'I tell you, the hardest thing I ever did there was clock in. Nobody did any work. We kipped through most of the nightshift. They even had fold-up beds for the men to sleep on, but we always got up in time to have a shower before the dayshift came on. I tell you it's not surprising they closed it down and no wonder British industry went down the pan.'

The brief tour of the Swan's site over, the group of former workers and I head back to the main gate, passing a series of windows, numbered 1-14, where workers used to collect their wages. In a nearby office building, a set is being built for the ITV cop show, 'Vera; this is the series' shooting base, and the latest in a long line of productions brought here by an enterprising partnership between North Tyneside Council and Northern Film & Media, the region's screen agency. So they do still make things at Swan Hunter's, but with celluloid, costumes and actors. Inward investment of another kind…

We return to the old railway line, but soon that walk peters out and we are obliged to walk along Hadrian Road, a thoroughfare unlikely to have been walked in triumph by a Roman emperor receiving the tributes of a grateful people. Eventually we find a haven of peace, passing through the gap left by a demolished railway bridge. Somewhere near here, 'a lad' Brian knew climbed onto a similar bridge on a somewhat uncertain journey home from the pub and fell through its crumbling walkway to die on the tracks below. A happier fate has befallen the lucky residents of Railway Terrace, with its pleasing aspect of the Tyne, lovely front gardens and a strong sense of community. A woman drinking coffee and reading her paper on her doorstep confirms the first impressions: 'It's so secluded just here. Cut off from the world, but in a nice way. It has one of the best views you can find anywhere on the river, and it's like the 1940s, people look after each other and if anyone pops out they just leave their doors open. We look after each other.' A little further, in the delightfully named Point Pleasant,

is now self-sustaining. Less surprisingly, according to Ian Lightfoot, there is very little resale in the UK, due to the steady reduction in the capacity of British foundries and mills.

'We used to supply the Laconby mill on Teesside, but now that it's closed, the vast majority of the products of our yards in the region go abroad.'

The significance of this trend is obvious, and as the walkers stand watching another scrap carrier loading, and the Ijmuiden ferry *King's Seaways* slip its moorings, blow its horn and head for open sea, it's echoed by the watching Brian as he reflects on our journey around Wallsend – and his exquisitely vivid memories.

'You drive up and down the river and it's full of memories, but I've realised how many of the places I remember have gone. You don't notice it, but it's happening all the time. People say it's changed for the better, and maybe in some ways it has, but in a big way it hasn't. I mean, there are no jobs any more, are there?'

This is a common perception; we've heard it many times on our walk, and seen it disproven almost as often, especially in the last few days. But as all Tynesiders know, it also contains a significant element of truth. As we prepare for the very last day of our Tyne Walk, in my mind I'm trying to reconcile the jumble of impressions and work out what I really think about the biggest issue of our time by the water:

What is the future of the Tyne and its communities?

⚓ TROLLEYOLOGY

I've given my life to these contraptions
so hope to answer all your questions
on why the Second Elizabethans
revered trolleys, enough to offer them
into the water that used to flow
along this valley you still call *Tyne*. I know,
as transport, they seem quite primitive –
let's not forget the people were limited
by their dependence upon the wheel –
and yet, as artefacts, trolleys reveal
the brightest glimpse we have of ancestors
who persistently failed to register
more than a scrap of their thoughts on paper.
When we read *Tesco*, or *Happy Shopper*
carved in plastic, we know the ancient tribes
were saying a trolley signified
where they belonged: it lent them a voice.
To give up a trolley meant sacrifice,
and yet the people were driven to it
for reasons we've now intuited –
it seems the Inter-Industrial Lull
shook people's faith in the Gateshead Angel,
driving them back to their northern River
where they attempted to gain its favour.
By giving it objects they most valued,
each tribe was asking the Tyne to renew
its bounty. Because we know what came next,
we must proceed with the utmost respect
ensuring our excavations focus
on trolleys, rather than all that bogus
Road Cone Theory or *Beercanology*,
for trolleys wield the most authority

⚓ ON THE WATER IX

A view of the Tyne from the 1960s: *Black River*

She's all things to all men, the bonny hinny or a noble flood, a twisty-faced old drab or a pay packet that's never quite fat enough. If no longer that 'cursed horse pond' of Captain Phipps, or the universal provider of host-men and merchant adventurers, or the limpid stream known to generations of boozy singers and brawling keelmen, she still does us proud. Stuck in a traffic jam on the Swing Bridge or at the foot of Pilgrim Street, we never pause to think that she's at the bottom of it all. Without her we'd be lost; indeed we wouldn't be here.

Lining up on the Low and High Lights for a clean run into the crab's legs of her piers she is home at last; and it doesn't take small sailors only to know that the Prior's Haven and Shields' sands are gifts of the gods. At the same time, perched on a catwalk in freezing rain and jockeying so many yards of ship's belly into place, or morosely considering an empty order book, or despairingly looking for one bit of grace in the chewed-up battlegrounds between the yards, slipways and workshops, you wouldn't give a couple of megs – that's a Tyneside tuppence – for her.

But she can be a beauty, especially by night, all of the 18 miles from the Boundary Stone, where an infusion of Cross Fell porter and Cheviot peat buffs against a tide probing all the way up from Spar Hawk and the open sea. Being at the bottom of the Tyneside cellar she pours on, inexorably, like lava, molten glass, or black treacle, under a triumphal arch of light and reflected light. Sentinels mark her way: cooling towers and the standards of transmission lines, the big brick cone of Lemington glassworks, pubs with impossibly high flood markers, cokeworks, gasworks, Armstrongs and the long lurch of Scotswood Road, the Shot Tower, then a concourse of bridges, including the big bow of the New Tyne all radiant in floodlighting. Stumps of Norman teeth look down on her, and the lantern of St Nicholas is warm against the sky, softer than the blazing portholes of multi-storey flats and big ships awaiting a tide. Shields way, beyond the crackle of electric arc-welding, there are huddled villages of ships, tugs and trawlers. The lights sweep round, and mast lights move like fireflies intent on business, not fun. You can only judge from the wash what kind of ship passes by, collier or butter-boat, grain-ship or coaster; looking down from the Spanish Battery all you get is an impression of one kind of darkness cutting through two others of air and water.

She can also be a beauty in daylight, best of all on a rare summer's day when sky, cotton wool clouds, and smooth water shimmer together, and when ships, buildings and buoys grow identical twins below a waterline of outrageous Mediterranean blue. Ships endow her with a momentary splendour – for instance when the drag-chains settle in a cloud of red dust and a host of figures borrowed from a Lowry painting throw up their arms and yell themselves hoarse at the sight of busybody tugs slowly turning another one of her bairns in line with the channel. Or when a luxury liner decked out in white tropical sails over the bar with her nose in the air. But simpler things will achieve the result – one rowing boat alone in the wastes off Bill Point. Or the sun setting on a packed congress of shipping at Shields. Or a pack of seagulls going up with a clatter as the Swing Bridge begins to turn on its axis, directed by a man in a glass conning-tower – facing upstream the Swing Bridge looks like a ship, the water cutting away from a bow that's anchored in Pons Ælii and maybe three other bridges. At these times you feel that there's something in being a son of the Tyne.

But beware sentimentality, the curse of this river. The noble old dame has a questionable past. For Ptolemy she simply didn't exist, or wasn't worth a stroke of the stylus. And with what name the Tigris boatmen cursed her as they ferried provisions to troops building some kind of Wall or other is open to conjecture. It was only when Bede was sent back to his native Jarrow (really Monkton, but we can stretch a point) that the old dame was christened, churched and named in the one great book to come out of County Durham. Then she became the moat behind the Marches; then another army marched in (or came as human ballast in the collier boats); and literature and learning gave precedence to millstone and grindstone (a friend of mine once saw a Kenton grindstone in the middle of Russia), salt, iron and ships, glass, coal and chemicals.

They couldn't help making a mess of it (we can) but those chewed-up bits of Sandgate, St Anthony's, Friar's Goose, Felling Shore, Wallsend (where miners dug the first tunnel under the Tyne), Hebburn, Percy Main and Chirton are enough to make a point: it must have been beautiful once, it could be beautiful again. The river needs not only landscape planners but men with green fingers. And noses. It would be grand to see children bathing bare-pelted, in tributaries where salmon and sea trout run once again.

This is not all. To see the river you have to foot it, and to see it is to realise how a great port has been strangled for want of good roads. The ground on both side falls steeply, sometimes near precipitously, ideal for the wagon-ways that ran down to the staithes with coal for the keels plying down to the colliers at the bar – sometimes as many as 500 hand of sail. Then the problem was to get coal out and nobody was bothered much about stuff coming in. The legacy can be seen in a criss-cross of moderate roads – the steep, cobbled outlets from the quays must have killed many a good horse, and a good lot of trade. The ferries are splendid (and one is splendidly free of charges) but too far apart and too slow, while the post-war foot tunnel at Howden amounts to little more than a toy, especially when you look at the steep escalators and the tiny echoing passage, then remember that this is the age of the car.

So the new bridges and the new big tunnel can't come too quickly. They will truly marry the two shores, but it's a pity the nuptials had to come so late in the day, especially in a region that grows miners and bridge builders like apples on the tree. What will she look like when all these plans have matured? As different again. We have discovered at last that even a black river can be coaxed into being something incomparably better. This one could be the wonder of the world.

Black River by Sid Chaplin
Written for the opening of the original Tyne Tunnel, 1968

DAY TEN

⚓ FRIDAY 29 JULY

On the last morning of our walk – sunny and bright, as it's been most of the way – we meet just downstream of Northumbrian Quay and the departure point for the nightly Ijmuiden ferry. For this final stroll – just a few miles to the tip of Tynemouth pier – we are joined, as we were on the first day, by Port of Tyne chief executive Andrew Moffat. As we wait for a final straggler to arrive (no names – after all, she does have to come all the way from Hexham), Andrew tells us of the growing popularity of the Tyne for cruise liners, which usually dock a few yards from where we're standing, an ideal jumping-off point for visitors to explore Northumberland and Durham. Perhaps the most exotic visitor of recent times, the month before our walk in fact, was a curious vessel called *The World*, at 644 feet, the largest privately owned yacht on the planet, divided into 165 private and extremely luxurious apartments. Since its launch in 2002, *The World* has continuously circumnavigated the globe, allowing its 'Residents' to wake up in an exotic new destination every few days. But I'm equally tickled by the annual pre-Christmas visits of the ferry *Norröna* from the Faroe Islands, most of whose population, it seems, fall on Tyneside's shops intent on taking most of their stock back to the North Atlantic. Chocolate is apparently an especially popular purchase.

As it happens, there are no liners present this morning, only a rusting Dutch trawler, the *Hanny*, being given a raucous welcoming fanfare by three juvenile common terns. Having reached full complement, we take a look at Royal Quay marina and note that besides numerous tied-up yachts and dinghies, there's another working-boat visitor, the lobster boat *Amadeus* of Folkestone. The interesting bell tower is a survivor of the marina's previous incarnation as the Albert Edward Dock, built in the 1880s around the out-flow of the Coble Dene primarily to service the coal trade. I fancy a cuppa in the floating bar/restaurant, the *Earl of Zetland*, which ferried crofters (and no doubt sometimes their sheep) around the islands of Orkney for 35 years, but there is no one about.

PREVIOUS PAGES
Beached buoy, overlooking mouth of Tyne at North Shields.

327

On the way down the Coast Road earlier, our esteemed chauffeur Brian remembered a story from pre-marina days when he dropped off a passenger here one night. The decidedly dozy old chap lived in an equally ancient fishing boat.

'He was more than a bit pissed and didn't notice that the tide was out, so he just stepped off the quay and fell 15 feet onto the deck of his boat. I ran to help – I thought he must have broken something, but he just picked himself and his bottles up and went below as if nothing had happened.'

We cross the marina's preserved lock gates and wander downstream past some hopeful fishermen to some forbiddingly high fencing and beyond, a vast site populated only by a few men in hard hats and high-visibility jackets. But there's no tedious detour this morning: I make a call and we are shepherded to the other side of the fence – and what was once the vast Smith's Dock…

The eponymous Smith, Thomas of that ilk, first went into the ship-building business in 1810, taking over William Rowe's shipyard at St Peter's, and then moved downstream to this site in 1851. One of the first ships to be launched at the yard was the *Termagent* in 1852. The company became linked with South Bank on the Tees after opening a shipbuilding yard there in 1907, with the North Shields Yard being used mainly for repair work, oil tankers in particular. The company headquarters remained on the Tyne. Well, I suppose it would, wouldn't it? In the 1930s it was the company's boast that Smith's was the largest ship repair yard in the world; indeed, they were often so busy they hired space in other yards.

One of the most memorable episodes in the Smith's story occurred during World War II, when the yard armed and converted many trawlers requisitioned by the Admiralty for the Royal Naval Patrol Service, including Her Majesty's Trawler *Amethyst*, and more notably, *HMT Arab*, in which Lieutenant Richard Stannard of Blyth won the Victoria Cross for exceptional bravery and endeavour in enduring 31 separate air attacks at Namsos in Norway in May 1940, and putting out a fire on a jetty later used to evacuate British troops. Smith's Dock was also famous for preparing the design of the Flower-class corvette, an anti-submarine convoy escort of World War II celebrated in one of my boyhood favourite reads, Nicholas Monsarrat's novel *The Cruel Sea*. (The film with Jack Hawkins is worth a look too; we watched it again recently – an absolute belter…)

A generation later in 1968, Smiths chalked up another shipping milestone, building the *Manchester Challenge*, the first British-built and -owned container ship, but much of its subsequent history, as the river's overcapacity in building and repair became ever more clear, represented a slow and inexorable death. Despite a merger with Swan Hunter, it finally closed in the 1990s.

As we saw a few days before, a vital pre-requisite for finding new uses for these abandoned yards is their clearance and levelling. The morning we arrive, this four-year process is evidently nearly complete, courtesy of the engineering company with a strong Tyneside track record (Volker Stevin also worked on the Millennium Bridge): the 30-acre site has been landscaped, roads put in place, two docks have been filled in, though three remain, one wet, for amenity purposes (basically the nice view), and two for car parks on top of which flats will be placed. The plan is for 800 new homes to be built by the developers Places For People on this gentle curve of the river with a fine view out to the piers.

As we stroll down to the water, there's a slightly autumnal edge to the wind. 'It's like that all year,' comments local resident Charles, cheerful as ever. By one of the empty docks, we chat to a workman, who's carrying, but apparently not using, a hammer. We note a row of dead rusting bollards on the bottom; someone has painted 'Smithy 07' on the side. He says they should have filled it with water and filled it with trout. When they emptied it, he says, they hoped to find a few salmon at the bottom, but all that was left were eels. He laughs. 'Story of my bloody life!' A seagull flies overhead making a sound like Tommy Cooper's laugh.

Leaving Smith's Dock we came across the last dead pub of the walk (I got to about 20 at the end of the first week and stopped counting): the evocatively named Crane House. Some of Tyneside's oldest inns stand along this shore, happily most of them still open, though thankfully not the bull-baiting ring that once drew bloodthirsty crowds. A ferry is just arriving,

mostly disgorging women whose full shopping bags suggest they've been buying at South Shields' popular Friday market. Further on is the Porthole pub, traditional sailors' haunt, and the porched entrance to one of Tyneside's most famous nightspots: La Continentale, AKA for reasons best left to the imagination, 'the Jungle'. One of the legends about this place is that the girls touting for custom here had the prices chalked on the soles of their high heels. In the car that morning, Brian stated definitively that they didn't. When asked how, he stated gnomically that he knew because he knew. More innocently, Brian remembered watching a BBC crew filming scenes for *When the Boat Comes In* on the dizzyingly steep Borough Bank; I was probably standing next to him. That morning he told another story: of driving two young lads with shopping bags to the spot on the Fish Quay where a rusting, holed hulk was moored. They told him they were being paid a tiny sum to deliver it to the Thames, despite having no marine experience and only the briefest of navigational directions: turn right outside the piers and keep going till you hit the Thames. It is not recorded what became of them. The Jungle also crops up in a legendary ferrymen's tale, about a well-cut drinker leaving his favourite watering hole to catch the last ferry to South Shields, only to find it leaving the quay. He took a run at a jump, but stopped himself, then tried again – and landed in the drink. Happily he survived, though was fined later for causing a public nuisance. I suppose you could say he had two bites at the ferry...

The fine Georgian block that once provided a bolt-hole for the Jungle's customers, as well as a sailors' home and customs house, is now divided into flats, and very nice they look too. This is a familiar story along the rest of the quarter-mile amble to the Fish Quay: residential taking over from marine and industrial. Rather pompous 80s flats descend the steep bank to the riverside, where they enjoy a water feature with a difference: the remains of a little dry dock used for many years by Tyne trawlers and light-ships, known locally as 'the Haddock Shop'. We pass the blue Cosalt tower (they supply marine safety equipment) topped by Tom Young's palatial pigeon cree (he sold his family sail-making business on condition he could keep his beloved birds there), with a quick visit to the Port's control room overlooking the river (Christy is especially intrigued), and find the Fish Quay also in the throes of change. At first glance nothing has changed: the fishing boat *Frem* is tied up on the public quay, plastered with Newcastle United stickers, and half a dozen boats along the Fish Quay itself; the Fishermen's Mission remains open, and the legendary marine grocer William Wilson continues to have humorous messages whitewashed on its windows. Today's text reads, 'Don't feel ripped off – everyone is.'

But there is change nonetheless: North Shields may be Britain's premier prawn port, but its days as a base for deep-water boats seem to be over. It's only seven years since the death of the Fish Quay's chronicler Tom Hadaway – he came to work here at 14 and eventually became a successful merchant before starting to write plays and films – but no doubt he'd be surprised at what's happened since. Then again, Tom had already seen many changes on the Quay in his lifetime; indeed he wrote about them to powerful effect, as when he described his pal 'Muts', a fish filleter: 'He could boast it took six polis's to bang him up, and he had the bruises to show, but a machine arrived that could cut fish faster than ten men, and this giant of a man was undermined.' This story inspired an early play, *The Filleting Machine*, mounted by Live Theatre and put on screen by Amber Films. In 1989 Amber also made a feature film of Tom's story *In Fading Light,* which recorded the lives of a group of Shields fishermen before, during and after a trip. For the filming Amber actually bought and manned the 63-feet anchor seine netter *The Sally* and during it the late Sammy Johnson was almost washed overboard by a big wave during shooting and was saved only by the quick reactions of fellow actor Dave Hill. It's rather an amazing shot: you wonder, how on earth did they do that?

IMPORTANT NOTICE

DOG AND WIFE MISSING

REWARD FOR THE DOG
See Staff for Details.

HOMEMADE SOUP
AND
BUN £1·60·

TEA, COFFEE AND HOT CHOCOLATE
To Take Away·
DON'T FEEL RIPPED OFF
EVERYONE IS!!

SAVALOY SARNIES
WITH ALL THE TRIMMINGS

WINNERS OF THE
BEST BACON BUTTIES
IN THE NORTH EAST·
2010

DO NOT FEED
STAFF·

OLD TRAWLER
COOK'S CHAIR
SIT ON IT
FOR GOOD LUCK
ALL DONATION'S
GO TO CHARITY

FRESH
COOKED
BACON
BUTTYS

NORTH SHIELDS
FISH QUAY
CRAB
SANDWICHES
MADE FROM FRESH
CRAB MEAT PRODUCED
ON NORTH SHIELDS
FISH QUAY

BEST H
FRESH
SCONES·
TE
BEST H
HOT CHO
H
HOT SOU

There are significant compensations to the current big changes sweeping the Quay, in the form of a regeneration scheme by North Tyneside Council and other partners, including the Port, which has spent £6 million strengthening and restoring the public quay and dredging its waters (not surprisingly, they came up with lots of net). I suppose the focus is gradually shifting from fishermen landing and selling fish to visitors eating fish and drinking beer. This isn't a criticism, by the way, more a statement of fact: I happen to do both, often at North Shields, as I do this Friday lunchtime in the Low Lights Tavern, the area's oldest and cosiest pub, in the company of local resident and entrepreneur 'Bertie' Forster.

'They reckon this place has been serving ale for about 400 years, but dealing in fish has been going on here for twice that long. But it's always been as much about outsiders coming in as much as fishermen going out to sea, and that's what we're seeing now.'

We've met Bertie before in these pages: brought up in South Shields, he was the son of a tug captain and dock-master at Tyne Dock. But like many of his generation, he struck out on his own, very different course. Much to his dad's bemusement, he became an auctioneer. This comes as no surprise: his dress is that of a dandy and he's a born story-teller.

'I've done all kinds. I worked for years in the auction business and then at Beamish Museum acquiring and cataloguing artefacts. I lived in Capheaton for a while and once set up a tearoom in the village hall. Then in 1999 I saw an ad in the *Journal* for a café on the Fish Quay. It had been a greasy spoon but I emptied all my junk into it and ran it as a 1920s tearoom. I called it 'Berteas'. I wasn't supposed to live in it, but I did, quietly. I did off-the-wall things – we put on some of Tom Hadaway's plays, for instance. It was good while it lasted but the problem was that the trade died in the late afternoon. Not any more. The Quay's developed a mixed economy of restaurants and bars and with the history of the place, its sense of community and the atmosphere of the fishing boats, it's become very attractive to visitors by day and by night. Just look at my old place – now Sambucca's restaurant – it's always packed.'

Bertie still lives on the Quay, above his old teashop.

'It has a great view of the river. What more could a chap ask for? I know it's changed a lot, but what can you do? Change comes but you can't resist it. You just have to adapt to it.'

⚓

OPPOSITE
High Light and Fish Quay,
North Shields.

We move on. Andrew points out the spot where as a boy he used to fish for whiting off a reel with his dad, and then pass another Low Light – not the pub, but the white tower that masters of sailing ships used to align with its

334

taller sister, the High Light, to guarantee safe entrance into the river. (Turner once drew it, perhaps while he was planning his wonderfully atmospheric watercolour *Shields, on The River Tyne.*) There are fine old buildings everywhere we look, most happily under restoration, including the remains of Clifford's Fort, built in the 17th century to guard against Dutch naval incursions. A more recent structure commands the hillside above us to the north: Knott's Flats, built in 1938. James Knott was the classic local-boy-made-good, a shipping clerk from Howdon who built up the Prince Line, the third biggest merchant fleet in the world with ships mostly built on the Tyne and Wear. But after two of his sons were killed in the Great War, he sold his ships and set up a charitable trust that remains vigorously active in the region to this day. Among our group, opinion is divided as to the architectural merit of Knott's Flats; I personally think it belongs to the Soviet brutalist school, but I have always admired its clock, and all those balconies. The father of a friend of mine, a retired seaman, used to spend his days on one of them, in all weathers, watching the ships come and go, listening to their chatter on his shortwave radio. One curious fact about the place: it was picked by the Nazi High Command to be a regional HQ once the formality of their invasion had been completed.

Standing on the charming little beach below Clifford's Fort, Charles takes photographs of waves breaking over the rocks, and seals, of the Black Middens, Christy goes looking for sea-glass and I ponder the place where another watcher used to perch: the wooden pier, mostly broken down now, from which the Tyne's shipping movements were observed and then despatched to Lloyd's of London. One misty night long ago, the watcher was observing his lonely vigil when he heard, but did not see, a Swedish sailing vessel approach.

'Who goes there?' he hailed.

'An-na!'

'I said, who goes there?'

'An-na!'

'What is the name of your bloody ship?'

'An-na!'

'Listen man, I kna' ye kna' but I need to kna' an' all!'

So far as I can make out, this is the only known joke about the Lloyd's lookout pier at North Shields. It seems appropriate that it was told me by a man with Swedish antecedents, who also knows how his forebears pronounced the name 'Anna'.

On the riverside path to the Spanish Battery, the Memorial to Northumberland's own Admiral Collingworld looms over us, precisely aligned in the direction of the site of the Battle of Trafalgar, where Collingwood assumed command of the British fleet from the dying Nelson, ensuring the greatest naval victory in the nation's history. A couple on swish bikes pass us and stop 100 yards ahead, at the official end of the 140-mile C-2-C route from Cumbria. Paul and Jo ask us to take their picture, their smiles as wide as the river.

As we crest the rise of the Battery and see the finish line on the end of Tynemouth pier, Andrew and I are ambushed by a Radio Newcastle reporter with his tiny recorder, plying us with questions. He kicks off with:

'What have been the highlights of the walk?'

Curiously, it turns out we're about to have one of the very best.

As we march along the pier, waves are just beginning to spray over the top of the seawall. Plovers are perched along the lower wall. A yacht is nudging between the piers. I take my life in my hands and peer north towards Blyth. It might sound strange, but somewhere out there is an area of sea that could provide a new, sustainable and jaw-droppingly significant source of energy for Britain, as well as a powerful engine for economic growth on the Tyne. It may seem as if the midday sun has suddenly got to me, but bear with me…

At the heart of it is the acronym UCG-CCS: Underground Coal Gasification – Carbon Capture and Storage, and it was explained to me by someone we first met on the walk in Hebburn, local boy and mining engineer Paul Younger, now pro-vice chancellor at Newcastle University.

'Actually, the UCG bit isn't new: it was first proposed here in the North East by Sir William Ramsay in 1913, but early experiments were left incomplete when World War I broke out. Lenin championed the technology and it was developed at industrial scale in the Soviet Union, but it was never going to be economic in a capitalist economy as long as conventional fossil fuels were cheap and abundant. But the price of petrol is on an inexorable upward trend, oil's getting less abundant and in a few decades it'll be so scarce, it'll be a luxury for the few. And that won't just be an issue for road transport, but for plastics and other synthetics on which our world now relies. In the meantime, 75 per cent of the coal in the North East and in most other coalfields is still in place underground. But what if we can convert this into fuel without further damaging the atmosphere in the process?'

This is the tantalising big idea. UCG now seems economically viable, not just because of the rising price of oil, but also the phenomenal recent advances in directional drilling and chemical engineering. As coal is turned into gas far underground – basically, by injecting oxygen and steam through one set of bore holes and extracting the resulting valuable gas from another set, UCG offers a cleaner source of coal-derived gas than the surface alternatives, as the 'nasty' residues like tars and ash all remain safely locked away hundreds of metres below ground. Here's where the CCS comes in: the CO2 arising from using this valuable gas will return into the deep underground voids created by this new mining, where it can remain till kingdom come, safely out of reach of the atmosphere.

'We've done the sums on all this, and it stacks up. For the last two years we've been putting together the technical and business model for a venture called Five-Quarter, named after a seam that lies under my house! We hope to break ground within a year or two – and the jobs created will be safe, clean and hi-tech, more like operating a chemical plant than a traditional coalmine.'

To test this process, Five-Quarter are currently seeking an investment of some £5 million. To go into production will cost barely more than ten times that – comparative chickenfeed. Yet the benefits are potentially immense: within the 400 square miles of the company's comparatively small first licence from the Coal Authority is an energy source equivalent to 75 per cent of the natural gas extracted from the North Sea since the 1970s. The benefits for the Tyne and its communities flowing from this industry of the future are considerable – as a port of supply – though it seems likely that access to these seams wouldn't be made at sea, but on land, a much cheaper alternative. It may not be the so-called 'golden bullet' that many have yearned for since the death of the monolithic heavy-industrial employers of the past. In that sense the world has moved on: by and large modern industrial processes require far fewer 'workers' and a small number of 'technicians'. Along with wind energy, UCG has the potential to bring huge benefits to the region – possibly even jobs in the tens of thousands – and the rest of the country. Five-Quarter's first licence to mine off the Northumberland coast could result in the gasification of two *billion* tons of coal. These figures are beginning to impress the politicians: Newcastle Central MP Chi Onwurah recently led a Parliamentary debate on clean coal and received cross-party support. UCG-CCS is perhaps an idea whose time has come. As the old North East miner's slogan puts it: 'The past we inherit, the future we build.'

Our guide for the last leg of the journey along the Tynemouth pier is watchman Dave Appleby. By a curious coincidence, his colleague Mel Powles, who saw us off from the South Shields pier, spends most of his time here too. He's worked for the Port since 2006, but is a boilermaker by trade. It turns out that he served his time at Smith's Dock and his grandad spent his working life on Tyne tugs and ferries. We pass four timbers standing clear of the pier – the remains of a ferry landing that once serviced excursion boats from Newcastle – and Mel waxes lyrical:

'I feel privileged. I love the job and being with the public. I especially love just walking along the pier and watching the boats go in and out. I've got to know the pilots and the trawler lads and the ferries and they all give me a wave. I once took a man up the lighthouse and he said, I've lived here all my life and now I can die happy – I always wanted to come up here!'

By now we've reached the vinegar-bottle shape of the lighthouse. Our friends from the Port have erected bunting and a finish line. As we cross it, the champagne corks are popped and a Tyne Tees cameraman films the toast, while a reporter from the Whitley Bay *News Guardian* scoops up our quotes. Everyone's happy – who could not be? Yet I'm reminded that sometimes people visit this place on rather sadder occasions. Mel regularly guides family groups who come to scatter the ashes of a loved one.

'Last Sunday eight people came from Doncaster to scatter the ashes of their mother at her request. They all say how beautiful these little ceremonies are and I have to agree, though I leave them to their private moments.'

I've come across this phenomenon before, meeting various people who've done the same thing, and one or two who've written touchingly about it. Most recently, I had such a conversation in my local paper shop with Gail, who runs it with her husband, Brian. She had chosen the river for her father's remains; not a special request, she just knew it was right. Quite unprompted, she then added simply: 'The Tyne, it's coming home, isn't it?'

Now for the special treat: Dave Appleby unlocks the lighthouse's many locks and we step inside. It turns out that he's a former lighthouse keeper himself, working on 32 lighthouses in all, including Lundy, Alderney and Sark before ending his days at North Foreland. Indeed, when he was based at nearby Souter, he visited this lighthouse in 1967. Two men tended but did not live in it at that time and inside the rooms at the lighthouse base there are signs of their occupation – an ancient fold-down bed, and in a creaking cupboard, ancient timesheets, a pamphlet entitled *How To Use Your Belling Cooker* and a paperback novel by Hal Debrett appositely titled *A Lonely Way to Die*.

We then climb exactly 100 steps to inspect the light itself, weighing five tons and floating on a quarter-inch bed of mercury, made by 'Barbier Bernard & Turenne, Constructeurs, 32 Rue Curial, Paris'. One or two chips are pointed out in the glass, courtesy of Luftwaffe gunners in World War II.

Finally we climb out through a hatched door onto a circular walkway. We find ourselves standing on the most easterly piece of Tyneside, on the very edge of England. We can see four other lighthouses – the Herd Groyne, South Shields pier, St Mary's Island and Souter; the wind turbines at Blyth and the Lynemouth smelters. Dave says on the clearest days he can see Coquet Island, the top of Cheviot, Hartlepool and occasionally even Whitby. There's a ship on the horizon, heading north. Below us, young guillemots are

paddling frantically in the water, calling out to their mother, a cormorant flies low over the water and a pair of terns hover and dive vertically into the sea: how strange and wonderful to be looking down on flying birds!

This is without doubt one of the most amazing views I've ever had. I look at my walking companions and they're all grinning at the sensory joy of it. I suppose I'm doing the same. It's good to be alive at such a time and in such a place.

Then I feel moved when I find myself thinking of other people and other times. It's impossible to stand on this spot and not think of all of the ships, and the men and women who built and worked them, to have passed this way over the last 2,000 years. Many were built on the river and sailed away to make their journeys and meet their destinies across the oceans and seas of the world. Many are recorded and remembered in books, the excellent websites devoted to the ships of the Tyne and the memories of those who once sailed in them or their descendants. Most are now forgotten, but of course a few are legendary, and have been remembered in various ways in this book. I think of some of them now: *Turbinia*, *HMS Kelly*, *Esso Northumbria*, the *Mauretania*, the *City of Port Elizabeth* – and the people who sailed in them, the lads who did the donkey work on the *Mauretania*, for instance – its firemen and trimmers.

In 1911 the writer Arnold Bennett was taken into the bowels of an Atlantic liner similar to the legendary ships of the Tyne. He was taken down steel ladders, past ramparts of machinery, jets of steam and the moving chain of

the steering gear, to the roaring red jaws of the ship's 190 furnaces. Here he watched the firemen and trimmers labouring to feed them. Stokers spaded coal from bunkers into barrows that the trimmers hurried to the furnaces, running at full tilt. They dared not slow down for they knew their mates were immediately behind them with more heavy barrows. They dodged blistering steam pipes and furnace casings, swerving dangerously as the vessel rolled or pitched. The firemen then spent seven minutes shoveling this coal into the scorching furnaces, seven minutes clearing white-hot clinkers with long slicers and another seven raking over the ashes. After 21 minutes they would rest and recuperate briefly until the remorseless cycle began again, for two shifts a day of four hours each. The men wore grey flannel singlets, which they would repeatedly wring out, their sweat instantly evaporating on the hot metal floor, and a sweat-rag around their necks, clenching it in their mouths to stop the urge to gulp down water, which caused severe and disabling cramps. Few of these men, lean as poplars, ate while they were at work – food was slopped down a 'swill chute' – but preferred to wait for the main meal of the day: usually something called 'oodle' – long-simmered beef with onions and carrots, sometimes spiced with titbits of fancier fare, no longer deemed presentable to passengers, from the so-called Black Pan. The men slept in dormitories holding 68 in two-tier bunks, trying to recover from the swirling coal dust, the sulphur fumes and the endless, killing nature of their work, dreaming of a temporary respite at the next port, where of course they got blind drunk. Above them meanwhile, as Bennett remarked, first-class passengers soared in lifts and confectioners delicately sculpted petits-fours.

Then I try to personify what I've read about the mariners of the Tyne and my memory settles on one name: Albert Edward Edwards, born in South Shields in 1900, a merchant seaman who made a total of 57 voyages around the world, ranging from a few days to months. His first voyage started on 27 June 1918 on the *Florentia*, boarding at South Shields and heading for Marseilles with a cargo of coal and two ships' boilers. It only lasted for two days: the ship was sunk by a U-boat torpedo two miles off Robin Hood Bay and three sailors were drowned when a lifeboat capsized. Albert's very last voyage was in World War II, beginning in South Shields on 10 February 1942. He boarded the *Empire Howard*, on its way to Russia via Iceland as part of Arctic Convoy PQ14. Heavily laden with tanks and trucks for the Soviet Army, the ship was torpedoed on 16 April 1942 and broke up and sank within 60 seconds. There was no time to launch lifeboats. Some 38 crew survived in the water, somewhat protected by oil released from the ruptured fuel tanks. Suddenly from out of the mist came the anti-subma-rine trawler *Northern Wave,* firing depth charges in an effort to trap the attackers. Only those at some distance lived to tell their story, the remainder dying instantly of internal injuries or broken necks. A naval history suggests that of all the epic sagas of the Russian convoys, this was the saddest. Only nine of the *Empire Howard*'s 54-strong survived; Albert Edward wasn't among them. He died aged 42, leaving a widow and two daughters back home in Shields. Like many sailors, he had never learned to swim.

Perhaps I ought finally to tell a story of another ship with a happier ending, and here's a riddle to go with it. See if you can solve it!

What ship left the Tyne after completion and never got wet?

While you're chewing it over, here's a literary clue. One of the many foreign engineers who came to the Tyne in the 19th and 20th centuries to learn about building ships was a Russian called Yevgeny Zamyatin. While he was here in the late 1910s and early 1920s, he planned and wrote a classic futuristic novel called *We*, based on his difficult experiences of his country's recent Bolshevik Revolution and the dystopian hell that was life in the middle-class suburb of Jesmond. And the ships whose construction he helped to supervise were… icebreakers.

So was the ship in my riddle: the *SS Baikal*, built at Armstrong Whitworth's Walker yard in the 1890s for the Manchurian section of the Trans-Siberian Railway, on which it carried trains across Lake Baikal, ice-bound for five months of the year. Thus the ship had to be simultaneously ferry and ice-breaker. This was just the start: the 4,500 ton ship had to be transported to the landlocked lake across the Baltic by sea and then 5,000 miles of Russian steppe by rail and barge. This entailed building the ship, then disassembling it, packing it into 7,200 crates of varying sizes. A detail I love: since the ship was a mirror-image of itself, the stem being exactly the same as the stern, they were painted in different colours to aid reass-embly. Black and white, of course. The presiding genius of this operation was a young engineer called Andrew Douie. It took four years of his life, mostly taken up by transporting the ship's components from the Tyne to Lake Baikal. He faced many problems, among them the pulling of barges up the fast-flowing rapids of the River Angara by teams of men and horses; the sight that beheld him where he arrived at the shore of Baikal and found that against his orders, all of the crates had been opened, their rusting contents sinking into the mud in a confused jumble; their eventual reass-embly slowed by bouts of epic drunkenness among the local workforce of Tartars, and the bad blood between them and better-paid craftsmen from

St Petersburg, which as he notes drily in his account of the project, 'caused a good deal of bad feeling resulting in occasional bloodshed and murder'. But eventually the *Baikal* was launched into service and the estimable Mr Douie came home, though sadly his ship was destroyed in the Civil War following the Russian Revolution of 1917. The moral, I suppose, is that a Geordie can always be relied upon to get the job done, even when it seems impossible. It's this inspiring thought about the quality and potential of the people among whom I live that lingers on my mind as I take a last look up the River Tyne and then climb back down the lighthouse at its mouth. We are done.

As we make our way back along the pier, the breaking waves have got higher and bigger. Dodging them is like a game of Russian roulette, but somehow it doesn't seem to matter that we get wet. Along the way we make a final discovery, standing back as Mel tells us the very last story of our journey. He points to a tiny gap in the stonework of the pier wall. Here the daughter of a builder was allowed to place a tiny doll's head. A kind of good luck charm, I suppose – and one taken at what you might call face value ever since. It's rather touching to notice that the combination of sea air and thousands of tiny fingers have erased much of the dolls' faces, though you can still just trace their rather ghostly features…

So we climb again to the top of the Spanish Battery, somehow reluctant to leave this matchless scene, and treat ourselves to an ice cream as we watch the DFDS ferry leave, many of its passengers leaning on the stern rails, basking in the late afternoon sun as they wave at the steadily disappearing Tyneside.

We get in Brian's cab and drive home.

You wear a shirt that's clean as light
and pilot this bank of machines,
to capture the Arctic storm in a graph
or summon Captain Sienkiewicz
on his slog through radio waves.
You throw him answers, marker buoy bright

but never look at the view or point
because you're in the business of knowing
everything out there's happened already:
in your mind's eye, that man
who's leaving the law courts now will jump
in the river, more likely than not;

the boatload of thugs and copper wire
will not be getting away with it;
Isolda's departed from Panama City,
soon to find out she'll have to wait
for the Tyne to deepen itself
enough to contain her berth.

You try to bear with the present,
place a little red frame round the date
and nudge it along each morning,
cover your desk with fragile cups
to remind you of the rest of us:
the tourists in your high office

who'll never know how N'8 = X
or how to move a whole bridge,
or just how much those years at sea
could make you long for land, your children,
the reason you moor your moods in the neap
and always address the uncertain as *Sir*.

AFTER

⚓ AFTER

It's been almost a year since my friends and I finished our walk up and down the tidal Tyne but its memories still sing inside us and, hopefully, in these pages too. We asked many questions on the journey, but some of the people we interrogated asked one question back: what have you learned on your journey?

It is a query that deserves an answer, but before I try, there's a bit of catching up to be done. If, as former Prime Minister Harold Wilson famously said, a week is a long time in politics, then a year in the life of a port is much more than a sequence of 730 high tides. Quite a lot has been going on down by the water, as you're about to discover...

At Fred Crowell's Aladdin's Cave of a boatyard in South Shields, the former Seaham Harbour lifeboat *George Elmy* is still on the stocks, but its restoration is nearing completion and it's due to be handed over in August 2012. 'It's got more extras than *Ben Hur*,' calls Fred cheerily down the phone, but he seems quietly happy with the job. His order book is full too, with new jobs on other wooden vessels, including retired fishing boats, pending. 'In fact I'm turning work away, so no plans to retire yet.'

Just upriver at the Customs House, director Ray Spencer is coping manfully with a cut in its Arts Council funding that led to 14 redundancies in April 2012, but remains optimistic in difficult times. 'We're just carrying on, but with a renewed determination to make the future as exciting and ambitious as we can.' In one respect, the future will be different: after the coming Christmas production of *Dick Whittington*, the venue's brilliant pantos will no longer feature the legendary partnership of 'Tommy and Dotty' (Ray himself as the former, and Bob Stott the latter). Bob, a management consultant with a difference, is hanging up his sparkly frocks for good. Oh no, he isn't, I hear you shout...

The window at which Ray works looks out over what was the Middle Dock, where his father worked for many years, and beyond, the yard where for some years McNulty Offshore had constructed and repaired modules for use in various of the North's energy fields. In February 2012 the company went into administration with the loss of 100 jobs. The cause was predictable: 'tightening global trading conditions'. A few months later there was a more positive development, as the ten-acre site was bought by the Port of Tyne, whose Tyne Dock base is immediately upstream. The purchase will allow McNulty's administrators to complete the company's existing contracts, maintaining around 60 jobs, and holds out the prospect of other

OPPOSITE
Tynemouth cliffs.

351

firms using the site for similar work, as well as signaling the continued growth of the Port's business and land holdings; its river frontage at Tyne Dock now extends to a kilometre.

Nestling by the water at Tyne Dock is the headquarters of Ford Aerospace, a business thoroughly rooted in Shields and apparently going from strength to strength. 'Things are going well, very well,' purrs Geoff Ford, 'but we can't be complacent. We're making a big push for export orders from the so-called BRIC emerging economies. In fact we've just won our first contract from Brazil and while conditions are challenging, they're very interesting.'

Geoff's landlord, the Port of Tyne, is sounding similarly positive notes in bucking the general economic climate. In fact, 2011 was a record-breaking year for the Port, by any measure: a 116 per cent increase in total tonnage of cargoes handled; a 30 per cent increase in turnover; a 130 per cent increase in profit after tax. This reflects growth across virtually all of the Port's activities, but in particular in the import of coal for the Drax power stations and the export of Nissan cars. Being a trust port, and therefore a public asset with no shareholders to whom to pay dividends, profits are invested back into the port's facilities. The figures for 2011, for instance, reflect previous investment in a new facility to handle wood-pellet fuel and the dredging of the river channel to even deeper levels, thus enabling 83 per cent of the world's bulk carrier fleet to use the Tyne. Even better, the auguries for 2012 seem just as positive.

Meanwhile at Jarrow, users of the Tyne Pedestrian and Cyclist Tunnel are getting used to a long climb. The last remaining working escalator broke down after our visit and is unlikely to be restored to full working order. A problem with the drive sprocket of the 'up escalator' at the Grade II-listed tunnel, which links Jarrow and Howdon in North Tyneside, had led to it being turned off for safety reasons. The last remaining working wooden escalators in the world are unlikely to be switched back on, though the vertical lifts are still in operation, though not half as much fun.

A&P, which operates the last major ship repair yard on the river, is managing to weather difficult market conditions. In May 2012 it was announced that the company was bringing the activities of its two North East yards, on the Tyne and Tees, into a single unit to create 'the necessary focus, flexibility and competitive cost base to meet existing and emerging market requirements'. It remains to be seen what exactly this will mean for the Hebburn yard.

On the west side of the Newcastle-Gateshead bridges, the most obvious change is to the skyline, caused by the gradual disappearance of the so-called Dunston Rocket. I can't honestly say that a nation mourns, or the sum of human happiness has been increased by the tower blocks of the 1960s, but at least this one had more character than most.

Sadder developments on the north side of the Tyne at Scotswood: in June 2012, BAE Systems announced the closure of the last survivor of the once-mighty Armstrong industrial mammoth with the loss of 330 jobs at the end of 2013, bringing an end to arms manufacturing in Newcastle's West End after 165 years. Once, warships, huge guns and tanks were made here but latterly the plant has specialised in Terrier engineering vehicles, deployed in the building of trenches and barriers, but demand for them has declined along with cuts in defence spending in the UK and the USA.

A little further up the Scotswood Road, a company with equally deep roots on the banks of the Tyne is surviving the downturn with rather more success. For a company making road surfaces, Jobling Purser might have struggled during the mild winter of 2011-12, but compensated for this and cuts in local authority spending by selling more abroad. Its managing director Tim Jobling-Purser sounds as chipper as ever. Hardly surprising, I suppose, for a man who runs a business from Paradise Yard...

On Newcastle's Quayside a pontoon has been put in place where visiting yachts can moor, so a new generation of sailors can enjoy the area's cultural offerings. A little way downstream, the piles that channeled boats under the highest section of the walkway on the Millennium Bridge have been removed, thus de-cluttering the visual impact of this breathtaking structure. Less welcome perhaps for the seals I've often seen hanging about here, taking advantage of the narrowed gap through which the river's salmon and sea trout had to pass. Yet as we've heard, there are plenty of fish in the Tyne. A little further down, the vast Spiller's Mill has disappeared and the Port of Tyne has sold the land to a housing association for development and the crew of the *Clearwater* will have to find somewhere else to dump the detritus they pluck from the river.

The striking growth we saw along the river in Walker at the Offshore Technology Park and the Neptune Energy Park continues with help from the Government's Regional Growth Fund, but essentially driven by newish companies mostly operating at the cutting edge of technology in the energy business. Duco are pressing ahead with a new £30 million plant to manufacture steel tubing for the North Sea and two flourishing companies in the same sector – SMD and Bridon – are moving into new factories nearby. This stretch of the river is proving a powerful engine of economic development.

The two men behind Shepherd Offshore, the catalyst behind this turn-around, have acquired another landmark property in the North East. The building once housing the old Museum of Science and Engineering in Newcastle's Exhibition Park (which generations of boys visited to operate the wondrous models of Tyne-built ships now in the Discovery Museum) has been bought by Bruce and Freddy Shepherd to house their collection of historic vehicles, including the Foden lorries used by their father in his haulage business.

One of the most striking contrasts of the journey was evident standing at the waterfront on the border between Newcastle and North Tyneside. Looking upstream was a kilometre of new factories, restored and busy quays, vehicles on the move, ships moored, men in hard hats and high visibility jackets: the future. Looking downstream there was what was once the mighty Swan Hunter shipyard, a barren terrain of cracked concrete, rusting metal, empty buildings and empty docks: the past.

But there are signs this may soon begin to change. The owner of the site, North Tyneside Council, is looking for a partner to help regenerate the yard as a hub of green energy and has applied for cash from the European Regional Development Fund for infrastructure work. As the land is designated as an enterprise zone, it will benefit from business rate relief, but the new units must be occupied by March 2015 for tenants to benefit. Everyone concerned will therefore need to get a shift on…

Meanwhile, costume racks will continue to be pushed around the former shipyard for at least another year: ITV has commissioned a third series of the detective series *Vera*, based on the novels of local author Ann Cleeves.

Just downstream, the rumours we heard of new work coming to the Hadrian Yard of Offshore Group Newcastle were confirmed in April 2012. With the help of a £600,000 grant from the Government's Regional Growth Fund, the company is embarking on a new venture to build steel jacketed foundations for offshore wind farms, which may create 1000 new jobs. Work should start on a prototype late in 2012.

Before we leave the Regional Growth Fund, it's worth recording that its predecessor in channeling public sector investment to regional projects in industry, media, tourism and other areas, the development agency One North East, whose HQ we passed by the river in Newburn, ceased to exist in June 2012, having been abolished by the Coalition Government. During its ten-year history, ONE invested a total of £2.7 billion. The Regional Growth Fund is currently evaluating 72 new bids from the North East to a total value of just over £350 million.

Not content with acquiring the McNulty's site at Tyne Dock, the Port of Tyne has also acquired two other riverside sites on the north shore, near the entrance to the Tyne Tunnel. Meanwhile the Port's chair for the last seven years, Sir Ian Wrigglesworth, who we met at Bill Quay to chew over issues of economic development, is stepping down, with his deputy Sir Les Elton to replace him. Continuing with the theme of departures, Professor Paul Younger, product of the Hebburn shore, hydrologist, mining engineer, folk singer and 'Tyne Tippler', is leaving Newcastle to take up a new post at the University of Glasgow. Many people up and down the Tyne, including this writer, will be sorry to see him go for reasons both professional and personal, but Paul is retaining many important links with home, especially his involvement with Five-Quarter, the new company pressing ahead with plans for the safe and sustainable development of the vast coal reserves lying under the North Sea off the Northumberland coast. It would be richly ironic, in a very good way, if the mineral that first stimulated the growth of Tyneside could be harnessed once again to power a second industrial revolution. This may sound like a pipedream – and how many false dawns have there been in the region in the last 50 years? – but I have a hunch it just might, providing it gets the political and financial support it deserves.

So we return again, metaphorically, to the end of the Tynemouth pier on that sunny Friday afternoon in July 2011, where the four Tyne walkers were asked that ticklish question: 'What have you learnt?'

Many things…

One of the first was to follow your instincts, and your nose, leave the path or the road and explore alleys and lanes, and knock on doors, even if they aren't open. The very first time I did this – walking along an unpromising cul-de-sac near the water in South Shields – we struck gold, in the form of Fred Crowell's boatbuilding shed. This was an object lesson, and we learnt it. Our motto became: be nosey, in a nice way.

When we did, what we experienced in every single instance except one (which will remain nameless) was a warm welcome and open house, teas and biscuits and on several memorable occasions, home-made cakes. More importantly, our hosts and the people we more or less bumped into gave of themselves, their attitudes, feelings and even more striking, their stories. These have enriched and, it might even be said, made this book, giving it a sense of real and sometimes difficult lives, in which problems are settled or at least eased by cooperation, friendship and humour. Sometimes in such conversations, the people we met would say something so surprising or profound, the listener would be brought up short. A relevant quote:

'I'm continually fascinated, obsessed, appalled, amazed and delighted by the infinite variety of human beings, especially by their capacity for courage, nobility and compassion… and if you think they are shallow, just talk to any ordinary Joe and find out just how deep an ordinary Joe can be.'

Spot on. I ended the walk with even more respect, admiration and affection for the people among whom I live, my fellow Tynesiders.

Back to that quote. When I started writing this book, I never expected to refer so much to, or in that latter case quote from, a person who died precisely 25 years earlier: my father, the pitman-turned-novelist and essayist

Sid Chaplin. I should have known better, for during the course of his 29 years living in Newcastle, Sid wrote a great deal about the Tyne and its communities, in the form of two fine novels and countless essays and pieces of journalism, which remain as fresh and vital as ever. When I was a boy, and later as a returning adult, we often walked by the river and I learnt much from him about its history and life. Fifty years later, on this rather longer walk, there were many times when it struck me how much my dad would have savoured that sight, or laughed at what that person said. I can never pass the Baltic without remembering the time a few months before his death when I took pleasure in showing *him* something – the kittiwakes which had recently taken up residence in the derelict old mill built for storing grain for the region's population of pit ponies. After our parents die, I suppose we all spend the rest of our lives looking for them in one way or another. Thus, though it wasn't intentional, our Tyne Walk partly became, to quote the title of John Mortimer's own family memoir, a voyage around my father.

A word more about the people of Tyne. Before we set out I had some understanding of the particular histories of some riverside communities, and how many had grown as a result of inward migration. What I hadn't appreciated was the scale of it: the Shetlanders and Yemenis of South Shields, the Irish settlers Charles Mark Palmer attracted to the booming Jarrow of the late 19th century, the hordes of Aberdonians Andrew Leslie brought with him to Hebburn. Time and again on our walk we met people whose family stories began in another place, mostly Scotland, Ireland and other parts of England, but sometimes much further afield. For these people and their descendants, Tyneside was a place of possibility and sometimes refuge, as in the moving story of Drag Milton who, after the horrors of war-torn Serbia, rebuilt his life in the little Tyneside village of Clara Vale. Others represent an amalgam of these movements, among them Paul Younger, whose parentage connects both ends of the Celtic fringe. Being a Chaplin – Durham miners but originally Suffolk farm labourers – I shouldn't have been surprised at the idea that modern Tyneside is almost as much of a melting pot as downtown Chicago, but I was. As a consequence of this history, our roots in this place are often shallow in terms of time, but consequently rather deeper in strength.

One of the other things we learned on the walk was easier to spot: marine and industrial use of the Tyne and its banks is now concentrated on a much shorter stretch than used to be the case: basically, from the piers to Hebburn on the south shore, and Walker on the north. This is partly the result of the ever-growing size of modern ships, which means that berthing facilities must be available at deeply-dredged quays in the final three miles of the river's passage to the sea – with growing hotspots of development at Walker and Tyne Dock – and the gradual retrenchment in traditional heavy engineering, especially above the Walker bend. Of course there are flourishing enterprises beyond this point – International Paint in Felling, for instance, and Jobling Purser in Scotswood – but they are welcome exceptions to the rule. Indeed on day four of the walk, from the Tyne Bridge to the point at which the Team enters the Tyne, we encountered almost no industry at all. There is of course an obvious upside to this: in many places the river banks are returning to nature, and quickly, as can be seen most graphically in the woods of Bill Quay, and it was a delight to us all to witness the richness of wildlife, especially wading birds and the more rarely seen but increasingly ubiquitous salmon. So let us glory in a cleaner river – and the idea that its shores in Newcastle and Gateshead are primarily now for Tynesiders to enjoy and increasing numbers of visitors to discover: a leisure experience, and also, in various places, a residential experience. After all, we all hanker after a room with a view. There is no environment more enduringly fascinating than moving water – how many people did we spot just gazing silently at the river?

It's interesting to speculate why this might be. My own pet theory: we all have an instinctive understanding of the importance of rivers to the very means of life; as the central mechanism of the 'hydrological cycle' by which rainwater falling on the hills is carried back to sea, where it evaporates into clouds which bring that water back to us again. But this summer of 2012, with yet another cloudburst lashing the windows a few yards from where I write, isn't perhaps the best time to rhapsodise about rivers and rain…

Everywhere we went on our walk, it seemed, we were confronted by a question whose answer proved elusive. Sometimes we asked this question, sometimes the people we met asked it of us. It became a recurring theme; if you like, the elephant in the room, if such a metaphor is applicable to a walk. Sometimes it was asked in sorrow, or bemusement, or even anger. The question was this: what happened to the Tyne's once-great industries in shipbuilding and heavy engineering? Various people offered us conflicting opinions: that management failure was to blame, specifically to invest in modern technology; alternatively, the unions were at fault, in their apparent resistance to new working methods. Others suggested the two sides shared responsibility for what was a stunning collapse, more or less within a generation – a plague on both their houses. But the more I listened and read, the more it struck me that many of these views lacked something – a bit of historical context. So, in all humility, here it is…

Just as Tyne shipbuilding expired quickly, it grew almost as rapidly. In the first half of the 19th century, 330,000 tons of shipping was built on the river, in the form of 2,700 vessels. Between 1850 and 1900, output exploded, reaching about 5,200,000 tons, and at least 7,800 much bigger ships. This included many warships, which became the speciality of such yards as

Armstrong Mitchell and Palmers. In 1893, the UK had 81.7 per cent of the world shipbuilding market, and of that the region's three rivers built half: the Tyne, Wear and Tees shared a staggering 40 per cent of the world market. Yet the seed of eventual decline had already been planted: in 1906 the battleship *Kashima* was launched on the Tyne, the last of a series of warships built by the company established by William Armstrong in Elswick. In future the ships of the Japanese Navy would be built in Japan.

Despite this, the impact of two world wars and a prolonged depression, the Tyne yards built some 7,600,000 tons during the first half of the 20th century. By 1950 British shipbuilders still accounted for 40 per cent of the world market, and the Tyne, Wear and Tees shared roughly half, building 22 per cent of the new vessels on the seas of the world.

But 40 years later, by 1993, within the working life of a riveter or caulker, there was no shipbuilding capacity whatsoever on the three rivers.

This postwar period actually began well, with full order books; in the 20 years to 1964 the North East built 45 per cent of the total UK merchant tonnage launched, but this masked another downward trend: the number of people employed in the yards on the three rivers fell by half in more or less the same period, from 130,000 to 65,000. The writing on the wall became harder to ignore.

The principal cause was obvious: foreign competition. In the 25 years from 1956 to 1981, nine countries joined Britain in reaching an annual output of at least a million tons: Germany and Japan in 1956, Sweden 1964, France 1971, Spain 1972, Norway 1973, Italy 1974, USA 1975 and South Korea in 1981. From 1968, Japan's output equalled that of the rest of the world combined. Orders stopped flowing like a high tide – they had to be fought for, even or especially at home, for another important feature of this postwar period was the failure of the British merchant marine to expand in the same way as the rest of the world. From being more than 12 per cent of the world's tonnage in 1966, it fell to less than 4 per cent by 1984. A thriving shipbuilding – and ship-repair – industry depends on the base of a strong national merchant fleet, but as we heard from Fred Newman and others on our walk, by the 1980s, seemingly in the blink of an eye, that was no longer the position in Britain.

In the light of growing foreign competition in the postwar period, there was obviously a growing emphasis on cost, but here too Tyne shipbuilders faced problems. One of these stemmed from Britain's pioneering role in the industry, and the ironic penalty of having won World War II. Foreign competitors built yards from scratch, using the latest and most efficient technology and processes, building ships, for instance in dry docks rather than on slipways, but on the Tyne it was not possible to switch to these more efficient layouts because of the restricted space occupied by the yards.

At Swan Hunter's Neptune yard, the awkward triangular shape of a long established site, for instance, meant that plating and fabrication sheds could not be placed at the head of berths, so they had to be positioned less effectively at the side.

Beyond these problems, it does seem to be the case that yard managements were reluctant to spend on new technology. The consensus of expert opinion suggests that there was some investment after the war but it was limited. If you watch, as I did, Amber's marvellous film *Launch*, made in 1973, one of its abiding impressions is of antiquated and worn-out machinery, symbolised by the ancient lighter pottering around the vast structure of the super-tanker *World Unicorn*. When foreign competition and market contractions really bit later in that decade, the fault lines in the industry began to show. In the past, yard bosses had exploited the separation of trades and the market system of hiring labour, arbitrarily reducing rates for particular trades and laying off workers when work dried up for a particular trade, which would not have been the case if the trade structure had been more flexible. Now though, the trade unions were blamed for the ills of the industry, with endless bad press about demarcation disputes. The truth was that it was fear of unemployment and a justifiable mistrust of managements, based on bitter past experience, that drove these disputes. In the end both sides seemed unable to find common ground – to change – and paid the penalty. As that wise man Benjamin Franklin once remarked: 'If we don't hang together, by Heavens we shall hang separately.'

There is a reason why I have – forgive me – written at such length about this issue and tried to offer a short but historically accurate and non-partisan perspective. It often struck me on the walk that many of the people we met had been deeply affected by the collapse in the river's traditional industries. Part of this is genuine bemusement – how on earth did it happen? – and part lasting hurt. This is obviously understandable for those who lost their jobs as a result, but there is also what mealy-mouthed generals term collateral damage: in my view, the process inflicted a much wider and equally heavy blow on collective confidence and local self-esteem, one reason perhaps why so many people assert that the river is 'finished' when it so patently isn't. Now that 20 years have passed since the last shipbuilding yard passed into history, maybe it's time at last to shrug off the communal trauma of the past: the shipyards and engineering giants have gone and aren't coming back, for reasons some of which were inevitable and others that weren't. Let's learn the lessons of the latter, and move on…

But move on to what?

Often during our walk I asked people we met what they thought about the future of the river. Sometimes the answers were pessimistic, most damningly when former Hebburn shipyard worker Ron French spoke five blunt words: 'Ferry trips, that's basically it.'

And here's another pessimist: Alan Reece, despite his part in establishing two of the Tyne's most successful companies, feels that the future in manufacturing of the UK, never mind the North East, is in doubt. He is scathing about politicians of all parties who he feels have sleepwalked through the gradual withering of the UK's industrial base, failing time and again to support it when they should have done. When I pointed out the recent statement of Prime Minister David Cameron that the British economy needed to be 'rebalanced' to support industrial innovation and become less dependent on the financial sector, Dr Reece's withering look provided eloquent enough answer, but he added, 'We're about to reach the point of no return with manufacturing. I hope our lords and masters wake up and start taking decisive action.' Also, I can't help but observe, that word 'rebalanced' makes a fundamental shift in the policies of successive governments sound easier than it surely is, and belittles the underlying truth that within my lifetime the British economy has tilted alarmingly away from manufacturing industry, with serious implications for us all. As Chris Mullin said in his last speech to the House of Commons before retiring as the Labour MP for Sunderland South in March 2010: 'I continue to doubt that there is a long-term future for an economy based on shopping.' Or banking, he might have added…

So after ten days by the water, whose camp am I joining? The pessimists like Ron French and Alan French, or the optimists like Ian Wrigglesworth and Bruce Shepherd? At the outset I feared the opposite, but I saw and heard plenty on our Tyne Walk, meeting as I did outstanding people with big ideas, to give me some confidence about the prospects of the river and its trading and industrial roles, particularly in existing and new energy fields – oil and gas, wind and wave, even coal, in both imported and exported form. I suppose you could say the Tyne made me believe again.

I call in further evidence the words of someone else I met on the walk, at the TEDCO Business Park on the Jarrow-Hebburn border. Actually, I'd seen Bob Stott before, on the stage of the Customs House in South Shields, giving his legendary annual panto performance as 'Dame Dotty'. Mr Stott is equally impressive in another guise, as a well-travelled and perpetually busy consultant in organisational change. In 2011 we began an email correspondence in which Bob offered sharp analysis of how and why he thought the region's political and industrial structures had failed in the past. I can't pretend to have understood everything in those emails, but its essence can be boiled down to just nine words: failure to recognise reality, and then act upon it. As I was approaching the end of this book, I wrote to Bob and asked him to send me a few more words, encapsulating his view of the Tyne's future. His reply came from Singapore, where with rich irony he is advising its port on a development strategy:

'The river will provide new ways of thinking, forestalling the problems caused by the old. It promises us a new vision and an economy driven by the production of new ideas, a creative networked community, and a strategy that will turn the challenges created by complex global trends into competitive advantage. Its strategy will grip the imagination; exciting things will happen as it leverages collaboration, creativity, collective intelligence and momentum, as it reinvigorates a sense of community and continuity.

'The river has no alternative, for we live in a complex, volatile and uncertain world, but by embracing complexity, the river will open up new opportunities and make decisions that benefit multiple stakeholders. The river will galvanise our future, a future described over a quarter of a century ago by the American physicist Heinz Pagels in his prediction, "The nations and people that master complexity will be the economic, political and cultural superpowers of the next century."'

If this is indeed what awaits us all, I'd like to be a part of it. It chimes with me, for this reason: at the start of our Tyne Walk, there were two things I *felt* to be true, for me and all the other Tynesiders, 782,000 of us; at the end of it, I *knew* them to be true: the Tyne is our past; more importantly, it is our future.

⚓ ACKNOWLEDGEMENTS

This book would not have been possible without the sterling and generous support and encouragement of the Port of Tyne. I would like to thank all members of its staff for their unstinting help, but wish to record my particular gratitude to the following:

Sir Les Elton, Chairman
Phil Lynch, Port Surveyor
Andrew Moffat, Chief Executive
Mike Nicholson, Harbour Master
Brian Reeve, Chief Technical Officer
Sir Ian Wrigglesworth, Chairman 2005-12

Susan Wear, Director of Corporate Affairs, and the following members of her staff – Lisa Donohoe, Lisa Liddell, Gillian Scott and the estimable Robert Fuller – who kept us on the road, and fed. I should also like to thank former Port employee Margaret Brooks for her invaluable help in deciphering and transcribing page after page of notes scribbled on the journey.

I would also like to thank New Writing North, its chief executive Claire Malcolm in particular, for guiding this slightly madcap adventure towards publication with their customary warm encouragement and expertise.

All of the contributors owe a debt to the book's designer, David McClure, who has sensitively wrought unity from its disparate elements, and copy editor John Adair for his diligence as well as sympathy with the subject matter.

I also wish to thank three greatly knowledgeable Tynesiders who took on the considerable burden of reading the manuscript and then offering vital corrections and helpful suggestions: the aforementioned Susan Wear, the writer and poet Tom Kelly, and Ian Whitehead, keeper of maritime history at Newcastle's Discovery Museum. I also thank Ian for his help in guiding me through the rise and fall of shipbuilding on the Tyne. My gratitude also to Dave Waller for his invaluable help in telling the fascinating story of the Tyne's tugs.

However, I should make it clear that any remaining errors of fact or interpretation rest solely with this writer.

It almost goes without saying, but nevertheless should be stated, that our biggest thanks go to the Tynesiders we encountered during and after our walk, who gave freely of their time, expertise, stories and memories. They are too numerous to list here, but they are of course named in the book and we thank them all for embracing the spirit of this book. On part of the walk we welcomed guest strollers who offered their own experiences (and often bought the beers), for which thanks to Charles Bowden, Jake Campbell and Andrew Moffat. I would also like to offer the thanks of all of the walkers to East Coast Taxis, and Paul Irwin in particular, for generously carrying us from point to point along the Tyne. I would like to acknowledge the help of staff at Newcastle's Central Library and the Lit and Phil in accessing printed material about the Tyne, and the use of information from the following books:

Time and Tide, A Celebration of the River Tyne, edited by David Archer
Maling and Other Tyneside Pottery, by RC Bell
Pictures of Tyneside, by JW Carmichael, edited by S Middlebrook
The Day of the Sardine, by Sid Chaplin
Titanic Lives, by Richard Davenport-Hines
Edgelands, by Paul Farley and Michael Symmons Roberts
Lost Shipyards of the Tyne, by Ron French and Ken Smith
The River Tyne, Its History and Resources, by James Guthrie
William Armstrong, Magician of the North, by Henrietta Heald
The Making of the Tyne, by RW Johnson
Armstrong's River Empire, by Dick Keys and Ken Smith
Tales of the Tyne, by Dick Keys and Ken Smith
Industrial Tyneside, by Henry A Mess
The Town That Was Murdered, by Ellen Wilkinson

Finally, as in all my enterprises, my deepest thanks and love to my wife, Susan Chaplin, who was not a companion on the Tyne Walk but was nevertheless with me every step of the way.

Michael Chaplin has written extensively for radio, television and the theatre, most recently scripting the film *Just Henry* for ITV and adapting the diaries of former Sunderland South MP Chris Mullin for Live Theatre's long-running production, *A Walk-On Part*. In 2011 he published *Come and See: The Beguiling Story of the Tyneside Cinema*. Brought up in Newcastle, by a tributary of the Tyne, he now lives there again after 30 years living and working in London. *Tyne View* is the culmination of three years spent as Writer in Residence for the Port of Tyne.

Birtley Aris was born in Sunderland now lives in Hexham, Northumberland. From 1946 he was a designer and craftsman in stained glass in Newcastle and London. Returning to the North in 1962, he has exhibited locally and nationally. His interests are the landscape and architecture of this region, and poetry as a basis for picturemaking. Collaborations with contemporary poets include *Storyville* (1992) and *Wild* (2004) with Linda France, *Night Train* (2009) with Sean O'Brien, and *Bobby Bendick's Ride* (2010) with Peter Bennet. He had a retrospective exhibition at the DLI Museum and Art Gallery, Durham, in 2007.

Charles Bell grew up in Newcastle upon Tyne overlooking the Ouseburn. After many years away in Leicester and London, working originally in social work and latterly in corporate real estate, he returned to his native Tyneside a few years ago.

Christy Ducker began life on Tyneside, and now lives in Tynedale. Her pamphlet, *Armour,* was a Poetry Book Society Choice in 2011. Her poetry commissions include residencies for English Heritage, and for Tyne & Wear Museums. She has received the Andrew Waterhouse Prize, and is currently writing a collection of poems about Grace Darling, as part of her PhD research at Newcastle University.

PORT

of

TYNE